# BUSTED!

*For the time will come when men will not put up*
*with sound doctrine.*
*Instead, to suit their own desires,*
*they will gather around them a great number of teachers to say*
*what their itching ears want to hear.*
*They will turn their ears away from the truth*
*and turn aside to myths.*

2 TIMOTHY 4:3 – 4

We want to hear from you. Please send your comments about this book to us in care of zreview@zondervan.com. Thank you.

*Busted*
Copyright © 2009 by Fred von Kamecke

This title is also available as a Zondervan ebook. Visit www.zondervan.com/ebooks.

This title is also available in a Zondervan audio edition. Visit www.zondervan.fm.

Requests for information should be addressed to:
Zondervan, *Grand Rapids, Michigan 49530*

**Library of Congress Cataloging-in-Publication Data**

Kamecke, Fred von.
    Busted : exposing popular myths about Christianity / Fred von Kamecke.
      p. cm.
    ISBN 978-0-310-28320-1 (softcover)
    1. Apologetics. I. Title.
BT1103.K36 2009
239—dc22
                                  2008036194

*Interior design by Sherri Hoffman*

*Printed in the United States of America*

09 10 11 12 13 14 15 16 17 18 19 20 • 17 16 15 14 13 12 11 10 9 8 7 6 5 4 3 2 1

# FRED von KAME

# BUSTED!

### Exposing Popular Myths about Christianity

ZONDERVAN®

ZONDERVAN.com/
AUTHORTRACKER
*follow your favorite authors*

*For Patty*
*You light up every room you enter and warm every heart you meet.*
*Walking with you on this journey is a joy.*

# CONTENTS

## MYTHS ABOUT THE CHRISTIAN FAITH

# FOREWORD

Humans use only 10 percent of their brains."

"A penny dropped from the top of a skyscraper could kill a pedestrian."

"Chicken soup can cure the common cold."

"Lightning never strikes the same place twice."

"A dog's mouth is cleaner than a human's."

"Animals can predict natural disasters."

"It takes seven years to digest gum."

Have you heard any of these claims before? My guess is that you have. At some point in my life I have heard each one of these ideas heralded as gospel truth. I even heard the claim that animals can predict natural disasters from one of my elementary school teachers, and my mom loved to repeat the last one about gum. As widely circulated as many of these are, the reality is that they are *all* myths. Yes, *myths*. I was certainly let down when I first learned this. Yet despite my disappointment, the reality is that they have little significance on my daily life (or yours, for that matter).

But what if we buy into myths about spiritual issues? What if we are wrong about God, Jesus, the Bible, or central issues of the Christian faith? Can we simply continue our lives as before? Clearly, when it comes to spiritual beliefs, much more is at stake. My father once said, "The resurrection is either the most vicious, wicked, heartless hoax ever foisted upon the minds of men . . . OR it is the greatest fact of history." There is no middle ground, either the resurrection is the greatest fact or it's the greatest farce. According to the apostle Paul, if Jesus' resurrection didn't happen, then faith in Christ is worthless—we are still in our sins (1 Cor. 15:14, 17).

While believing the myths listed above ultimately matter very little, it's hard to underestimate the consequences of believing myths about God. Our spiritual beliefs have not only eternal implications, but daily consequences as well.

This is precisely why I so enthusiastically endorse *Busted*. Fred von Kamecke tackles the most commonly cited myths about God, Jesus, the Bible, and the Christian faith that abound in both the culture and, sadly, many times in the church. Whether it's through the influence of popular movies, the Internet, TV, or word-of-mouth, crazy ideas about God are everywhere. Yet Fred is up to the task. He is a first-rate scholar who writes in an engaging, conversational style that is accessible (and interesting) to the nonspecialist. Fred follows the lead of the apostle Peter, who insisted that the case for the Christian faith is solid: "For we did not follow cleverly devised myths when we made known to you the power and coming of our Lord Jesus Christ, but we had been eyewitnesses of his majesty" (2 Peter 1:16, NRSV).

There has been a huge need for a user-friendly resource that helps people wade through the many spiritual myths pervading our culture. *Busted* has hit the nail on the head. Whether you are a Christian who wants to go deeper in your faith or a skeptic weighing spiritual options, *Busted* is an indispensable resource. It's ideal for individual study, small-group discussion, or even the classroom setting. I highly recommend it.

**Sean McDowell** is a teacher, speaker, and the coauthor
of *Evidence for the Resurrection* (Regal, 2009) and
*Understanding Intelligent Design* (Harvest House, 2008).

# ACKNOWLEDGMENTS

No book is written in a vacuum and I am deeply grateful for the input of so many people in my life. I want to thank my parents, Ralph and Elizabeth von Kamecke, as well as my brothers, Phil and Tom, and sister, Nancy, for their encouragement and comments on early drafts, or just cheering me on. Other family members gave encouragement and helpful input: Elizabeth and Sam Lirones, Dave and Michele Doucette, Karen and Fritz Richards, Chris and Debbie Wing, Gus and Nancy Wing, and Linda and (Uncle) Doug Wing.

I want to thank my friends and colleagues at The Chapel: Ashley Roberts, Dave Thompson, Arnie Gentile, Alex Chlewicki, Tami and Hal Cook, Tammy Chapman, Holger Bucks, Lisa Stueckemann, Susie Krueger, Stephanie Schreiber, John Spears, Joy and Jim DeLaere (and her friend Virginia Lange), John Bruss, Andy Burns, Becky Cappelli, Mike Eichstadt, Ron Shaw, Bo Johnson, Kathy Chapman Sharp (and her daughter Beck), Stacia Gibson, Bekah Layton, Barb Robinson, and Walt and Amy Roberts. I owe special thanks to my grammar Nazis: Debbie Veltman, Jen Jao, Michelle Habrych, and John Toner. Other friends also weighed in, among whom are Ben and Heather Letto, Kelly and Dawn Paterson, Chad Meister, Jared Niedermeyer, Dan Daniszewski, Jeff Newby, Tulsi Becker, and Cindy Drake. I am truly thankful for all concerned for their helpful comments, as well as rescuing me from countless typos and a variety of blunders. Special thanks are due Sue Mihalovic for her clairvoyance in finding the precise cover photo I had in mind.

The godly instruction and challenges provided by my professors at Southeastern College (now University, in Lakeland, Florida), Reformed Theological Seminary (in Orlando, Florida), and Trinity Evangelical Divinity School (in Deerfield, Illinois) have left an indelible mark on my life. I am deeply grateful for the blessed, though at times hair-raising, education these people provided.

Many of the themes in this book were hammered out in classes I taught as an adjunct professor both at Trinity, and to a greater extent at North Park University. I am particularly grateful for my interactions there with Linda Bellville, Scot McKnight, Klyne Snodgrass, and Steve Graham. I thank Pastors Scott Chapman, Jeff Griffin and The Chapel board of elders, not to mention Pastors Brent Davis and Rick Egbert, for graciously allowing me sabbatical time to focus on writing, and Fred Heald for covering for me during that time. Jamie Wamsley deserves special mention for coming up with the title for this book. I am grateful for David Frees and Zondervan for all their assistance, especially taking a chance on an unknown author.

I want to thank my lovely wife, Patty, who read through the manuscript and gave me so much valuable feedback. I could not have done this without your loving patience. Finally, I thank the Lord Jesus Christ, who gave me the idea in the first place. May your Word find open ears and willing hearts.

# ABBREVIATIONS

**Bible Versions**

| | |
|---|---|
| ESV | English Standard Version |
| KJV | King James Version |
| NASB | New American Standard Bible |
| NET | New English Translation |
| NIV | New International Version |
| NKJV | New King James Version |
| NLT | New Living Translation |
| NRSV | New Revised Standard Version |

**Dictionaries**

DJG — *Dictionary of Jesus and the Gospels*, edited by Joel B. Green and Scot McKnight (Downers Grove, IL: InterVarsity Press, 1992)

DPL — *Dictionary of Paul and his Letters*, edited by Gerhard F. Hawthorne and Ralph P. Martin (Downers Grove, IL: InterVarsity Press, 1993)

DLNT — *Dictionary of the Later New Testament and Its Developments*, edited by Ralph P. Martin and Peter Davids (Downers Grove, IL: InterVarsity Press, 1997)

# MYTHS ABOUT THE BIBLE

# Chapter 1

# SETTING THE TABLE

What an incredible age this is. We live in a time of technological marvels with new advances announced nearly every day. Computers and iPods are outdated before they can be shipped and earth-shaking innovations in cell phones and BlackBerries are passé before we can make the first call. Information comes at us from all sides in a relentless barrage. One would think in a day such as this that myths, misconceptions, and falsehoods wouldn't stand a chance of surviving without instantly being exposed, with clear-headed truth taking their place. One would be wrong.

Everyone knows someone who knows someone who has a friend (who wouldn't lie) who knew a guy who bit into a hamburger from (any fast-food chain) and found half a cockroach! Or, perhaps you've heard that "the infamous atheist Madalyn Murray O'Hair has recently petitioned the FCC to outlaw Christian broadcasting" (a particularly heinous affront since she's been dead for years). If anything, the information age has increased the opportunities to pass these myths on, as well as countless others like them. It also raises the opportunity for someone to take myths head-on and expose them for what they really are. This is precisely what some Hollywood special effects experts decided to do.

## ENTER THE MYTHBUSTERS

In a popular cable TV series, a few inventive souls with way too much time on their hands set out to debunk perennial urban legends. The show is called *Mythbusters*. Sometimes the daring investigators actually wind up validating a myth or two, but they more often declare them "Busted." Can someone really be sucked out of a pressurized airliner if a window is shot out at 30,000 feet? (*No, but he'll never be the same.*) Could Ben Franklin really have performed the kite in the lightening storm experiment? (*No, unless we want to say his last achievement was inventing toast.*) Can a soloist really shatter a crystal goblet by hitting the right note? (*Yes, actually, but don't try it at home, ever!*) The claims may continue in the culture's collective consciousness, but the false ones are, as far as the record goes, shown to be false. The truth just needs the same amount of press as the nonsense.

This book is written in the same spirit of honest inquiry and desire to expose bogus claims, but with a different focus. While watching *Mythbusters* one day, it occurred to me that Christianity has its share of myths, legends, and outright lies attributed to it. People say a lot of things about the Bible and Christianity that are simply not true. Such statements are spoken as if they are take-it-to-the-bank facts, even though they've been debunked a million times (give or take a few) in scholarly literature. The myths are common knowledge; the responses are not. This book is about getting some of these responses into your hands.

## IT'S NOT JUST THE CULTURE

Sometimes the attacks aren't coming from the culture per se, but from biblical scholarship itself. Skepticism dominates the universities and permeates the media. The claims these scholars make are often just as bogus as the urban legend variety, but they have the weight of credibility owing to the prestige of those making them.

Please don't misunderstand. I am not casually dismissing every view I disagree with as a myth. Scholarly discussions can be very involved and often result in new insights and discoveries. Conservative scholarship would be impoverished without the influence of challenging, and sometimes correcting, opposing perspectives. There is, however, a level of skepticism that is empty. It has nothing to offer except venomous attacks on traditional Christian faith that, in fact, run contrary to the evidence.

As is the case with urban legends, this level of intellectual skepticism has been actively engaged on many fronts. Many of these skeptical claims have been soundly refuted, in some instances, several decades ago. You wouldn't know that, however, from watching PBS specials on the "real" Jesus, or perusing the articles that recycle this or that discovery casting doubt on the Bible. Skeptical scholars attacked; Christian scholars decisively responded, but the TV anchor didn't get the memo. This is why I would like to bring you up to speed on some issues that were settled long ago and tell you about some of the arguments that are currently being engaged.

## REASONABLE FAITH

This topic gets a little dicey since we're dealing with issues of faith. There are among us those who insist faith is fine, as long as you keep it to yourself. They are also adamant that faith has no business interacting with the realm of facts. However, it is important for us to know that there are reasons for believing the Bible's testimony — there are facts that back it up. We definitely need to have faith, as the Scriptures make clear (Hebrews 11:6), but we don't need to be intimidated when someone points out that "It all goes back to faith." Of course it does, but it is not *blind* faith.

A central theme of Christianity is that God invaded history in the person of his Son. Jesus lived, died, and rose again in an occupied country full of strife and rival claims. In the same way, this faith continues to unfold in the real world, with Christians striving to make the case that the gospel message is "true and reasonable" (Acts 26:25). It is not an issue of "faith versus fact." No, it's an issue of the facts pointing the way to a reasonable faith.

If you've been around Christian circles for a while, you may recognize that I am talking about "apologetics." As it relates to Christianity, apologetics is the discipline of offering a rational basis for the Christian faith — a defense, if you will. In fact, the New Testament itself has something to say about it. For instance, Peter tells Christians: "Always be prepared to give an answer to everyone who asks you to give the reason for the hope that you have" (1 Peter 3:15). When Peter mentions "answer" (some versions translate it "defense"), he uses a term that winds up in English as "apology." Normally, an apology relates to smoothing over a tiff with your sweetie, but the word didn't mean that in Peter's day, and today it has an additional meaning. An "apology" in this technical sense refers to making a defense for a particular view.

You may not be accustomed to hearing the term as such, but we do apologetics all the time. "My favorite football team is clearly the best for the following reasons," or "There's only one correct way to cook a roast, and here it is." (Anyone suspecting I might have had sexist categories in mind in these last illustrations has never seen my buddy's wife come right off the couch like a screaming banshee every time her team fumbles.) What we're doing in these instances is defending a viewpoint. It's no different with Christianity. The Christian faith self-consciously presents itself as a truth capable of rational defense (Acts 1:3), one worth standing up for (Jude 3).

## THE NERVE

That last line is bound to raise some folks' hackles if spoken too loudly. Maybe you've heard a time or two that the Bible just can't be trusted. After all, it's been translated too many times. How could it be a sure guide to anything? While we're at it, you may be asking yourself if *any* of this is really important. Isn't truth simply relative, just a matter of convention? By contrast, if you *do* decide to stand up for what you believe, aren't you really just being pigheaded? Some folks seem to believe that either going along or being a pain are the only available options.

Our culture has rightly highlighted the need for patience, dialogue, and tolerance; there is much to be said about avoiding needless offense. But those very things, especially tolerance, are too often used like a club in an attempt to silence Christians. Anything goes in our society—anything, that is, except the gospel. It must be silenced as a divisive and unscientific collection of fairy tales. It is interesting that Christians are often singled out as intolerant and insensitive toward other beliefs, but I never hear anyone in the culture or the media complain about those who level their attacks *against* Christianity. Have you?

## A LOST ART?

We as Christians are often put in the position that something needs to be said in response to the barbs of the skeptics. But many Christians have gotten a little rusty when it comes to defending the faith, rusty enough that a book like this could be useful. It wasn't long ago that pastors and Christian authors waged a "battle for the Bible" against this onslaught, seeking to equip their people with answers to these attacks. The average churchgoer had enough knowledge about what was going on to be able to stand firm. In our day, the drumbeat of attack continues, but, for too many people, it has simply become background noise. Few are paying any attention, and those who *are* aware of the issues are reluctant to say anything. There are many reasons for this, but let me highlight three of them.

### Whatever

One reason for the reluctance to engage such a topic as defending the faith is that we are in the "Whatever" generation. We may try to address a commonly held myth, but we are met with apathy. Usually uttered with a roll of the eyes, "whatever" is spoken with an air of exasperation mixed with a touch of condescension. It is uttered as the final word on the subject, or at least that's the impression we are to take from it.

"You don't really believe that Jesus rose from the dead, do you?"

"Well, yes I do, and there are some good reasons to believe it's true."

*"Whatever."*

### Avoiding the Battlefield

Another reason for the reluctance to defend the faith is that the whole thing sounds so militant. It's the natural outcome of talking about a *battle* for the Bible, *attacks* on it, and a *defense* of it. These all are terms taken directly from the battlefield. It's easy to conjure up an image of a grim-faced soldier taking the hill. Closer to home, imagine an obnoxious zealot pointing out to friend and foe alike that if you don't follow his narrow interpretation, "you are all going to hell." Far too many Christians opt for such an approach, and many people have been turned off as a result. It is completely contrary to the attitude Christians are commanded to have. Before going on to the third reason, let's explore this one a bit further to get a better picture of what I'm talking about.

The New Testament encourages us not only about defending the faith, but also gives clear instructions about *how* to do so. After Peter tells his readers to "give an answer" for their faith, he tells them to do so "with gentleness and respect, keeping a clear conscience," all the while maintaining "good behavior in Christ" (1 Peter 3:15 – 16). Here is a call not just to convey spiritual truth, but to do so in a spiritual manner.

Let's take Paul's familiar challenge to Timothy as another example. "Do your best to present yourself to God as one approved, a workman who does not need to be ashamed and who correctly handles the word of truth" (2 Timothy 2:15). The application is usually that Christians need to be engaging in Bible study; we need to have the facts of the Scriptures firmly in mind in order to be able to hold our own in any discussion about it. Now this is all true as far as it goes, but if we read this verse in light of some other things in the wider context, we gain a better perspective of what Timothy was facing.

Timothy was a young pastor put in charge of a rowdy congregation, concerning which Paul writes two letters. The first one starts off with a reminder that it was Timothy's duty to "command certain men not to teach false doctrines," nor to "devote themselves to myths," nor to get entangled in a variety of controversies that detract from God's truth (1 Timothy 1:3–4). Paul and Timothy were the first "Mythbusters."

In his second letter to Timothy Paul tells the young pastor to stand firmly in God's grace while entrusting the gospel to faithful teachers (2 Timothy 2:1–3). Conflicts were inevitable, so Timothy must brace himself and plunge ahead regardless, with the gospel firmly in mind (2:3–8). Timothy needs to be a bit of a broken record when it comes to preaching and teaching it, but here's the rub: he has to warn people not to get into picky little quarrels (2:14).

Verse 15, then, comes in the midst of this conversation; it is set in contrast to being argumentative. Make it your goal, Timothy, to know God's Word. The very next thing Paul tells him is to "avoid godless chatter," followed by warnings about some specific troublemakers (2 Timothy 2:16–18). He warns Timothy once again to avoid "foolish and stupid arguments" because they just lead to quarrels (2:23). "The Lord's servant," we are told, "must not quarrel," but must address these issues with kindness, ability, and not even a trace of resentment (2:24). The key point here, and the alternative to arguing, is a godly disposition: "Those who oppose him he must gently instruct, in the hope that God will grant them repentance leading them to a knowledge of the truth" (2:25). Our failures to address issues in a kindly manner only underscore that God's way is the right way.

Coming up with reasons to trust the Bible is an issue of information. Discussing those reasons in an attitude of humility and compassion, not to mention a genuine concern for people, is a matter of godly character. God's Word needs to be shared in God's way to have any God-honoring effect. We cannot be satisfied with the cold facts of a hard-as-nails argument. We need the warm embrace of faith, God's very breath to bring the facts to life. As you read this book, please don't mistake my comments aimed at people's views as personal attacks on the people themselves. They are not. It would be a disservice to all involved if this book is used merely as fuel for an argument.

As a contrast, let me offer a word about the style in which this book is written. I've tried to keep the tone friendly and approachable throughout the book. I've also made every effort to write in a conversational style, weaving together strands of serious discussions with a touch of humor. There are many excellent works on apologetics on the market. Some are fairly technical and beyond the reach of the average churchgoer. Some are written with a bit of an edge. I want to avoid name-calling and stick to the facts as I see them. I don't rant and rave. (Why rant and rave when a simple rant will do?) I am not making fun of people who hold views with which I disagree.

I do however, have a lot of fun with the *views* they hold, namely, the *attacks* leveled against the beliefs the church has held sacred for centuries. It is akin to the old saying that God hates sin but loves the sinner. In a similar fashion, I'm not attacking the skeptics, but their public comments are fair game.

So let's look again at Paul's advice. Without a hint of contradiction, he tells Timothy to be kind and gentle (2 Timothy 2:24–25) right on the heels of comparing some false teaching to "gangrene" (2:17). One could imagine Paul talking with Hymenaeus and Philetus (the false teachers named in the passage) with Timothy looking on. Paul models all of his gracious character, mixed with an unblinking appeal to the gospel, as he strives to win them over. These are people he's trying to rescue from a demonic snare (2:26), so his compassion is appropriate. When it comes to their teaching, however, he considers it gangrenous. It's the stench of death spreading through the extremities of the body of Christ. Unchecked, the body will die, so radical treatment becomes a necessity. Love the false teachers (hope for their redemption); hate the false teaching (call it what it is, and ask the nurse for a saw). His compassion, you see, shifts from the false teachers to the victim of the teaching, the church.

There are many such attacks on the church today. The issue here is defense. I'm *defending* a heritage that stretches back to the little churches in the Roman Empire, to the sandy shores of the Sea of Galilee, to the slave quarters in ancient Egypt, to the call of Abraham, God's friend.

### Tools of the Trade

Now, to recap, apologetics is avoided because we often meet up with apathy; it is also avoided due to its perceived militant nature. The third reason people are reluctant to engage in apologetics is that Christians don't feel up to the task. They just don't think they're equipped to get into a discussion with an out-and-out skeptic. This book is all about giving you some equipment.

In the following pages I focus on some frequently recurring myths and misconceptions about Christianity. These misconceptions all have the same undercurrent: Don't worry about Christianity; it's nothing special and pretty much all made up anyway. My approach is to give a brief summary of a given myth, followed by an explanation of why it isn't so. You'd expect that, of course, but I'm focusing more on the biblical and historical evidence than you usually encounter in such books. These select myths are addressed primarily by giving the Bible a fair reading, situated in its own time frame.

## DUSTY SANDALS

A recurring theme throughout this book is the need to transport ourselves from the cluttered highways of cybernet-technoville to the dusty streets of ancient Galilee and Jerusalem. We need to walk with Jesus in his world and see him through the eyes of the people he encountered, friend and foe. We need to hear with fresh ears how the young Jew's message would have sounded to Jewish ears and to marvel with the people at his astounding miracles. We need to recoil in horror as spikes pierce his limbs and stand transfixed as we witness that poor man's slow, agonizing death, his blood soaking into the parched Jerusalem ground. We need to feel the rush of emotion, awe, and wonder as we talk (and eat!) with the Master three days after his death. So don't be surprised if we take frequent journeys to that ancient world as a means of attempting to get a handle on ours. An extra pair of sandals is recommended.

## MY INTENDED AUDIENCE

I am writing this book for the average Christian (or interested seeker) who has not had the opportunity for formal study in a Bible college or seminary, but senses the need for some solid information. I am writing for people who hear these myths, have a feeling they're wrong, but don't have the tools to address them. This book can also be used as an evangelistic tool. Give it to friends or family members and pray that God will open their eyes. The issues raised here could spur on some lively conversations.

Over the years I have encountered numerous arguments raised against Christianity in general, and the truthfulness of the Bible in particular. Yet, I have never encountered an objection raised that can withstand a clear, reasoned defense. When the facts come to light (and sometimes it's a long wait), they always validate what the Bible has to say. I am unaware of any discovery that proves the Scriptures to be in error. With such a track record, in situations where the jury is still out, the Bible really deserves far more of the benefit of doubt than it is usually given.

Still, the debates continue and are endless and technical, and they often require an extensive background in the field to even follow the discussion. Relax; we're not going to go into such depth here. For those of you who *do* want to delve deeper into these topics, I've included a "Going Deeper" section for each chapter, with some suggested readings to get you started.

The myths I deal with in this book fall into four main categories: myths about the Bible, myths about Jesus, myths about God, and myths about the Christian faith. We will go from making the case for the trustworthiness of Scripture, to clarifying its testimony about the identity of Jesus and the triune God, which then puts us in a position to discuss the Christian faith more accurately. Finally I will offer some concluding thoughts.

## JUST A FEW MORE DISJOINTED ITEMS

Throughout this book I refer to the biblical writers by their traditional identities without entering into debates about authorship. A quote from the gospel of Matthew, for instance, may be introduced as "Matthew says," or a quotation from Ephesians may be "Paul writes," without further comment. I refer to the Bible extensively, so you'll want to have one handy to check things out for yourself (as noted on the copyright page, I am using the NIV).

Throughout this book, I am not using the Bible as proof, per se. Rather, I am using it as evidence. Particularly when you consider the New Testament, the writers made incredible claims about the life, death, and resurrection of a carpenter from Nazareth. Their claims about Jesus had the effect of painting a bull's-eye on their brave foreheads. Their preaching sealed their fate, and many of them met with cruel deaths. This leads me to ask why they would say such things in the face of this kind of hostility. The only satisfying answer is their encounter with Jesus, both before and after his crucifixion. At the very least, these first-century documents deserve a fair hearing.

I also need to say something about the sources I've used for this book and the lack of extensive citation. Unless I'm directly quoting someone or am filling in some necessary details, I've opted to forgo endnotes. This is not a formal scholarly work for a theological publication; it's a popular-level book written pretty much the way I talk. I'm not terribly concerned if I end a sentence with a preposition (those little words you're not supposed to end a sentence with).

I may be prone to occasionally split an infinitive, or transgress any of a hundred rules of formal writing. But, this is not formal; it's colloquial. It's not a research project or a theological treatise. I am writing this as if we are having a conversation in a coffee shop. You are sipping a fresh-brewed Kona, and I am just exploding myths, exposing lies, and generally making a nuisance of myself.

Having said that, the attentive reader who *is* familiar with the literature will easily discern how heavily influenced I am by it. So let me just openly declare my flagrant plagiarism of the giants in the field and point you to select readings so you can further investigate the extent of my transgression.

For now, we have some more pressing issues to attend to. So, grab a cup of coffee and find a cozy corner. Let's do a little myth busting of our own.

## GOING DEEPER

Here are four general books on apologetics you may find helpful: Mark Mittelberg, *Choosing Your Faith* (Carol Stream, IL: Tyndale, 2008); Lee Strobel, *The Case for Faith* (Grand Rapids: Zondervan, 2000); Kenneth Samples, *Without a Doubt: Answering the 20 Toughest Faith Questions* (Grand Rapids: Baker, 2004); and William Lane Craig, *Hard Questions, Real Answers* (Wheaton, IL: Crossway, 2003). For more in-depth treatment of the topic see the essays in *Reasons for Faith: Making a Case for the Christian Faith*, edited by Norman Geisler and Chad Meister (Wheaton: Crossway, 2007). For a classic treatment with a philosophical bent see Ron Nash, *Faith and Reason: Searching for a Rational Faith* (Grand Rapids: Zondervan, 1988).

# Chapter 2

# YOU CAN'T TRUST THE BIBLE BECAUSE IT'S BEEN TRANSLATED TOO MANY TIMES

The Bible's testimony plays a central role in addressing all of the myths and misconceptions in this book. That being the case, it won't hurt to establish at least some measure of trustworthiness for it before we proceed. It is all the more important to do so since the Bible is not always considered trust*worthy*. In fact, debates have been continuing for centuries on this very topic with scholars of every description launching salvos at each other.

Critics raise objections and advance theories that regard the Bible as merely a collection of deeply held beliefs that bear no resemblance to reality. Others respond with evidence and arguments designed to blunt these attacks. However, one thing none of the critics advance as an assault on the Bible is the claim that it's been translated too many times to know what its message really is. In other words, that is just not an issue among scholars. It is, my friends, simply a common myth in the popular culture.

Essentially, the myth claims the Bible has been translated over and over into hundreds of languages throughout the course of the centuries, so today nobody knows what it originally said. Although this statement seems to have a ring of truth, it is actually a classic logical fallacy known as a *non sequitur*. This is just a fancy way of saying "You can't draw that conclusion from your premise; it does not follow." (Or, as New Englanders would prefer, "Ya can't get there from here.") The logical problem itself is a bit of a setback, but this particular myth also encounters another problem. It doesn't fit the historical picture.

The first part of the statement, by the way, is true; the Bible *has* been translated numerous times over the centuries. It's true, but irrelevant. It's been translated repeatedly but *it does not follow* that its message is therefore forever lost in translation. For this to be so, the process of translating would have looked something like this: Paul writes a letter in Greek (the common language of the empire) to a church in Rome. This letter is known today as *Romans*. All is well and good, but eventually someone translates it into Latin. Now everybody knows that no language can be precisely translated into another without losing something, so we're one step removed from the original. Next the Latin version is translated into, say, Ethiopic (we lose something else); the Ethiopic version is translated into Arabic, then Spanish, then countless other languages. We quickly get too far away from the original to have any hope of recovery. (Jesus didn't *die on the cross between two robbers*; he was *cross because someone dyed his two robes*.)

Did you notice the scenario assumes something without ever saying it? When the Latin translation was made, the Greek one was tossed; when the Ethiopic one was made, the Latin was pitched, and so on. If that were the case, the result would be that no standard of comparison survived and we'd have to agree with those who make the claim. The historical situation, however, was very different.

## ANCIENT "PHOTOCOPIES"

Today we can go to bookstores and buy as many Bibles as we wish. Men's Bibles, Women's Bibles, Youth Bibles, Study Bibles, Left-Handed Dyslexic Red-Haired Plumber's Bibles, you name it. I've lost count of how many English versions are currently available, but you can get anything from very Old English (*predating* the KJV) to the folksy Cotton Patch Version, to the somewhat stilted NASB or ESV (with apologies to these otherwise fine products). In the ancient world, however, it was a little different. If you wanted a copy of the Bible, you copied it yourself, or you paid a trained scribe to copy one for you. (The printing press wasn't invented until the 1400s.)

Pushing back a little further in the past, we need to consider what it would've been like to be a Christian at the time the New Testament was being written. Let's continue using Romans as an example. Paul wrote it late in his ministry, around AD 58 or so. It was the common practice of that era to send a letter by a personal courier, who would then read the letter to the intended audience, in this case, a home church in Rome. Before being sent to another church, a copy would be made. This was not only common, but sometimes explicitly commanded (Colossians 4:16; 1 Thessalonians 5:27). Keep in mind, this is the only New Testament they have, a stunning letter (or two) written by the former persecutor-turned-apostle. As word got around that Paul was writing other letters, they too were copied, collected, and eventually began circulating as a collection (perhaps as early as AD 100).

All this copying was still in Greek, the original language, but this changed as time went on. Eventually Latin became the trade language of the western part of the empire, and as people gradually lost their proficiency in Greek, there was a growing need for a Latin translation. No one knows when the first translation was made, but what we call the Old Latin version appeared in North Africa around the late second century AD (at least translations of the Gospels and some Old Testament books). Latin translations of Paul's letters may have been that early, maybe a little later. Whatever the case, we are left with at least a century of copies being made and distributed in Greek (some of which survive to this day) before the Old Latin surfaces.

It's important for us to realize that the first Latin translation occurred at a time when Greek texts were still plentiful. Did the Latin translation lose a bit in the process? Maybe — *go check the Greek manuscripts that predate it.*

## FAR AND WIDE

This was the case with all of the New Testament books. Initially sent to local churches (and individuals in a few instances), copies were made before passing the writing along. As with Paul's letters, it wasn't long before the Gospels were bound together and made the circuit as a fourfold unit (sometimes along with the book of Acts); likewise, the other letters began to circulate. Many of these made it as far as Alexandria, Egypt, by the early third century AD. At least one fragment consisting of a few lines from John 18 dates to as early as AD 125, perhaps even 115. When *translations* of New Testament writings into other languages started showing up, they did so in a world awash with Greek manuscripts.

As the centuries progressed, literally thousands of Greek manuscripts were produced. Of these, over five thousand survive to this day, ranging from mere scraps or a single page, to collections of several books, to complete, or nearly complete Bibles (Greek Old and New Testaments). Besides the Old Latin, other ancient versions were made in Syriac, Coptic, Gothic, and Ethiopic. As Christianity spread, the need for translations into local languages and dialects increased, a process that continues to the present.

It is true that in many instances, translations were made from an existing translation (Latin and Syriac were the foundations of several ancient versions). Sometimes a given version was the result of a translation from a translation of a translation. This was not always the case, of course, and when the Reformation dawned in sixteenth-century Europe, there was a renewed effort to go back to the original languages, which led to a demand for printed Hebrew Old Testaments and Greek New Testaments. These texts in the original languages became the foundation for fresh translations. Even in those instances in which the practice of starting with a Latin translation persisted (as was the case for the first several English versions), it was done in a world that preserved Hebrew and Greek manuscripts. So, *manuscripts in those languages existed side-by-side with translations of them, and do so to this day.*

Incidentally, a related common myth making the circuit today is the conspiracy theory that the New Testament was worked over by church leaders in the fourth century. They transformed the simple Nazareth peasant preacher into the mighty Son of God! I'll have more to say about this in chapters 5 and 16, but I just want to point out something at this stage of the conversation. By the time there *was* a church leadership powerful enough to do such a thing (assuming they had a mind to), the New Testament manuscripts and translations were already scattered throughout the empire, many of them already buried in sweltering Egyptian sand or hidden away in little church storage rooms. In other words, they were safely out of reach from would-be interlopers.

## THE MANUSCRIPT EVIDENCE
### Conniving Christians

Speaking of buried treasure, the history of the Old Testament has an interesting twist. Most conservative scholars maintain that the last book written, 2 Chronicles, was finished around 400 BC (others will argue that some of the psalms and the book of Daniel were written as late as the 160s BC). In any case, the first five books of the Bible were translated from Hebrew into Greek around 250 BC. This became known as the Septuagint. Eventually the rest of the Old Testament was translated into Greek as well and came to be known with the same name.

Stay with me here. As the centuries wore on manuscripts wore out and were replaced, and so we found ourselves in an interesting position by the early twentieth century. The earliest *surviving* manuscripts of the Septuagint dated to the mid-fourth century AD, while the earliest *surviving* Hebrew manuscript in existence dated to the early ninth century AD (known as the Masoretic text, the basis for our current English translations). Who could say if the Septuagint is a good translation of earlier Hebrew texts? The only *surviving* Hebrew texts were later. Maybe the Septuagint botched it, or worse, was intentionally changed in the early Christian era. Perhaps the later Hebrew manuscripts of the medieval period just reflect that altered job.

### Prior to Qumran Discoveries

| | BC | AD | | |
|---|---|---|---|---|
| 1400 – 400s Hebrew texts written | 250 Septuagint translation | 300s Earliest Septuagint manuscripts in existence | 800s Earliest Hebrew manuscripts in existence |

Some medieval Jewish scholars made just such a charge concerning a prophecy in Isaiah 52 – 53. If you've never read that passage, take a moment to do so. The medieval scholars accused the Christians of doctoring it up to make Jesus fit the prophecy. It sure looks suspiciously specific. Who could say whether or not somebody changed things? The Jewish scholars knew that the Greek translation, the Septuagint, had been in Christian hands for centuries, so obviously they manipulated the text in favor of a Christian interpretation. Subsequent Hebrew manuscripts were then influenced by it. It had been translated so many times, you see, that no one really knew what it originally said.

### Goats and God's Word

Fortunately, in 1947 a young Bedouin shepherd brought clarity to the situation. While looking for his lost goat he tossed a stone into a cave and heard pottery shatter, inadvertently discovering what has become known as the Dead Sea Scrolls. Several jars of ancient manuscripts were discovered in a series of caves in an area known as Qumran on the northwest shore of the Dead Sea. Among these manuscripts were copies of the Old Testament Scriptures in Hebrew, Aramaic, and some Greek, which were subsequently dated between 150 BC and AD 70 (with most of the biblical texts on the BC side of the spectrum). The Hebrew texts turned out to be remarkably close to the Masoretic text, the most spectacular example being the Isaiah Scroll dated to around 100 BC (differing from the Masoretic text only in terms of a handful of inconsequential variations in spelling).

This ancient manuscript of Isaiah had the same astounding prophecy found in the Septuagint, the one about the execution and resurrection of the Lord's Servant. It is reflected in later Hebrew manuscripts and is the same as we find in our current English Bibles. Medieval Christians were exonerated (at least on *that* score).

This incredible episode validated the oft-stated claim about the painstaking precision with which the Hebrew scribes approached their task. With the toss of a stone, Old Testament texts came to light that are a thousand years older than what was previously known. This means our current English translations of the Old Testament are based on a Hebrew text that has existed remarkably unchanged for over two thousand years. The burden of proof is on those who argue that the same degree of care was *not* exercised in an earlier phase.

Today there are many English translations; do they faithfully reflect the Hebrew? Some do better than others; *just check out the Hebrew manuscripts that predate them.*

### Discoveries after Qumran

| | | BC | AD | |
| --- | --- | --- | --- | --- |
| 1400 – 400s Hebrew texts written | 250 Septuagint translation | 100s Earliest Hebrew manuscripts in existence | | 300s Earliest Septuagint manuscripts in existence |

### Where Are the Originals?

There is much more to this issue, as any specialist would readily tell you. But as I said in the Setting the Table chapter, my target audience is the nonspecialist, so the innumerable side issues, endnotes, clarifications, objections, and validating arguments must be left to your own study. Still, this chapter raises some other issues that need to be addressed briefly, namely, the existence of the originals and the accuracy of translation.

First, the issue of manuscripts and original languages immediately raises the question of where the originals are located, that is, the actual manuscripts Moses, David, Matthew, and Peter, to name a few, wrote so long ago. The technical term for the original is an "autograph." The bad news is none of them have survived. Someone could conclude from this fact that, since there are no originals, it's anybody's guess what the Bible originally said. But that brings us to the good news. The wealth of existing manuscript evidence (not to mention all of the translations and citations from rabbis and early church fathers)[1] allows for a high degree of certainty that the original text is represented within the wealth of manuscripts we now have.

The art and science for determining the original text from the existing evidence is called "textual criticism." It is the process of sifting through the manuscripts, comparing and scrutinizing them and applying well-worn methods to recover the original text. The issues surrounding the Dead Sea Scrolls demonstrate the care with which the Old Testament was preserved; the situation with the New Testament, however, is a little different.

As I said earlier, there are thousands of manuscripts of the New Testament, but no two are identical; all of them have what are called "variants." This might sound a little unsettling, but it is what one would expect from the process of hand-copying lengthy portions of Scripture (or any document for that matter) initially by untrained scribes. Yet, since there is such a wealth of manuscripts and since scribal practices are well known, not to mention that variations tend to be localized, textual critics from all points of the Christian spectrum maintain that the certainty of recovering the original wording is high indeed (always in the high 90s percentile). The vast majority of variants involve spelling, grammar, harmonization, and the like, most of which are easily identified.

The variations that *do* occur are tenacious. Once a variation is introduced into the manuscript tradition, it continues as a piece of evidence. The other manuscripts, of course, don't disappear, so there is a continuing testimony of what one manuscript records, existing side-by-side with others that do not share that particular reading.

You should know that, regardless of the variations, no central doctrine of Christianity is threatened. There is no variant reading that denies the resurrection, makes Jesus less than the exalted Son, or questions his power to save us. Any central doctrine that *is* affected by a textual variant still has ample support from other texts. In other words, "the content of the message and its theology are not in question."[2]

Once the text is reasonably established it becomes an issue of translation. That, of course, introduces another set of wrinkles.

## A REAL MINDBLOWER

A former student of mine from Russia told me about a missionary's visit to his church in Siberia. The missionary was preaching up a storm and his interpreter was holding his own admirably. At one point the missionary said that something or other really "blew my mind." The interpreter thought for a second and said, "His brains were splattered all over the walls and ceiling." Perhaps something was lost in the translation.

There is no use denying that landmines aplenty await anyone taking a statement in one language and attempting to render it in another. (Can you imagine what a French, Samoan, or Chinese interpreter would do with "preaching up a storm," or what "landmines" have to do with translation?) Is it any different with the Bible? Taking three ancient languages and translating them into modern English is bound to produce some mindblowers.

Fear not. Translating ancient biblical idioms has been going on for a long time. Our current translations (again, existing side-by-side with ancient manuscripts) are truly excellent and only get better with new discoveries and advances in theories of linguistics. There are indeed problem verses, and it's simply a fact that idioms, puns, artful literary devices, plays on words, and the like don't precisely carry over into English. Often the "punch line" just doesn't work. The issue, however, isn't whether someone can render a snappy line from Greek into snappy English, but if the meaning of the Greek can be expressed in such a way that it makes good sense in English. The "punch" may be lost, but the basic meaning can still be conveyed. Piece o' cake.

Apart from learning the languages yourself (a continual source of delight for seminary students), you really do have to trust the experts, but it's not blind trust. No one who is informed on the issue of Bible translation, whether a staunch conservative or an equally staunch liberal, ever advances a theory that our English versions *fail to correctly translate* the original languages. True, the versions differ, but a broad sampling of versions will quickly show how much they are alike! Listen carefully to the critics the media puts forth from time to time. The attacks are not aimed at whether or not you can trust a translation, but *that you can't assume what is written is true.* No one claims the New Testament really doesn't say Jesus rose from the dead, but many *do* claim that such a (correctly translated) statement is simply a fairy tale.

Whatever you might consider the worst or best translation, they all present the same overall message without any variation to the central themes: God created a beautiful world, but its caretakers rebelled against him, plunging the world into sin and chaos. God formed a nation to be the world's light, gave it his law, and settled it in a Promised Land. From this nation he brought forth the promised Savior and Messiah, who died for all, that all might live through him and be reconciled to God the Father. He raised this Savior from the dead and exalted him to a place of glory and power, ruling all heaven. One day he will return to rule the earth. This Savior sent the Holy Spirit to earth in order to testify to this wonderful message and empower its witnesses. All who believe in him are adopted into his family and receive forgiveness and a renewed life that will outlive this planet. These and other core teachings are intact, no matter what version you are reading.

## SUMMING UP

Can you trust a Bible that has been translated a million times? Yes. Since we have a wealth of reliable manuscripts in the original languages, we are able to establish the original text to an impressive degree. What we have is essentially what Moses, Luke, James, and all the rest wrote so long ago. Also, since we are dealing with biblical languages that have been studied for centuries, rendering them into the various languages of the world is a discipline that has been incredibly fruitful. How many times it happens is irrelevant.

## GOING DEEPER

For further reading on textual criticism, I suggest you begin with an introductory book like David Allan Black, *New Testament Textual Criticism: A Concise Guide* (Grand Rapids: Baker, 1994); Black also edited a collection of essays on the topic called *Rethinking New Testament Textual Criticism* (Grand Rapids: Baker, 2002), which will be useful after you get a little more reading under your belt. A standard in the discipline should be read next: Bruce Metzger, *The Text of the New Testament: Its Transmission, Corruption, and Restoration* (Oxford: Oxford Univ. Press, 1992; updating his 1964 original).

For the Old Testament I suggest starting with Ellis R. Brotzman, *Old Testament Textual Criticism: A Practical Introduction* (Grand Rapids: Baker, 1994), which is the companion work to Black's *Concise Guide*. A valuable follow-up would be Walter Kaiser, *The Old Testament Documents: Are They Reliable and Relevant?* (Downer's Grove, IL: InterVarsity Press, 2001); see particularly the discussion about the Isaiah scroll on pages 45 – 46, 164. A new resource that handles textual issues in both Testaments is Paul D. Wegner, *A Student's Guide to Textual Criticism of the Bible: Its History, Methods and Results* (Downer's Grove, IL: InterVarsity Press, 2006). Most of these books include extensive bibliographies for more in-depth study.

For an interesting interchange of both sides see the skeptical presentation of Bart Ehrman's *Misquoting Jesus: The Story Behind Who Changed the Bible and Why* (San Francisco: Harper Collins, 2005), and the conservative response by Timothy Jones, *Misquoting Truth: A Guide to the Fallacies of Bart Ehrman's "Misquoting Jesus"* (Downer's Grove, IL: InterVarsity Press, 2007).

# Chapter 3

# THE GOSPELS AREN'T RELIABLE: TOO MANY YEARS WENT BY BEFORE THEY WERE WRITTEN

Have you ever played "Telephone"? Start with seven or eight people seated in a circle and whisper a short phrase to the person to your right. The phrase makes its way around the room, whispered quietly from person to person, until it finally comes back to you. Everyone messes it up along the way so that, by the time it reaches you again, it is all but unrecognizable. (The fun part is assigning blame to whoever messed it up the worst.) This may work well as an icebreaker, but when people point to it as the way the Gospels were put together, it's more than a problem. It's actually a myth.

Here's the way it plays out: everybody knows that the Gospels (Matthew, Mark, Luke, and John) were written down decades after the fact. Since the stories were passed down by word of mouth over such a long time, they became increasingly fantastic as the life of Jesus had more and more legends added on, not to mention placing on Jesus' lips things he never said. It is "Telephone" writ large.

There is an element of truth here; that is, decades passed before Matthew and the others put pen to paper. It is *not* true, however, that the Gospels are *therefore* unreliable. You hear this in the popular culture, but this particular myth also has the backing of some New Testament scholars. Also, we are not dealing with a *non sequitur* here (as in chapter 2) since the claim is not a *logical* problem. It is, however, an *historical* one. It assumes there were no eyewitnesses around when the Gospels were penned, so the first Christians were able to just make things up as they went along. Stories made their way around until finally being written down *with absolutely no safeguard, continuity, or a previous person in the chain having any oversight or even knowledge of what was said and finally written. Everyone else just blithely went along with the grossly distorted account about a Jesus that never existed.*

Before filling in some details, let me calmly suggest that what actually happened did not remotely resemble such a haphazard process. When we take account of some other factors, this type of reconstruction of the Gospels just doesn't fit the evidence.

## THE SPOKEN WORD

Unlike modern America, much of the ancient world greatly valued one's ability to hear, retain, and recite large quantities of spoken material. It was mostly an oral culture, and at that time, there was something known as an attention span. Disciples sat at their master's feet as he (the majority of ancient teachers were male) expounded his views. It was not at all uncommon that the teacher himself never wrote anything down; a disciple would eventually do so, but only after the teacher had passed off the scene. Socrates comes to mind here. He never wrote anything that anyone knows about. That task fell to Plato, one of his pupils, who did so after Socrates' execution.

Similarly, Jesus never wrote anything we know of (beyond some doodles in the sand), but he took three years to instill the essence of his teaching in his disciples. He taught them publicly (Matthew 7:28; Luke 5:3) and privately (Matthew 13:36; 24:3; John 13–17) — we could even venture "repeatedly" — but always by word of mouth. He sent them out in pairs to proclaim his message, "the kingdom of heaven is near" (Matthew 10:5–7).

What could the apostles use to explain this message to their fellow Israelites? Perhaps they repeated the same illustrations Jesus constantly used and painstakingly taught them. It is reasonable to assume that this teaching was a fair representation of what they spent so much focused time learning (Matthew 10:27), and it's likely that some of them took notes. When the time came for the apostles to instruct the fledgling church in the months following Jesus' crucifixion and resurrection, it is also reasonable to assume that this teaching was the essence of what Jesus spent years instilling in them (including forty days after his resurrection).

## THE SKEPTICS AMONG US

Unfortunately, there are those who deny this. In their minds, what Jesus originally taught is forever lost in the shuffle. Rather than taking the Gospels as accurate reflections of the words and deeds of Jesus, skeptical scholars begin with an assumption of doubt. These scholars maintain that all we have is a record of the musings of the early Christians—what they thought and believed, but *not what actually happened*. If we were to believe the imaginative reconstructions of these skeptics, the process of going from the events of Jesus' life to the writing of a gospel may have been something like this:

Someone named Jesus, about whom we do not and cannot know much for certain, had a short-lived ministry in Israel. He said some snappy things, gathered some followers, and was inspiring in some hard-to-define way. Apparently, he had some inflated notions about himself and somehow ran afoul of the authorities, who promptly killed him. Poor Jesus. After his death, his enterprising disciples either made up the story of his resurrection, were deluded into thinking he rose from the dead, or were really just writing pithy, poetic metaphors that ignorant people took literally.

Some skeptics assume that the Gospels are a result of prophets speaking in church services. The anonymous community, not bothering to distinguish between a prophet's message in their day and the things Jesus said years earlier, just kept collecting these sayings until someone finally wrote them down. Far less charitably, others view the early Christians as fabricating the story to fit their needs. Problems with divorce, taxes, relationships with the synagogue? Just make up a story about Jesus; put words in his mouth that address the situation and voilá, no more problem.

As long as we're making things up, why not make Jesus more wonderful with each successive telling of the story? While we're at it, why not just say he's God? (Someone will eventually have to connive with other like-minded souls to come up with the Trinity, but that's what smoke-filled rooms are for.)

### Do You See What I See?

Maybe the process went something like this, so these skeptics reason: After Jesus' death, James breaks the brooding silence by saying, "He's dead, *sigh*, but at least his words live on." Then Peter adds, "I can still hear him, just like he's still here." "I can too," John replies, "I can just see him in my mind's eye." Matthew nods pensively, but Thomas says, "I don't hear nuthin'." Suddenly Peter exclaims, "I ... I can see him; he's right there!" In the emotion of the moment, not to mention their guilt for having abandoned him, the others *see* him too.

The tortured emotions and intense longing of these followers of Jesus produced a powerful hallucination. The emotional scene makes such an impact that the story of those sad days after Jesus' death is told and retold. It isn't long before whole crowds, victims of this mass hysteria, can *see* him. Jesus is alive! In fact, he's the Lord who ascended to heaven in a cloud of glory and will return to judge the living and the dead! ("We talkin' 'bout the same Jesus?" asks Thomas.)

The problem here is that hallucinations are experienced by an individual's private perceptions and cannot be shared. But according to the New Testament, many people experienced the same thing over a forty-day period. Jesus was alive again, proving by his tangible, physical presence that he was really alive. "Mass hypnosis" theories won't fly either. Jesus appeared repeatedly, to different people in different locations, and often munched on a bit of fish. A hypnotist that could've pulled that one off would be the real wonder-worker of the first century.

## When All Else Fails, Blame the Greeks

Some claim the simple Jesus was transformed as the church spread into the Greek-speaking world. This was a world rife with stories of powerful beings and gods coming to earth, having their way with women, and producing heroes with incredible powers. The Greeks didn't have much use for *messiahs*, but had a lot of room for *lords*. Layers of mythology were slowly added to the simple carpenter's story. Jesus became an exalted Lord, a Son of God, not unlike Hercules. Why, he can even take a little bit of food and feed five thousand people with it! He can walk on water!

One recovers the original, unadorned Jesus by stripping off these layers. The Gospels must be minutely examined; anything that remotely smacks of the supernatural cannot be historical. Remove the fake stuff and reconstruct what *really* must've happened. Once this is done, the familiar carpenter-turned-sage returns.

## There Must Be an Explanation

Another aspect of this skepticism is to try to find out why the story developed in the first place. The miracles recorded in the Gospels are either outright denied (the Christians just lied) or explained away. There was no miracle involved with the feeding of the five thousand; it's just that a little boy decided to share his lunch. This touched everyone's heart, so they decided to share theirs as well—it was a miracle of sharing. Jesus didn't walk on the water; he was walking on a shallow sandbar. It just looked like water from the disciples' perspective on a dark night. (Were there sandbars halfway across the Sea of Galilee?)

Sometimes the miraculous is taken as poetic symbols for expressing religious ideas (the resurrection symbolizes human triumph over adversity). Jesus certainly did not rise from the dead. (Dead people don't do that, you see.) He never healed blind people. What he did was open our eyes to lofty truths (which I guess was something like, "be nice to mean people and pay your taxes").

The Gospels, as the skeptics say, tell us almost nothing about the actual person, ministry, and fate of Jesus of Nazareth. What they *do* tell us, and *all* that they tell us, is what first-century Christians *claimed* about Jesus. This account, passed down as it was by word of mouth for decades, transformed the humble and meek carpenter into a divine, miracle-working Son of God, the Lord of heaven and earth.

I'm left wondering why the disciples were willing to die for a man who walked on sandbars and got folks to share their snacks.

## RESPONSES TO THE SKEPTICS
### Were Peter and Paul Asleep at the Switch?

Does any of this fly? These inventions and embellishments had to have occurred in the first century (since even skeptics acknowledge that the Gospels were written by the end of the first century). Don't miss this point. These skeptics expect us to believe that, while Jesus' disciples, enemies, and countless eyewitnesses still lived, nameless people transformed the simple Jesus, meek and mild, into a miracle-working, sinless Son of God who conquered death. This was all done when there were plenty of folks around to put a quick kibosh on any Jesus fairy tales. There were just too many people around to say, "Wait a minute, Jesus didn't *say* that; he didn't *do* that, and he wasn't *like* that. I was there."

By way of analogy, we are currently around sixty years removed from the Holocaust. Also, unfortunately, there are many people today who insist it never happened and who then concoct various theories as to what *really* happened. Their theories, however, run into a bit of a snag—Holocaust survivors (not to mention volumes of physical evidence). Someone could well say, "I find your claim that the Holocaust never happened fascinating, but *I was there; I saw it with my own eyes.*" Such a theory as denying the Holocaust is rightly assigned to the nut fringe since so many eyewitnesses are around to testify to their experiences. This is the situation some would-be spinner of Jesus fairy tales would encounter in the first century.

## Why Follow *This* One?

First-century Jews would not have followed, at great personal cost and certain danger, an executed false messiah they knew to be a failure, regardless of the stories folks were making up out of whole cloth. There *were* false messiahs showing up from time to time, but their movements died with them (Acts 5:35 – 37). By way of contrast, three days after Jesus' death some women reported they had seen him alive. Though the other disciples did not believe them at first (Luke 24:10 – 11), by the next week several encounters were reported. Thomas resolved his doubts. James, Jesus' skeptical brother, and Saul, the rabid persecutor, both became staunch worshipers of the Galilean.

What on earth could have caused these first-century Jews to make such a claim about the carpenter, Jesus of Nazareth? Why insist that he fulfilled their Scriptures, performed miracles, and was the Messiah who conquered death? Why launch a movement dedicated solely to him as God's exclusive representative, insisting on spreading the message throughout increasingly hostile territory? Why die for this man who was executed in Israel as a seditious criminal?

The skeptics answer that the Jesus of the Gospels was just invented to fit the need. I guess people in those days felt the need to be persecuted.

## Let's Try This Again

As you would expect, the skeptics haven't convinced me, so let's look at this from another perspective. I propose that the following better fits the biblical evidence as well as the testimony of the early church fathers and various early historians.

The ancient Jews treasured their Scriptures, but not everyone could read. There was also a large body of teaching that was passed on by word of mouth. Rather than whispering snippets from person to person, the process was much more involved. A rabbi, having invested a lifetime in memorizing large blocks of Scripture and instruction under the watchful care of *his* rabbi, would teach his disciples *over the course of years*, making sure they were proficient at reciting it flawlessly. The sect that came to believe Jesus was the Messiah also attached great importance to their Master's teaching.

The apostles, hand-picked and intensively instructed by Rabbi Jesus, proclaimed his teaching and deeds. When the time came to fill the gap left by Judas's defection, the replacement's qualification was that he had to have been with the apostles from the time of Jesus' baptism all the way to his resurrection and return to heaven. In other words, he had to be an eyewitness to the whole saga of Jesus' life and ministry (Acts 1:21 – 22).

We are told specifically that at the beginning of the church's life, the believers in Jerusalem "devoted themselves to the apostles' teaching" (Acts 2:42), which was an oral teaching of what Jesus said and did. The churches that sprang up did so under the watchful eyes of the apostles, whose credentials were that they were eyewitnesses of the events (his ministry, death, and resurrection), and "ear witnesses," if I may coin a term, of his teaching (John 19:35; 21:24; Acts 1:4; 2 Peter 1:16 – 18; 1 John 1:1 – 5).

### Keeping a Keen Eye on Things

Skeptics are notorious for denying the Gospels were written by Matthew, Mark, Luke, or John, but the early church fathers were unanimous in affirming them. It is likely that Mark actually wrote first, providing us with a summation of the preaching of Peter (again, according to the church fathers).[3] Mark's gospel was written just before Peter's death in the mid 60s. Current scholarship maintains Matthew and Luke wrote theirs after this time (later 60s, 70s, possibly 80s), and John wrote his gospel after his exile to Patmos (sometime in the late 80s or into the 90s). In every case, the Gospels were written at the end of the lives of those who had access to first-hand testimony. They safeguarded the teaching of Jesus, faithfully passing it on to others.

As the church spread, the Christian community crossed over ethnic boundaries. Even though we must admit to local flavor and emphases, the early Christians were remarkably consistent in their core proclamation. This is so because they had such great respect for the teaching the apostles handed down to them (1 Corinthians 15:1 – 3; Hebrews 2:3; Revelation 3:3). The message they proclaimed was understood to be the powerful word of God himself (Galatians 3:5; Ephesians 1:13; 3:2 – 3; 1 Thessalonians 2:13), so there was great care taken in passing it on intact (Philippians 4:9; 2 Timothy 1:13; 2:2; 1 John 2:24).

Rival movements also developed, which made accountability and oversight all the more important. When Philip evangelized Samaria, Peter and John paid a visit to see for themselves (Acts 8:14). Paul checked with the Twelve to make sure his message was on target (Galatians 2:1 – 10). Peter visited sites where Paul ministered (1 Corinthians 1:12; Galatians 2:11), and Paul even corrected Peter when he started to slide off base (Galatians 2:11 – 14). Peter later affirmed that Paul's letters testified to the true gospel, even putting them on the same plane as the Old Testament (2 Peter 3:15 – 18).

The historical situation just will not maintain a "Telephone" theory of passing on the story of Jesus. The message we have is what the first apostles proclaimed. Before pressing on to the next chapter, however, there are some further points to consider.

## ADDITIONAL ISSUES
### Who's on First?

The New Testament at first seems to follow a chronological sequence. The four Gospels present the life of Jesus; Acts records the birth and spread of the church, giving special attention to the conversion and missionary ministry of the apostle Paul. Next is a collection of letters by apostles (mostly Paul) or associates, and finally Revelation. Now, all that is truly chronological here is that the *events* recorded in the Gospels were followed by the *events* of Acts (the letters both coinciding and postdating these events). It is the question of who *wrote* first that raises some interesting issues. It wasn't the gospel writers, as you would think. The honor and distinction actually goes to Paul.

The apostle Paul was converted in the early 30s and immediately began to proclaim Jesus as the Son of God (Acts 9:20). He wrote his first letters in the late 40s or early 50s, and continued to write until he was beheaded in Rome around the mid-to-late 60s (which we know from the early church fathers). Mark was composed around the same time. This means that most (if not all) of Paul's letters were written before any of the Gospels were.

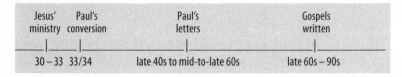

| Jesus' ministry | Paul's conversion | Paul's letters | Gospels written |
|---|---|---|---|
| 30 – 33 | 33/34 | late 40s to mid-to-late 60s | late 60s – 90s |

## Lord from the Start

Here's why this chronology is important. Paul's view of Jesus, from his earliest letters, is that of the divine exalted Lord, the risen Messiah, who is enthroned in heaven and who will return in glory. Paul's Jesus brings eternal life and rescue from sin and divine wrath. There is no merely meek and mild Jesus to be found.

Paul addressed issues as they arose. He made frequent reference to his conversion and his call to be an apostle, carefully distinguishing what he learned by revelation from Jesus (Galatians 1:11 – 12) and what he had received from other apostles (1 Corinthians 15:1 – 3). He also distinguished between what Jesus said in his earthly ministry and what Paul felt to be appropriate in light of his own situation. A good example concerns marriage and divorce. "To the married I give this command (not I, but the Lord): A wife must not separate from her husband" (7:10). He made this distinction because he was aware that Jesus had addressed the subject (later recorded in Matthew 5:31 – 32; 19:3 – 9). Then Paul adds, "To the rest I say this (I, not the Lord): If any brother has a wife who is not a believer and she is willing to live with him, he must not divorce her" (1 Corinthians 7:12). He put it this way because Jesus didn't address that particular issue, *and Paul didn't feel free to put words on Jesus' lips.* It just wasn't done.

Paul wrote from his experience as a convert enamored with his exalted Lord. He was filled with the Holy Spirit, powerfully testifying to the realities of the new covenant. He did not talk at length about Jesus' earthly ministry, *because it was not his experience; he didn't know him then.* He had enough on his plate concerning how to make Jesus intelligible to Jews and Gentiles (everyone who is not a Jew) throughout the Roman Empire, a task he pursued with incredible energy and focus.

## They Could Have Made Life Easier

One of Paul's main battles concerned Gentile converts and the Old Testament law. The big issue was circumcision, which received considerable attention (Acts 15:1 – 31; Romans 2:25 – 29; 4:9 – 11; 1 Corinthians 7:19; Galatians 2:12 – 21; 5:6; Philippians 3:3, etc.). Since the Gospels were written after much, if not all, of Paul's ministry, and if it's true, as the skeptics say, that early Christians created a Jesus to fit their needs (decades later), why is it we don't see Jesus addressing the issues that so vexed the early church? We never read about Jesus saying, "Verily, all Gentiles who confess my name will be counted as righteous apart from the law and don't need to be circumcised." The same could be said for the transition from synagogues to home churches, the relaxing of dietary laws, the shift from the traditional Sabbath (the seventh day) to "the Lord's Day" (the first), and a host of other issues that so vexed the early church. It just doesn't happen.

We also don't see a central focus on the resurrection in the Gospels as we see in Acts and Paul's letters. It is clearly predicted (Matthew 16:21; Mark 9:31), and all four Gospels end with the declaration that it had occurred. The fact remains, though, that the resurrection is not the central theme in the Gospels that it becomes in the rest of the New Testament. The Gospels focus, rather, on the earthly ministry of Jesus prior to his death and resurrection. Jesus was the Messiah proclaiming the coming of the kingdom of God, puzzling people with parables, and astounding them with miracles. If the Gospels are merely made-up stories that reflect the life of the early church, why don't the gospel narratives all revolve around the resurrection in explicit detail? The reason is simple. Paul wrote from his experience; the gospel writers wrote from theirs. They all strove to accurately portray their own time.

The gospel writers show remarkable restraint in doing precisely the opposite of what the skeptics allege. They present Jesus as they knew him prior to his suffering and death, and they are honest about their own inability to understand so much of what he said. Jesus rebukes them for simply not getting it, for being dull, even for having hearts as hard as unbelievers (Mark 7:18; 8:17). The central miracle of the Christian faith blows right past them. Jesus warns them of the coming crucifixion and the resurrection to follow (Matthew 16:21; 17:22; Mark 9:31; Luke 9:44), but they are baffled as to what he could possibly have meant (Matthew 16:22; Mark 9:10, 32; Luke 9:45). If you were making the story up, wouldn't it be better to present yourself in the best possible light?

The gospel of John is a classic case in point. When Jesus said he would raise up the temple in three days, he was not referring to the physical temple, as was thought at the time. He was predicting his resurrection (John 2:19–22). Nobody caught it then, nor did they have a clue about the rivers of living water (7:38–39), the triumphal entry (12:16), the meaning of the foot washing (13:7–9), the command for Judas to get on with it (13:27–28), or the resurrection itself (20:9). John, like the others, didn't have the freedom to simply read his own situation (and mature understanding) back into Jesus' earthly ministry. It just wasn't done.

**Layers of Legends?**

There is simply no evidence of a slow development by the apostles of seeing Jesus as purely human, then a great prophet, next a mighty miracle-worker, then a semi-divine being, and finally as a God Almighty Jesus. The first-century accounts present him as Lord and Christ at his birth (Luke 1), the Creator who came from the Father's presence (John 1; Philippians 2; Colossians 1) and who returned upon completion of his task (John 17). This is the *starting point* for any discussion of the Jesus we find in the New Testament.

## SUMMING UP

What the critics assert just doesn't fit the evidence. We *can* trust the Gospels as faithfully passing on the teaching of Jesus through his apostles. He carefully instilled his teaching in them and commissioned them to teach it to the world. As the church spread, there were safeguards in place, and great care was exerted to pass the message on to faithful people. The Gospels were all written at the end of the writers' lives, all of whom were eyewitnesses or relied on eyewitness testimony. We can safely label this little myth "Busted."

## A POSTSCRIPT OF SORTS

In the spring of 2006, we were treated to the juicy news that an ancient manuscript from an obscure Christian sect had been discovered. It is from the fourth century, written in a Coptic (Egyptian) dialect known today by only a few scholars, and it retells the gospel story in such a way as to make Judas out to be the hero! Suddenly the objection leveled at Christians that the Gospels were written decades after the fact, and are for that reason unreliable, disappears. Here's a text, centuries after the fact, that contradicts the traditional gospel story, and it is immediately embraced as the whole truth. Interesting!

Also, within weeks of this discovery, *The Da Vinci Code* movie premiered. Based on the best-selling novel, it had already stirred up a bit of controversy (and has spawned numerous spin-offs and responses). Here's a movie based on a novel that contradicts the traditional gospel story, *millennia* after the fact, and it is immediately embraced, just in time for Easter. So very interesting!

## GOING DEEPER

For further studies you may want to start with the standard introductory books, like Donald Guthrie, *New Testament Introduction*, 4th edition (Downer's Grove, IL: InterVarsity Press, 1990), or D. A. Carson and Douglas Moo, *An Introduction to the New Testament* (Grand Rapids: Zondervan, 2005). Speaking of Carson, you can read more about the way John dealt with historical issues in "Understanding Misunderstandings in the Fourth Gospel," *Tyndale Bulletin* (1982), 59–89. The classic treatment of this topic (as well as that of the previous chapter, for that matter) is F. F. Bruce, *The New Testament Documents: Are They Reliable?* (Grand Rapids: Eerdmans, 2003). A good introduction to the parables is David Wenham, *The Parables of Jesus* (Downer's Grove, IL: InterVarsity Press, 1989), or Robert Stein, *An Introduction to the Parables of Jesus* (Philadelphia: Westminster, 1981). My indebtedness to Larry Hurtado, *Lord Jesus Christ: Devotion to Jesus in Earliest Christianity* (Grand Rapids: Eerdmans, 2003) will be immediately obvious to anyone familiar with it.

Since writing this chapter a couple of books have hit the shelves that I have found immensely helpful, but I have to admit that I broke into a cold sweat when I read them. Both Timothy Paul Jones, *Misquoting Truth: A Guide to the Fallacies of Bart Ehrman's "Misquoting Jesus"* (Downers Grove, IL: InterVarsity Press, 2007), and Mark Roberts, *Can We Trust the Gospels?* (Wheaton, IL: Crossway, 2007), address issues much in the same way as I have. Ever mindful of the charge of plagiarism, especially since I joked about this in Setting the Table, I want to make sure I clear the air. We have read the same authors and hammered out our views based on traditional evangelical responses to the skeptics. It is no wonder that we have followed similar lines of reasoning and circled around the same portions of Scripture. What we have here is an instance of all of us fishing from the same pond.

# Chapter 4

# SCIENCE HAS PROVEN THAT MIRACLES DON'T HAPPEN (SO THE BIBLE IS A FAIRY TALE)

No two snowflakes are exactly alike. We can't be the only life forms in this vast universe. Science has proven miracles don't happen. These statements have one thing in common: they're put forth as scientific statements, but they are not. The first is a statistical, though unprovable supposition; the second is a value judgment; the third is a myth.

For the first statement to be true scientifically, every snowflake would have to have been examined and catalogued to demonstrate the absence of any duplicates. This would require a comprehensive sampling, from the first moment they started falling gently on the planet, through every flurry or ferocious blizzard, until the last little crystals fall in the indeterminate future. It's not that I think the statement is *false*. It's just that no one can ever *prove* that it's *true*. All that can be said is, so far, every snowflake that has been examined is a unique specimen, so it's probably correct to presume that all the rest are unique as well. It is probable, even likely,[4] but not a demonstrable fact.

The second statement may wind up being validated one day. We just don't know at this point. We may be all alone in the universe in the absence of irrefutable evidence to the contrary (apologies to the Hangar 53 believers), but who's to say what tomorrow may bring? As it stands, the statement merely expresses the *notion* that it *ought* to be the case that we're not alone. This is not science; it's philosophy.[5]

Now, on to the third—science has proven miracles don't happen. What we have here is really a flat lie. The first problem is you cannot prove a negative, but beyond that is the bigger issue of what we mean by *science*. We need to consider its Christian heritage, the popular secular rendition, and a more realistic (and humble) secular version.

## A CASE FOR CHRISTIAN ROOTS

It is a given in our culture that while science is based on facts, Christianity is based on faith, fit only for the weak and gullible. Faith is seen as a crutch for those who can't handle the facts of our existence and would rather cling to outmoded beliefs. So it may be surprising to learn that modern science likely descended from a Christian worldview. Here's the way one Christian scientist[6] puts it: "That the universe is intelligible to us is a basic assumption of science ... an assumption that stemmed in part from the Christian doctrine of creation." For Christians, "God was a God of order," so we'd expect "to see laws in the universe." Since humans are in God's image, "there was the expectation that we could understand that order." The notion that there was only one God led to the conclusion that "there would be a consistency of the laws of physics throughout the universe."[7] This, then, is a universe worth exploring.

You are not likely to hear this message on any PBS special in the near future. It goes against the grain of the popular narrative. According to *this* view of science, God created everything, so there is no inherent problem in asserting that he intervenes in our affairs from time to time, like performing a miracle or two. Stating this position is no substitute for proving it. I offer it merely as a plausible counter-explanation to the way science is usually pictured.

## NO ROOM FOR GOD

A second view of science is what I call the popular secular version. According to this outlook, science arose something like this: There was a time when people viewed the world and the starry heavens as being richly populated with various gods. These mysterious entities were held responsible for all the good things in life: health, babies, and bumper crops. They were also behind its darker aspects: sickness, famine, and every menacing bump in the night. Getting along in life was dominated with appeasing them. The Jews and Christians were no different; they just focused the conversation on God in his conflict with the Devil and his minions. Judaism and Christianity were nothing more than the natural development of religion, slowly progressing from superstition to the novel belief in one true and supreme God.

Primitive people sought solace through religion because they lacked the skills for critical thinking as well as the tools to be able to examine the reality behind their bizarre experiences. What they considered as miraculous was really just the outworking of the laws of nature. The benighted souls needed the light of reason and clarity of thought to deliver them from such superstitions.

A shift occurred in the way people viewed the world, as the story goes, in the seventeenth and eighteenth centuries, first in Europe and then in the New World. It was a time of discovery, invention, and speculation. This climate nurtured a point of view that, in the inclusive use of the word at that time, "man," not God, "was the measure of all things." The starting point for this idea was the conviction that there was no God, afterlife, miracles, heaven, or hell. All that existed was the natural order—our observable universe. People no longer needed gods or demons to explain origins or earthquakes. Apparent miracles were just that—apparent. All appeals to the supernatural realm were merely outmoded superstitions, and anyone so befuddled as to actually take the Bible at face value was simply shrouded in darkness.

This shift to highlighting rationalism and logical precision later came to be known as "the Enlightenment." Modern science was supposedly a direct result.

Science quickly earned a reputation for producing phenomenal results, instilling a notion in the collective consciousness of our culture. Not too long ago I heard something like this on the news. "Your mother always told you that chicken soup is good for a cold, but now science has shown that it's true." So, what your mama told you isn't *really* true until science says it is. This notion extends into an all-encompassing view of life: "If something cannot be proven scientifically, it isn't valid," or even, "I won't believe it until I see it."

Such statements demonstrate the close connection between science and philosophy, a line that often gets crossed without anyone noticing. The underlying philosophy is the *belief* that scientific discovery is able to account for everything in the natural realm. This is a notion, a conviction *about* science. It is not in *itself* science.

## Failing on Many Levels

There are some more problems with the statement, "If something cannot be proven scientifically, it isn't valid." First of all, it fails its own test because no one could ever scientifically demonstrate that the statement *itself* is valid.[8] Not only is it logically inconsistent, it simply does not fit the facts of life on our planet. For instance, science cannot "prove" the existence of love. One can prove that teenagers get goofy around the opposite sex, that mothers protect their young, or that couples can remain devoted to each other for a lifetime. One can describe how an old man sat at the edge of his dying wife's bed for hours on end, holding her emaciated hand in his arthritic grasp. We could describe countless actions and responses such as these, but we could never *scientifically prove* that any of this is love. Even so, only a fool would doubt that there is such a thing.

Or, obvious kidding aside, no one can prove the existence of the mind, or more specifically, of *thought*. Instruments can measure electrical activity in the physical brain, but we cannot prove the elusive and intangible category known as thought. Thinking proceeds unobserved, and there is no way to directly examine it. Only a fool would then conclude there is no such thing (even in an election year). Incidentally, anyone holding out with "we can't prove it *yet*" is simply responding in *faith* that science one day will deliver.

Our culture has enshrined this notion of science. As worthy of acclaim as it actually is on some levels, it is still ill-fitted to deal with all kinds of phenomena in our world. It just may be the case that there are realities that defy scientific explanation and are true nonetheless. Could miracles be included on the list?

You should know something about this "enlightened" view—it is not the end result of a reasoned argument with scientific proofs to back it up. It is *the starting point*. Once again, this is not science; it is philosophy.

At any rate, here's how the scientific method developed, according to the popular notion. It begins with an observation leading to a *hypothesis* that such and such is the case. By developing strict controls, experiments either rule out the hypothesis or demonstrate that it's a likely explanation based upon the available evidence. After repeating the experiment and building up a track record of results, the hypothesis progresses to the level of a *theory* that seems to best fit the evidence. As further experimentation validates the theory, corroborated by peer review, a theory can then be deemed a *fact*.

Keep in mind that, for a hypothesis to progress to the level of fact, you have to be able to present the evidence in such a way that it can be verified through repetitive testing. Results need to be confirmed by peers within the scientific community. In science, people are not taken at their word; what counts are the repeatable results of carefully crafted experiments.

### Where's the Proof?

When people say science has disproved miracles, all we really have before us is an unexamined assertion. There is no proof offered. If science has debunked miracles, then who performed the experiment demonstrating such a conclusion? What was the exact nature of the experiment? When and where was it carried out, and under what conditions, controls, and variables? In which scientific journal was this experiment recorded, and who performed the peer review to validate the claims? Where is the literature interacting with this experiment? Others should be able to gather the data, perform the experiment, and, assuming its validity, receive the same results.

The problem here is that there is no such proof. There has been no experiment; there are no results. All we have is a philosophical statement about how naturalists view the universe, a baseless assertion people often hear and accept uncritically. In other words, it's accepted on the basis of *a leap of faith.* Some may chafe at such a conclusion and say the impossibility of miracles is simply a given in this modern age. *This is the age of science, so we don't need God; therefore, miracles don't happen.* With such a statement, we've simply circled back to the philosophical starting point. It is still nothing more than an unexamined and unprovable assumption.

*This* view of science makes a claim it can't back up. It fails by its own standards. The next one we'll look at is a more realistic and nuanced view of science.

## SCIENCE WITH HUMILITY

The third view of science brings a little more realism into the discussion with a frank recognition of its own limitations. The humility I refer to here is the direct result of discoveries over the past decades, casting the conversation in a different hue.[9]

The popular version of science is driven by the outmoded notions that held sway in the nineteenth century, that of a mechanistic and deterministic universe. The universe was compared to a clock; it was static (unchanging) and predictable, and would conform to mathematically precise description. It was also seen as eternal.

The twentieth century witnessed several advances, particularly in physics. We now know the universe is expanding, so it's neither static nor infinite. The galaxies are moving away from each other and accelerating, which led some scientists to theorize about the point of its beginning. If this is all accurate, that we exist in a universe that began (with a bang?) and has been expanding ever since, then our universe has borders. What is on the outside? What are we expanding into? How can we even conceive of the edge of space? These are unanswerable questions by our current knowledge.

At the other end of the spectrum is the fascinating world of quantum physics. Matter at this subatomic level behaves in ways that defy description for those unfamiliar with the discipline. (Since this includes me, I'll just make a few brief comments and move along.) In our everyday experience we can easily determine where something is and, if it's in motion, how fast it's moving. I can see a baseball on the ground, so I know where it is. I toss it to a rookie pitcher, and he throws his best fastball, which according to the radar unit, clocks in at 90 mph. Not bad for a rookie. There it is; there it goes; here's how fast.

Old notions of the universe would lead us to believe it would be the same at the level of the atom and its smaller components. It's not. At the subatomic level, you can talk about the position of a particle, or its speed, but you can't precisely determine both. The reason for this is that any means of observation directly affects, indeed, *changes* the particle's position or velocity. This is known as the Uncertainty Principle.[10] It was the rejection of this principle that elicited Einstein's famous comment, "God does not play dice."

So, on the one hand, we live within a universe that is rapidly expanding, the borders of which defy our ability to describe or even imagine. I'm not suggesting that God is on the other side with a catcher's mitt. On the other hand, we have the incomprehensively tiny world of quantum physics, which refuses to behave in any predictable manner. The very building blocks of the universe yield far more puzzles than answers, but I'm not suggesting that God is hiding out behind a quantum particle. What I am suggesting is that our ability to comprehend and accurately describe the natural world has serious limits, which honest scientists readily acknowledge. We are finite creatures with finite minds living within a finite bandwidth.[11] Should we be surprised if elements of the supernatural world elude us?

Compared to the popular version of science, Stephen Hawking has a different take on theories and facts. "Any physical theory is always provisional, in the sense that it is only a hypothesis: you can never prove it." The problem is that it doesn't matter how many times experiments agree with a theory; "you can never be sure that the next time the result will not contradict the theory." Yet, "you can disprove a theory by finding even a single observation which disagrees with the predictions of the theory."[12] The universe is a puzzling place in which God, though he's likely not throwing dice, "still has a few tricks up his sleeve."[13]

Honest scientists cannot say that miracles do not happen; they can only say they haven't witnessed any. Who knows what tomorrow may bring?

## IS THAT ALL THERE IS?

Science is the means by which the physical universe is explored and explained. Its tools are designed to measure, quantify, identify, and investigate the natural realm. As such, it has nothing to say about any *super*natural realm. It really can't say anything about a realm of existence beyond the physical universe because it lacks the tools to investigate that.

This is the great irony of the science versus God and miracles debate. How can scientists say *anything* about a realm they cannot examine? How can they so confidently proclaim God doesn't perform miracles if their tools aren't designed to go beyond this universe or perceive any spiritual intervention within it? So when scientists do aim their tools at the physical universe, which are specifically and exclusively designed to explore the physical universe, are you terribly shocked that the physical universe is all they find?

## SOME PERSISTENT OBJECTIONS

"If I were God I'd leave some real proof." This seems to make sense, but the truth is it only reveals the darkness of our human souls. It is a demand for God to meet *our* standards and perform *for us*, immediately, if not sooner. The Lord Jesus heard this many times, but he refused to perform when challenged (Matthew 12:38 – 39; John 6:30). He encountered this attitude in his hometown, so "he did not do many miracles there because of their lack of faith" (Matthew 13:57 – 58). When Jesus was on trial, he endured a little side trip to Herod's court. Herod was thrilled, waiting for Jesus to perform a miracle or two. The Galilean stood silent (Luke 23:8 – 9).

As it was in the days of Jesus, so it is today. A lack of faith is not rewarded with displays of God's wonder. God is not going to stoop to performing magic tricks for a country doing its best to banish him from the public square. It's a miracle this country is even still here.

Others object: "Miracles happened all the time in the Bible, but they don't happen in our day," implying the writers just made them up. It's often missed, however, that miracles were emphatically *not* an everyday occurrence in the Bible; they tended to occur at key points as God unveiled his plan of redemption. Miracles showed that God was, once again, intervening in earthly affairs. Times like Israel's exodus from Egypt (Exodus 1 – 12), the conquest of Canaan (Joshua), or the ministries of Elijah and Elisha (1 Kings 17:1 – 2 Kings 13:21) were all times of great demonstrations of God's power. The ministry of Jesus was a profound example of this, to say the least. But there were times of drought when God wasn't doing much of anything that anyone could tell.

The nation of Israel languished in slavery for centuries before God showed up (Genesis 15:13; Exodus 3:7). The angel of the Lord greeted Gideon by saying, "The LORD is with you." Gideon replied, "If the LORD is with us, why has all this happened to us? Where are all his wonders that our fathers told us about?" (Judges 6:12 – 13). God was about to move, but only after a long stretch of divine inactivity. The prophet Habakkuk cried out to God to do the things he had heard about, but had never seen (Habakkuk 3:2). The turbulent time between the Testaments saw scattered interventions (the miracle of Hanukkah comes to mind; see *Shabbat* 21b in the Babylonian Talmud), but God seemingly just let things run their course. The period is known as the "Silent Years," not because nothing much happened, but because the prophets were silent and God was so aloof. In the same way, church history is replete with revivals, but is also full of long stretches of dismal dry spells.

Something else to keep in mind is that when God did something incredible in one corner of Israel, it didn't mean things were happening everywhere. Many events, in fact, occurred in rural areas or small towns or were of a totally private nature (1 Kings 17:9–16). The plains of Bethlehem thundered with the praise of angels (Luke 2:14), but all was quiet in Jerusalem. The localized nature of miracles explains why revivals tend to be known by their locations (like the Welsh revival of 1904). God may have been rocking Wales, but he wasn't making a peep in the Hebrides. If you hear about some incredible things happening in Asia or Africa, don't worry if nothing much is happening in your neck of the woods. God gets to select the what, when, and where of performing miracles.

## THE ROLE OF MIRACLES IN THE BIBLE

The ancient world was full of magical rites and reports of astounding feats, so the miracles of the Bible get lumped in the same category. However, one glaring difference is that ancient magic usually involved elaborate rituals and incantations, the purpose of which was to implore unseen powers to provide aid or protection, or to bring down a curse on one's enemies. The wonders performed were, for lack of a better term, for selfish reasons. The miracles of the Bible always had a central point: forsake error and turn to the living God. In other words, there was always a moral component, directing one's attention away from the self and false gods to focus on the one true

God behind the wonder. Let's look at two examples, the exodus narrative and the ministry of Jesus.

### So, Ya Wanna Worship Flies and Frogs...

The narrative about the Ten Plagues (Exodus 5 – 12) is known as a "polemic," an attack on an opposing view. In this case, it was the false gods of Egypt. When Moses confronted Pharaoh with the command "Let my people go," it was prefaced with "This is what the LORD, the God of Israel, says" (5:1). Pharaoh himself was considered a god, the son of Ra, the sun god. He responded in the next verse, "Who is the LORD, that I should obey him and let Israel go? I do not know the LORD" (which was his first mistake) "and I will not let Israel go" (which was his last).

Not only was Pharaoh a "god," but so was the Nile, frogs, various bugs, and so on. Each of the Ten Plagues targeted one of them. It's as if God said, "So the Nile is your god? Let's see what happens when I turn it to blood." *Whack.* "Frog gods strike your fancy?" The place was suddenly hopping with them, which soon died, leaving piles of bloated amphibian carcasses turning rancid in the Egyptian sunshine. The stench alone must've been a treat.

"You want to worship the sun?" *Whack.* The land was overcome with a deep darkness, a darkness that could be "felt" (Exodus 10:21). The final blow was against all the firstborn of the land, including the heir to the kingdom in Pharaoh's household. They all died in one night.

The plagues were miraculous events, but their purpose was not so Moses could outdo the court magicians. They were to demonstrate to all interested parties that the Lord, Yahweh, was God. All of the miraculous acts of deliverance (the splitting of the sea), provision (manna), and guidance (the pillar of smoke and fire) that followed the exodus were for the same purpose.

By the way, as this episode demonstrates, miraculous interventions can take on a negative quality for some of the parties involved.

Unbelievers demanding a sign from God should be thankful for the times he withholds one.

## Should We Be Looking for Another?

When John the Baptist first identified Jesus as the promised one, John enthusiastically pointed Israel in his direction. John recognized Jesus as the agent of God for the end time (Matthew 3:11–12), to whom God had granted an unlimited endowment of the Holy Spirit and power (John 3:34). This conviction gripped his heart until the day he found himself languishing in Herod's prison, facing a dim prospect for the future. It was in that dark period that he sent messengers to Jesus to make sure he had pointed out the right one! "Are you the one who was to come, or should we expect someone else?" (Matthew 11:3). John was likely looking for a conqueror and judge, but Jesus was preaching love and mercy *for Israel's enemies*. With Herod seeming to have the upper hand, doubts were setting in. The response was vintage Jesus:

> Go back and report to John what you hear and see: The blind receive sight, the lame walk, those who have leprosy are cured, the deaf hear, the dead are raised, and the good news is preached to the poor. Blessed is the man who does not fall away on account of me. (Matthew 11:4–6)

This response is more than a summary of Jesus' miraculous ministry. It is a compact drawing together of several strands from Isaiah's prophecy about the day when God would restore the fortune of his people (Isaiah 29:18, 19; 35:5; 42:7, 18; 61:1). It's as if Jesus told John, "Don't fall away, my friend. I'm doing the works of God in the midst of his people, just as he promised so long ago." The miracles of Jesus attested his claim to be the Messiah.

The crowning miracle of Jesus was the resurrection. Whenever I am discussing the subject of miracles with a skeptic, I first try to acknowledge the difficulty people have believing in such things.

But rather than spending a lot of time and energy on the sun standing still (Joshua 10:12–13) or an axhead floating (2 Kings 6:5–6), I bring up an empty tomb on the outskirts of old Jerusalem. This brings us quickly to the heart of the issue. That miracle is the sole reason for Christianity in the first place.

## SUMMING UP

None of these explanations is likely to persuade a diehard skeptic, but people on the receiving end of a miracle have no doubts whatsoever that God still performs them. I've had my share, and I've heard the testimonies of others through the years who have witnessed them. Skeptics are certainly within their rights to withhold judgment until they directly witness one. If a skeptic did witness some extraordinary event, it is by all means appropriate to use the tools of science to ascertain some of the facts surrounding it. (Was she really sick prior to being prayed for? Is she really cured now without any medical reason for it? Are there any before and after medical records and test results?) My guess, though, is that doubts would linger.

Miracles are special occurrences by definition. We shouldn't be surprised if we don't see them everywhere, every day. The reason we don't may be the same reason they didn't constantly happen even in the biblical narratives—a pervasive lack of faith.

My goal here has not been to prove miracles exist, but to dispel the myth about the role of science in the discussion. The skeptic can still say: "I don't believe in miracles." What can't be said with any credibility is that science has proven they don't exist.

## GOING DEEPER

A good case for the credibility of Jesus' miracles can be found at www.4truth.net/site/c.hiKXLbPNLrF/b.2902069/k.2CD7/The_Credibility_of_Jesus_Miracles.htm. For more on multiple attestation see www.christianorigins.com/miracles.html and the sources listed there. A good overview of magic in the ancient world may be found at www.st-andrews.ac.uk/~www_sd/magic.html. For a quick reference concerning the targets of the Ten Plague polemic see www.bible-exposition.org/Ten%20Plagues.htm. Extrabiblical sources concerning Jesus' miracles can be found at www.freerepublic.com/focus/f-religion/1304954/posts. Special thanks are in order for John Spears and Jim Runyon for their helpful feedback on early drafts of this chapter.

# Chapter 5

# POWERFUL POLITICAL AND CHURCH LEADERS CHOSE WHICH BOOKS TO INCLUDE IN THE BIBLE

This chapter deals with a myth about the "canon" of Scripture. A canon, in this context, refers to a "rule" or "standard." In biblical studies, it refers to the books that form our Old and New Testaments. Settling on this list was, in fact, a long process with several disagreements, some lasting to this day.[14] Contrary to popular myth, the process was not the result of a nefarious cabal in a dimly-lit, smoke-filled lodge. Usually the culprit is an emperor, some nameless pope, or, as one current scholar maintains, one brand of Christianity just muscling out the competition.[15]

The upshot is always the same: somewhere along the way, powerful people chose which books to include in the Bible for their own political reasons. In the worst version of this myth, a selection committee in the fourth century, led by Constantine, *invented* a new and improved Jesus in the process. The merely human king of the Jews was transformed into the divine Son of God. This is a view taken by Dan Brown in his novel *The Da Vinci Code*.[16] These theories (and many more like them) make the same basic point: the Jesus of the New Testament is a fabrication, nothing more, nothing less.

## HERE ARE THE PROBLEMS
### Facts Need to Be Denied

For this myth to work we have to deny some facts that even skeptical scholars affirm—all of the New Testament documents were written in the first century and were widely circulated by the fourth. Of course, Constantine could still have attempted to gather everything together for his grand rework. He could have ordered that his version replace all the others and made sure the competition was destroyed. New, divine Jesus in; old, merely human Jesus out. With everything safely replaced, the church could have gone its merry way with its made-up prophecies and stories about a wonder worker who rose from the dead. But such an attempt could never have succeeded.

Keep in mind an important point from chapter 2 — by the time anyone held enough sway over the affairs of the church to monkey with the New Testament, hundreds of Greek manuscripts, not to mention Latin, Syriac, Coptic, and Ethiopic versions, were being used in weekly services throughout the Roman Empire. They were read and cherished, stored and copied. Older, worn-out manuscripts were already buried in the hot Egyptian sands (only to be discovered in the 1800s). The fourth century was way too late to try to doctor up the text and make Jesus into someone or something he wasn't.

In our day, on the heels of centuries of discoveries of manuscripts dating to the second and third centuries AD, Constantine's supposedly new and improved Jesus would exist side-by-side with the so-called *original* Jesus. Where are all the writings that tell us all about this Jesus, meek and mild, the one who did no miracles and was nothing more than a nice man from Nazareth? The astute student of Christianity could reply by calling attention to the existence of fragmentary gospels and selected references in the church fathers that do, in fact, present a purely human Jesus (*The Gospel of the Nazareans, The Gospel of the Ebionites*, etc.). More on them in a moment, but discussions about rival gospels miss the point. My question is this: where are the so-called *original* manuscripts of Matthew, Mark, Luke, and John that display no knowledge of a supernatural Jesus?

*All* New Testament manuscripts, faithfully representing the first-century documents of the early church, present the same Jesus. He is always Christ, the Lord; he is always presupposed as the divine

Son of God who proclaimed God's kingdom, who died for our sins and rose again. Even the oldest manuscripts give us a Jesus who is worthy of our devotion, with no rival in sight.

Remember also that Constantine would have had to gather up and rework the Old Testament as well. But by the fourth century, the Dead Sea Scrolls had been buried in caves for around four hundred years. The scrolls of the desert community from around the first century BC (and into the Christian era) reveal the same God and aspirations for the Messiah as do our modern English translations.[17] Any theories that the Old Testament was doctored up in the fourth century with phony prophecies foretelling a phony Messiah are forever put to rest. Someone needs to tell the skeptics.

**Other Troublemakers**

In addition to this, Constantine would've had to track down all of the writings and sources that reported what Christian beliefs were. He would've needed to collect everything actively written against them, including the Gnostic literature of the second century (see below). There is also the issue of the church fathers, who were at pains to describe Christianity accurately to demonstrate why following Jesus posed no threat to the empire. They quoted the New Testament writings so extensively that even if all of the manuscripts were suddenly to disappear, the New Testament (and much of the Old Testament) could be virtually reconstructed from their writings. Assuming Constantine could even find these sources, he would also have to change them — *all* of them.

Well, let's grant the point. Constantine pulled it off and all previous gospels and pertinent literature were successfully replaced, never to be recovered, not even a scrap. The churches were instructed to begin worshiping Jesus as the Son of God, someone they knew to be nothing more than a nice man, a wise teacher, perhaps even a king. That just raises another question about this choice of religious leader.

## Why Jesus?

Let's assume Constantine released his list of approved Scriptures with a transformed Jesus and the empire accepted it all with a shrug of the shoulders. Let alone the extreme improbability of that even happening, why were they following Jesus to begin with? What made him so "bloomin' attractive"?[18] The Dan Brown version of this myth even assumes the existence of the church, replete with a leadership and faithful followers. Why this organized following for the nice man from Nazareth? What does a Jewish carpenter turned rabbi have to say to the Gentile world in the first three centuries? It is puzzling what attraction he would have in a Gentile empire as a mere, humble human. That the masses would suddenly shift to *worshiping* him as a god is, frankly, bizarre.

Keep in mind, as the myth goes, it isn't that Constantine commanded it and the people begrudgingly acquiesced. No, the people were just jazzed with this brand new belief about Jesus and accepted it wholeheartedly, a belief that survives to our day.

Also keep in mind that if this reconstruction is true, then another theory (myth?) of the rise of Christianity suddenly disappears — the notion that the teaching about Jesus developed very slowly as the church pushed on into the Greek-speaking world, with layers of legends increasingly transforming the simple carpenter into a glorious Lord. The critics need to make up their minds on this one. Was Christianity a slow development of legends (as skeptical scholars maintain), or was it the sudden innovation of power-hungry elites (as in this popular myth)? One can't have it both ways, can one?

## WHAT ABOUT BART?

I hope you can begin to sense that this version could not have happened. It is utter nonsense. A more sophisticated approach was recently put forth by Bart Ehrman, an agnostic biblical scholar. Does his view fare any better?[19]

Ehrman points out that modern Christianity has several competing expressions. That is certainly true, as you consider everything from formal liturgical services to folksy sermons in a rented storefront. Ehrman also adds groups like Jehovah Witnesses to the list. His point in so doing is that even though many would deny a group such as this as being genuinely Christian, the Jehovah Witnesses themselves certainly claim to be. No one, then, can claim to hold the truth to the exclusion of others. What's more, all of these views are just variations of a made-up belief system. He then presses the point that it has always been so, back to the very beginning.

Just who was this Jesus of Nazareth?

- Some people in the ancient world thought he was genuinely human and nothing more (the "Ebionites," an early Jewish-Christian sect).
- Others affirmed his humanity, but then said that he was adopted as God's Son at his baptism, given special powers, and absorbed into the Godhead after the resurrection ("Adoptionists").
- Still others claimed he was genuinely God and as such wasn't really human at all; he only *seemed* to be human ("Docetists," from the Greek, *dokei*, "he seems").
- A related group viewed all physical matter as inherently evil; salvation came by attaining to the secret knowledge of our own divinity, releasing the spark of the divine in all of us. Jesus is the path to that knowledge of salvation (hence, they're known as "Gnostics," from the Greek word for "knowledge," *gnosis*).

These are just a sampling; there were, in fact, all kinds of variations. One odd little group even said Jesus was God in the flesh, Lord and Christ at his birth, whose death and resurrection formed the center of their preaching.

I call this last group "historic Christianity." Ehrman denies any such category, preferring instead to call them "proto-orthodox." By this he means they held to beliefs similar to what *became* "orthodoxy" ("right beliefs") around the fourth century. This group gained the upper hand over all the others due to political maneuvering and shrewd marketing. According to Ehrman, they were adept at navigating the several currents of thought concerning Jesus. They affirmed the purely human Jesus found in the gospel of Matthew *and* the purely divine Jesus of the gospel of John, which, in effect, incorporated two opposing views (Ebionites and Gnostics, respectively).

Ehrman, however, is ignoring the other side of the coin. Matthew's Jesus is certainly human, but Ehrman ignores his divine origin and virgin birth (Matthew 1:18–21; 2:1–6), the fact that his title is "God with us" (1:22–23), and that he assumes divine prerogatives, like forgiving sins (9:2–6) or being worshiped (14:33; 28:17). John is unsurpassed in his vision of Jesus' divine glory, but does Ehrman forget the Divine One "became flesh" (John 1:14), grew weary and thirsty, as we humans are prone to do (4:6–7), and died a brutal death (19:1–30)? Even granting certain groups favored one gospel over another, both Matthew *and* John were, in fact, early favorites throughout the empire.

However the proto-orthodox faction managed to stay ahead of the game, it took the likes of Constantine and powerful church leaders to turn the tide and finally make it official. Yes, we're back to our friends, but they weren't tasked with inventing a new religion and Scriptures, as Mr. Brown would have us believe. Ehrman presents them as a selection committee, giving the yea or nay on the volumes of competing writings that had been circulating for centuries. These sources differed only in terms of who Jesus was and what he did. None of them had any bearing on actual events, none of them true in any sense of the word—just religious beliefs with no bearing on reality.

In order to assess this view, we need to consider some other pieces of the puzzle. What we'll find is that even though Ehrman's reconstruction seems more plausible than Brown's, the historical record just will not support it. Also, we're still left with an unanswered question even in Ehrman's view. With all the bewildering interpretations of who Jesus was (all, half, or not human at all), why were people grappling with his identity in the first place? Why get so worked up over the nice man from Nazareth?

What we find is that powers beyond the earth *did* have a hand in the development of the canon. The testimony of the risen Son of God is the key.

## THE TEACHING BEFORE THE TESTAMENT

The development of the canon is a detailed, centuries-long process that defies easy description in the short space available. So, I'll limit myself to a sketch of some of the more important milestones along the way and elaborate some key points.

The most important thing to realize is that, before there was a New *Testament*, there was a new *covenant*. By this I mean that a group of people came to believe the ancient promises of God's renewal (Ezekiel 36:24 – 28) and the promise of a new covenant (Jeremiah 31:31 – 34) had occurred in the death and resurrection of Jesus. He stood as the fulfillment of all the hopes of ancient Israel, a conviction that dawned slowly through his ministry, found specific expression in the Last Supper, and was sealed by the powerful presence of the Holy Spirit. Before ink met papyrus, the disciples' entire way of thinking and believing had been radically changed by this encounter. They clung to deeply-held convictions and core doctrines. Theirs was a theology of the new covenant, with Jesus as the focal point. It's what they preached; it's what they lived.

The only Bible the early church had was what we call the Old Testament, interpreted thoroughly in light of Jesus. These Scriptures provided the context, language, worldview, and validation for their new convictions. When the apostles did begin to write, the new covenant writings were deeply and richly interwoven with Old Testament quotes and allusions. Deuteronomy, the Psalms, Isaiah, and Daniel were early favorites, with select passages coming to enjoy a certain prominence (like Psalm 2; 8; 22; and 110; or Isaiah 53 and 61). By doing this, they testified to the world that they still embraced the ancient Scriptures, though seen in a new light.[20]

Through the course of time as the church branched out into the Gentile world, rival views about God and Jesus surfaced. Ehrman would have us believe rival claims coexisted from the beginning, with a bewildering array of portraits of Jesus each competing for attention. Not so. Within the borders of Israel there were two main factions: those who saw Jesus as merely human and those who said he was the divine Son, God in the flesh. Both sides affirmed his humanity *because they knew he was born, lived, and died on native soil*. The group that affirmed his humanity *and divinity* did so as a response to God's self-disclosure. These were the apostles and the wider circle of Jesus' disciples.

## Handed Down, Not Made Up

The rival groups that denied Jesus' full humanity arose decades after the resurrection, all on foreign soil. Some enjoyed a local following, while others gained wider recognition, but they all bore the stamp of having sprung from paganism. The views were foreign to the Jewish followers of Jesus and the next generation of believers taught by those followers. The Christians had no room for these competing ideas, not because such views didn't agree with their version, cramped their style, or threatened their political standing, but because they were not true. They received their message from Jesus' apostles, those who had lived through the incredible, unforgettable drama.

The testimony about Jesus, initially delivered and guarded by the apostles, was carefully preserved. That is why the biblical writers used technical terms for passing on an oral tradition, whether translated as "passed on" (1 Corinthians 11:2), "handed down" (Luke 1:1–2), or "entrusted" (Jude 3). In 1 Corinthians 11:23 and 15:3,

Paul clearly distinguishes that which he "received" from the Lord and what he "received" from the apostles. In both cases he "passed on" this teaching. The New Testament writings are the end product of the process.

This is also why the church fathers referred to that which was "handed down" as the only message worthy of following in the churches. Two of the apostolic fathers, in fact, may have been disciples of the original apostles: Clement of Rome (possibly a disciple of Peter) and Polycarp (definitely a disciple of John). This eyewitness testimony formed the core of the early church's faith; it was the foundation on which they stood.

## Marcion's Muddle

The process of defining a canon was likely set in motion when a man named Marcion left Asia Minor (modern-day Turkey) and showed up in Rome about the middle of the second century. He had some novel ideas about the God of the Old Testament, whom he viewed as inferior to Jesus, and drew up a list of books he viewed as authoritative. Essentially, he rejected the whole Old Testament, accepted only a severely shortened version of Luke, and only ten of Paul's letters (also severely edited). His is the first known attempt at a canon of the New Testament. The response to it (and to him) likely set the ball rolling for further developments.

It should not be missed, however, that Marcion's shortened list, and the negative reactions to it, presupposed the existence of other books already in wide circulation (like the Gospels and Paul's letters). Also, he didn't advance any Scriptures of his own, but sought to make his point from within the core of books already in wide circulation. Marcion's attempt to gain a hearing by trying to piggyback on the sacred writings failed.

The church in Rome rejected him because his views weren't in line with the testimony they'd already received. One man's views surfacing eighty or ninety years after Jesus' ministry, which contradicted every major doctrine passed down through the apostles, could not overthrow their testimony.

## Rising to the Challenge

That the formation of the church's canon was reactive should not surprise us. In the same way that much of the New Testament was written specifically to counter error creeping into the community of believers, rival claims spurred the church to clarify which books were authoritative.

It wasn't that the early church fathers had any church-wide power; they clearly didn't. Rome's prominence was still in the future. The fathers were elders ("bishops") over their respective areas, but had no real say in the affairs of other areas. What they had to say to churches outside of their sphere of influence came by way of exhortation and appeals to live according to the Lord and his gospel. That, you see, is the rub. What is the true gospel from the Lord? By the second century, the rivals began to appear prompting the church to clarify this very question.

The second-century fathers did not respond to the rival groups with a closed canon (a set list of approved books); they responded instead with a "canon of truth."[21] Here are the determining questions. Did a given book or belief conform to the gospel as it was passed down from the first century? Also, was it penned by an apostle (or associate), and did it come from their era?

Contrary to the popular image, the church fathers were not a governing body seeking to *confer* a given book's authority; they sought to *recognize* it. They tried to discern the presence and authority of the Son of God revealed in the books handed down to them, and they came to remarkably consistent conclusions with only minor variations.

## Some Other Factors

Such a quality of authority may have been in play in the churches' response to the emperor Diocletian. In the early fourth century, just before Constantine's rise to power, Diocletian issued an edict demanding that the entire empire return to ancient Roman paganism. Christians were ordered to hand over their religious literature so it could be burned or face the flames themselves (or worse). In the face of such a threat, it really came down to a simple question: What am I willing to risk death for, and what can I hand over with nary a qualm? Picture a young Christian grappling with keeping either Matthew or *The Apocalypse of Peter*. If this were the situation today, it would be like our wrestling over parting with a gospel or a volume of *Left Behind*.

When Constantine managed to consolidate his power and set up shop in the East, he issued an edict putting a stop to the persecution of Christians; he then issued an edict making Christianity the state religion. Contrary to the several versions of myths surrounding this emperor, he didn't have a say in the selection of a canon. What he *did* do was commission Eusebius, bishop of Caesarea, to supply fifty sets of Scriptures for his new capital, Constantinople. Constantine was trying to bring stability to an empire in chaos. It is likely that Eusebius's selection, combined with Constantine's official backing, assisted in standardizing the canon. Still, disagreements persist.

**Early Favorites**

It is not often recognized in evangelical circles that the formation of the canon has yet to yield 100 percent agreement across the entire Christian world. That might seem a little unsettling to some, but it demonstrates an important point: there *never* has been a governing authority powerful enough and widespread enough to make the entire Christian world toe the line on its canon. That said, it only makes it all the more amazing when we see how much agreement there actually is.

First to be recognized as authoritative, forming the core of the New Testament canon, were the four Gospels (Matthew, Mark, Luke, and John), the book of Acts, Paul's letters (all thirteen, from

Romans to Philemon), 1 Peter, and 1 John. These were never in dispute. Think for a moment about the picture of God, the way of salvation, and the instructions for holy living that emerge from these writings. These form the backbone of the church, both in terms of beliefs and practice. If this were all we had, the gospel message would remain intact, but there's more.

The books that took the longest to achieve widespread acceptance were Hebrews, James, 2 Peter, 2 John, 3 John, Jude, and Revelation. They were disputed in some areas and accepted in others. The problems they faced were questions about authorship or origin (Hebrews and 2 Peter); some were questioned because they seemed to oppose Paul (James). Though some churches still do not accept many of them (the Syrian church disputes 2 Peter, 2 John, 3 John, Jude, and Revelation), their inherent quality of authority was the determining factor for including them in the vast majority of the Christian world.

Think again about the picture of God, the way of salvation, and the instructions for holy living these writings contain. Do they in any way contradict the gospel message as seen in the core books? There is tension, to be sure (such as one finds comparing James with Romans), but their message reinforces the central themes as seen in the core. If we didn't have these books, our knowledge of God would suffer loss (especially if we had to part with Hebrews), but we could still get by.

Other books, such as *The Didache, 1 Clement,* or *The Wisdom of Solomon,* were included in the canon in some areas simply because they were teaching the same gospel as the core (though there were some oddities here and there). The church never reached any consensus on these books, again, because of questions of origin and authorship. Some were just too recent to make the list. Still, they were at least universally regarded as valuable reading. Why? Because the God they presented and the Jesus they proclaimed were the same as in the Scriptures.

## A Clear Contrast

Contrast this to a set of books from the second century and beyond: the Gnostic Gospels and letters. These include works such as *The Gospel of Thomas* (although the earliest Greek manuscripts of this work may not reflect the same tendencies as later Coptic texts), *The Gospel of Peter*, *The Gospel of Philip*, and many others. They all present a Jesus and a gospel message distinctly different from that of the core books. The church fathers never recommended these rivals, never cited them favorably, and never included them in any bound manuscripts. Why? They depicted a different God, Jesus, and gospel message. These gospels depict Jesus revealing secrets to his disciples that bear no historical resemblance to the events that occurred under Pontius Pilate's reign. They line up very well with ancient Eastern mysticism and pagan philosophy, but not with the message that was handed down. *That's why they were rejected.*

It is a fact, historically speaking, that all of the New Testament documents that were finally acknowledged as deriving from the apostles retain the essential connection to the Old Testament and intertestamental Judaism. These are the ones accepted into the canon because they present a Jesus like the one encountered in the church's proclamation, the Jewish Messiah who was the Savior of the world. Contrary to the protests of the skeptics, there was a clear and unbroken chain of tradition that passed from the preaching of Jesus, to the preaching of his apostles, to the final product of Gospels and letters from their hands.

These are the titles of the documents that emerged from that era: the Muratorian Canon (mid-second century AD), Eusebius's *Ecclesiastical History* (early fourth century AD), and Athanasius's famed *Festal Letter* (AD 367). The last of these was the first time that an ancient canon spelled out exactly the now familiar twenty-seven books that comprise the New Testament. Further councils and controversies served only to solidify the now centuries-old conviction. These are the books through which the Spirit of God speaks.

## SUMMING UP

Well before the fourth century even dawned, the core of New Testament writings enjoyed unquestioned and widespread acceptance as the testimony of Jesus and his apostles. The books that did struggle for recognition ultimately found acceptance in the vast majority of the Christian world because of their agreement with the core, as well as their inherent authority. All of this was done apart from any one governing body, whether an emperor, a pope, or shady church curmudgeons. It was simply a matter of the church tuning her ear to heaven.

## GOING DEEPER

My comments on the development of the canon follow the discussion in D. A. Carson and Douglas Moo's "The New Testament Canon," in *An Introduction to the New Testament* (Grand Rapids: Zondervan, 2005), 726–42, and the article on "Canon" in *DLNT*, 134–44 (see *Abbreviations* for full bibliographic info). For a thought-provoking summary of the rise of the canon and the weaknesses of (some) current evangelical reconstructions see www.bible.org/page.php?page_id=689. Handy summaries on the early church fathers can be found at www.britannica.com/bps/topic/30282/Apostolic-Father, and www.ritchies.net/p1wk3.htm.

For a quick reference guide to the distortions in the *Da Vinci Code*, check out Darrell Bock, *Breaking the Da Vinci Code* (Nashville: Nelson, 2006), or Lee Strobel, *Exploring the Da Vinci Code: Investigating the Issues Raised by the Book and Movie* (Grand Rapids: Zondervan, 2006), or go to rense.com/general71/davincicode.pdf. An interesting refutation from a Jewish perspective that Jesus is mentioned at all in the Talmud (and thus may be an entirely mythical figure) can be found at www.angelfire.com/mt/talmud/jesusnarr.html. (Does that mean I should stop writing?) A site after my own heart, which takes on the myths about the Council of Nicea in glorious myth-busting fashion, is www.tertullian.org/rpearse/nicaea.html.

# MYTHS ABOUT JESUS

# Chapter 6

# JESUS WAS JUST ANOTHER GURU WHO LEARNED HIS MAGIC ARTS IN INDIA

One of the trends in our current culture is the attempt to downgrade Jesus to manageable levels. After all, an exalted Lord who knows the *real me* and demands I surrender and follow his godly ways can be a little intimidating. It is easier to rule out all supernatural elements from the outset and regard Christianity as nothing more than one (mistaken) branch of the natural development of religion.

How, then, does one explain all the wonderful things said about Jesus? Few would argue that he was at least a wise man; perhaps he picked up some tricks along the way. He could also have discovered some deep, dark secrets. Maybe he went somewhere, like India, and learned the mystical ways of the gurus, or perhaps it was from Buddhist monks. Upon his return to Israel, he wowed the crowds with his new-found wisdom (and sleight of hand).

Several years ago a book called *The Lost Years of Jesus* made a bit of a splash, asserting just such a case (from supposed ancient documents).[22] The claims it makes have no historical basis on any measure; but, as usual, they have found their way into the common culture. One of the main points is that the New Testament is *supposedly* silent about the years between Jesus' adventure in the temple when he was twelve (Luke 2:42–50) and his baptism by John when he was about thirty (3:23). Where was he for those seventeen years in between? Well, in India, of course. This myth (and several like it) holds up pretty well as long as you ignore the scriptural evidence, not to mention the entire social, religious, and historical background in which the gospel narrative unfolds.

## GLIMPSES INTO THE LOST YEARS

First, let's look at the Scriptures. You will notice "supposedly" is italicized in the previous paragraph. It is not true that the Bible is *completely* silent about those years. A more accurate statement is to say the Scriptures are *virtually* silent about those years. Now before you accuse me of hair-splitting, "virtually" means "almost," "just about," or "nearly." To be sure, there is not much, but what *is* recorded needs to be considered.

The first glimpse of these "lost years" is in Luke 2. After the account of Jesus' birth, circumcision, and dedication at the temple, Luke concludes the scene with a summary: "And the child grew and became strong; he was filled with wisdom, and the grace of God was upon him" (2:40). This leads right into the story about Jesus at the temple when he was twelve years old. The family went to the Passover feast in Jerusalem, "according to the custom" (2:42). When it was time to return to Nazareth, Mary and Joseph apparently thought he was with someone else in the extended family. (It was customary to travel in large groups, both for fellowship and for safety's sake.)

The startling discovery of Jesus' absence led to a frantic search, finally ending up back in the temple. They found the boy Jesus conversing with the power elites, commendably holding his own. Mary blurted out a what-were-you-thinking sort of remark. His unflappable response amounted to "Where did you think I would be?" After this, Luke tells us, he returned home to Nazareth with his parents "and was obedient to them" (Luke 2:51), instead of saying he then went off to exotic lands to learn magic arts. Then the story concludes: "And Jesus grew in wisdom and stature, and in favor with God and men" (2:52).

Did you notice the refrain, the repeated comment that moves the story along? It's as if Luke says, "Here's the account of his birth," and then "*he grows in strength, wisdom, and grace with God.*" "Here's a glimpse of his childhood," and then "*he grows in stature, wisdom, and favor with God and people.*" What was Jesus doing during those seventeen years? He was growing up in Nazareth, getting taller (like kids generally do), becoming wiser, and staying out of trouble both with God and people. He was a good kid growing up into a good man.

Another glimpse occurs in an incident several years later in his hometown (recorded in Luke 4). After a preaching tour in area synagogues Jesus returned to Nazareth "where he had been brought up," and entered the synagogue one fine Sabbath "as was his custom" (4:16). Since he was in his hometown and had a custom of synagogue attendance, we can probably safely say that, so far, there is nothing remarkable in the story. He did this all the time. The plot thickens when he was chosen to read from the prophets. In response to his sermon — long-delayed hopes now fulfilled in his ministry (4:17 – 21) — all the people "spoke well of him and were amazed at the gracious words that came from his lips" (4:22).

Most of the Jesus movies get the story wrong at this point. The synagogue does not erupt when he claims to fulfill Isaiah 61. No, the crowd is still hanging on every word. It is the repeated reference to God's grace extending to the Gentiles that riles them up enough to throw him off a cliff. Even before that, the turning point, if you will, is the crowd's snapping back into the reality of the moment. As they marvel at his wisdom, it's as if someone says, "Hey, wait a minute! Isn't this little Jesus? That's Joseph's son, right?" (Luke 4:22). Jesus essentially ignores the question and picks a fight with them, exposing their arrogance and prejudice.

Matthew and Mark add some more details to the story. All of the people in the scene know his mom and dad (at least they're polite enough to regard Joseph as his papa); all his brothers and sisters are still hanging around (Matthew 13:55 – 56). They all know him as the apprentice carpenter following in Joseph's footsteps (13:55; Mark 6:3). They are simply perplexed: "Where did this man get this wisdom and these miraculous powers.... Where then did this man get all these things?" (Matthew 13:54, 56). It was precisely because of his normal upbringing in full view of family and friends in this tight-knit Jewish community that they were so perplexed.

By way of summary, let's tease out the hints we can glean from this episode about Jesus' early years. Luke tells us he returned to Nazareth "where he had been *brought up.*" We have a glimpse of the town in which Jesus was reared. We also have the added insight that going to the synagogue "was his *custom,*" his usual way of doing things (Luke 4:16). The strong reaction from the crowd is precisely because *Jesus' upbringing was so ordinary.* It's a classic "Who do you think you are?" moment. Matthew and Mark add details concerning the family with the strong implication that Jesus was there all along, working as a carpenter. Both conclude with the same sort of "Who do you think you are?" comment.

The scandal here is that the little kid who grew up in Joseph's footsteps is getting a bit high and mighty with the town folk. But notice what nobody says: "I know why he's so special now. He's a guru; yep, went to India."

## WHAT IF WE GRANT THE POINT?

That's pretty much the extent of the sketchy reconstruction of the so-called "lost years." It *is* enough to say that if Jesus had been absent for seventeen years, no one in his hometown was aware of it. If he returned as a guru, no one made an issue of it. But let's just grant the point for a moment. Let's say he *did* wander off, learned the ways of the Buddhist mystics or Hindu gurus in India, and returned to enlighten Israel with his new-found knowledge. This is where the social, religious, and historical background becomes so crucial for busting this myth.

Those who cling to this myth would have us believe a whopper. Specifically, that Jesus sauntered back into Israel after an extended absence and launched a new ministry based on a Gentile religion (or *religions*) that had nothing to do with Judaism, and in fact contradicted it on every major teaching.

To Jews of the first century, the Gentiles were regarded as outside of the covenant. At best, they were seen as distant candidates for one day joining God's people. They could be marginally tolerated or simply shunned. At worst, they were seen as repulsive, vile sinners shrouded in darkness, sometimes seen as no better than smelly pigs or mangy dogs. So if Jesus claimed to be a teacher of Gentile (pagan) wisdom representing Gentile gods and practicing Gentile magic arts, he would have been stoned on the spot. Remember, they wanted to throw him off a cliff just for insinuating that God *likes* Gentiles (Luke 4:27 – 29).

The actual storyline of the *Lost Years* is somewhat different from the popular myth, but it still will not hold up under scrutiny. The focus appears to be that Jesus tried to instill his teaching among the peoples of northern India. Putting aside the total lack of evidence for such a journey, the story completely lacks credibility in the claim that his teaching came from Hindu and Buddhist scriptures.

There are two problems here. First, a faithful Jew would not leave the Promised Land to seek spiritual training that was not based on the Old Testament. Anyone who did such a thing would be branded an apostate (someone who had turned his or her back on God). Second, that which Jesus allegedly taught in the *Lost Years* scenario bears little resemblance to Hinduism or Buddhism (from which he supposedly learned it), and bears little resemblance to what we know of Jesus' teaching elsewhere. In this scenario, Jesus' supposed message is a soft mishmash of vague spiritual sensibilities that is actually just an attempt to dress him up in Eastern mystical garb. The authors of such notions will have nothing to do with Judaism or Christianity. Instead, they want Jesus to embrace *their* religion.

Other "lost year" scenarios make even more grandiose claims, but the unifying theme seems to be that there is one grand spiritual reality, of which individual religions are simply varied expressions. Jesus is then presented as the spokesman for this or that religion. It is fascinating to note the lengths people will go in their attempts to include Jesus in their belief systems. Jesus just refuses to cooperate.

## A JEWISH STORY

Jesus was a Jew. He said Jewish things in a Jewish context to fellow Jews. There were, of course, many expressions of Judaism in the first century (Pharisees, Sadducees, etc.), but all of them were staunchly monotheistic; that is, they believed in one God. The central creed then, as it is to this day, was: "Hear O Israel: the LORD our God, the LORD is one" (Deuteronomy 6:4). They were a people in covenant with Yahweh, the God of the Old Testament, who had given them the land of Israel and taken up residence in their temple in Jerusalem. They all regarded their Scriptures as God's Word to, for, and about them. The real arguments concerned which group held the legitimate claim to represent the "true Israel." That is, which group could claim to be the true heir of the Law and the Prophets, the one that would embody the victory of Yahweh over all of his enemies? Disputes could be heated, even deadly.

If Jesus had truly been trained in India, we would expect him to take his disciples there for a little sub-continent training as well. Yet, Jesus and *his* little band never ventured farther than neighboring countries and territories (like Tyre and Sidon, or "beyond the Jordan"). Instead of venturing into the Gentile world, he focused on his homeland, traveling extensively in his home province of Galilee, with several journeys in and around Jerusalem. He based all of his teaching squarely on the Jewish Scriptures, constantly quoting from them and alluding to them. He claimed, like any other leader of a first-century Jewish sect, that his teaching alone was the true expression of God's will for his people. He claimed the Scriptures were fulfilled in his person and ministry (Matthew 5:17). He affirmed Israel's central creed (22:36–37). He upheld the highest standard of piety, so much so, his enemies could never accuse him of even a single sin (John 8:46; 9:31–33).

Yet, they killed him.

He irritated the leaders to no end by insisting he alone had the right interpretation of the Sabbath (Matthew 12:1–8; Mark 3:1–5), dietary laws (Mark 7:14–15), forgiveness (Luke 18:12–14), mercy (Matthew 23:23), and on and on. He went out of his way to show love and compassion to outcasts and "sinners," all the while exposing the hypocrisy of those who opposed him. His righteous gaze on their guilt-ridden faces was too much to bear, as were his exalted claims to be the one who alone speaks for God.

It took roughly three years for the Jewish leadership to have enough of the Jewish carpenter-turned-prophet-and-teacher who claimed to fulfill Jewish hopes and scriptural promises. In Jewish land, they convened a Jewish court and hastily condemned him for claiming to be the long-awaited Jewish king. Three years, it took. How long do you think he would have lasted if he showed up one day and said something like this? "Hey, y'all, I'm back. Forget about the Scriptures, one God, Abraham, Moses, and all that 'people of God' nonsense. I've been studying the Vedas and now know we are *all* gods. There's billions of gods, yet we're all one (*Ommmm*). There's no such thing as sin; in fact, nothing we see is real at all. It's all an illusion. So, if you just follow this path of enlightenment...."

He'd last about twenty minutes. The truth is that the evidence points toward Jesus having grown up in Nazareth and experiencing resistance to his astounding claims for that very reason. If Jesus took a trip to the Far East, no one seemed to notice. If Jesus taught religious concepts utterly foreign to Judaism, no one ever mentioned it. In short, if Jesus was a guru, I'm Rex the Wonder Horse.

## SUMMING UP

The scanty evidence of Jesus' early years will not allow for a visit to India. If it *did* occur, nothing in Jesus' teaching remotely resembles that of Hinduism or Buddhism. The only way Jesus and his teaching can be understood is in the light of his ancestral home and religion. The bland routine of his upbringing only heightens the shocking nature of his ministry, and provides a clue for why he was rejected by his own people.

## GOING DEEPER

For those of you who would like to examine this more closely, the best way forward is first to gain a working knowledge of the background of Judaism in the first century. The next step would be to gain some insight into the beliefs of major world religions. Finally, one needs to grapple with the distinct claims of Christianity. This is obviously a tall order, but here are some accessible resources to get you started.

For ancient Judaism (and Christianity), an excellent overview is Everett Ferguson, *Backgrounds of Early Christianity* (Grand Rapids: Eerdmans, 1993) or F. F. Bruce, *New Testament History* (New York: Doubleday, 1969). Also, a sample of writings from the period is collected in Walter Elwell and Robert Yarbrough, *Readings from the First Century World* (Grand Rapids: Baker, 1998). It would not take long to see how foreign the "lost years" myth really is to the first-century world.

A good beginning text on world religions is Lewis Hopfe and Mark Woodward, *Religions of the World* (New Jersey: Prentice Hall, 2006); see the Going Deeper section in chapter 13 for more sources.

Lee Strobel, *The Case for Christ: A Journalist's Personal Investigation of the Evidence for Jesus* (Grand Rapids: Zondervan, 1998), is a fine entry-level book for exploring Christian claims; a little more in-depth are Gary Habermas, *The Historical Jesus: Ancient Evidence for the Life of Christ* (Joplin, MO: College Press, 1996) and *The Risen Christ & Future Hope* (Nashville: Broadman & Littlefield, 2003). The place of Deuteronomy 6 in the teaching of Jesus is explored by Scot McKnight in *The Jesus Creed* (Brewster, MA: Paraclete, 2004).

# Chapter 7

# JESUS NEVER CLAIMED TO BE THE MESSIAH

As skeptical as people can be, I just don't think the average person on the street would ever doubt Jesus claimed to be the Messiah. To get *that* messed up takes a scholar. Jesus' messianic nature is so ingrained that the title has essentially become his name: Jesus Messiah, or to put it in the much more familiar Greek version, Jesus *Christ*.[23] Why would someone claim otherwise? It is yet another example of skeptics' attempting to knock Jesus down a peg and run roughshod over his followers.

To discuss the myth that Jesus never claimed to be the Messiah, let's first examine two assertions from a skeptical viewpoint drawn from the study of the Gospels. One concerns a feature of Mark's gospel, and the other concerns the sources Matthew and Luke used to write their gospels. These are both pretty technical items, but you'll probably run into them sooner or later in a PBS special or *Newsweek* Easter edition.

## CAN YOU KEEP A SECRET?

Around a hundred years ago a skeptical scholar by the name of Wilhelm Wrede called attention to something peculiar about Mark's gospel. Jesus kept telling people (and demons, for that matter) to cool it on the Messiah business, including not making a fuss about any miracles. After driving out demons, Mark tells us that Jesus "would not let the demons speak because they knew who he was" (Mark 1:34; 3:12). He healed a leper (1:44), brought a little girl back to life (5:43), healed a deaf mute (7:36), and ordered all of the people involved not to tell anyone. Select disciples witnessed the transfiguration (the scene on the mountain when he suddenly shined brighter than the sun), but on the way back "Jesus gave them orders not to tell anyone what they had seen until the Son of Man had risen from the dead" (9:9).

Time and again, Jesus preferred to keep the fact that he was the Messiah under wraps. Wrede referred to this as the "messianic secret," and he concluded from these (and many more) details that Jesus' messianic identity was only applied to him after his death. Wrede theorized that Mark (along with others in his community) reworked the original portrait of Jesus as a wise teacher to make him into the divine Messiah.

However, Wrede had to concede that even in Mark's account, the secret slipped out. Jesus commanded the Gerasenes demoniac to return to his family and friends "and tell them how much the Lord has done for you, and how he has had mercy on you" (Mark 5:19). When Jesus was on trial the high priest asked him point blank: "Are you the Christ, the Son of the Blessed One?" Jesus answered, "I am," and warned his accusers they would one day "see the Son of Man sitting at the right hand of the Mighty One and coming on the clouds of heaven" (14:61 – 62). When the governor asked if he was king of the Jews, Jesus answered plainly, "Yes, it is as you say" (15:2).[24]

This skeptical theory reemerges from time to time. At best it's a clumsy attempt to rid the Gospels of any trace of Jesus' messianic consciousness. And it still fails to account for the claim that did arise after Jesus' death and the central role it plays in the entire New Testament. Why would anyone want to invent that notion that Jesus was the Messiah and build the Gospels around it if it wasn't so?

The resurrection might tip the balance in Jesus' favor, but even that falls short. If rising from the dead was all it takes, why didn't anyone bother to make a messiah out of Lazarus (John 11:43 – 44), the widow's son (Luke 7:14 – 15), or for that matter, the little girl (Mark 5:41 – 42)? No, as N. T. Wright puts it: "There was no reason to regard a recently crucified man as Messiah, even if he had been raised from the dead, unless he had shown signs of claiming that status beforehand."[25] The record in the Gospels only makes sense when it traces the messianic claims back to Jesus himself rather than reflecting the religious musings of later Christians.

## A SOURCE IS A SOURCE

Another theory that denies Jesus' messianic nature concerns a discipline known as source criticism—that is, the search for the material the gospel writers used to write their gospel. That they used such sources is beyond dispute, as was readily acknowledged in Luke 1:1–3: "Many have undertaken to draw up an account of the things that have been fulfilled among us.... Therefore, since I myself have carefully investigated everything from the beginning, it seemed good also to me to write an orderly account."

Matthew and Luke likely used the gospel of Mark as a source, since Matthew includes 90 percent of Mark's material and Luke uses 55 percent. But the material Matthew and Luke share that is not found in Mark adds an interesting wrinkle. Many scholars theorize this was an independent source, referred to as Q (from *Quelle*, the German word for "source").

For those of you hoping for a point, I'm almost there. That there is material common to Matthew and Luke (like the Sermon on the Mount, or Jesus' assessment of John the Baptist) is just a fact. Some scholars believe this material was passed on orally, but others take it to the next level and see Q as a written source that has since disappeared. Still others go so far as to imagine the kind of people who produced it and what their religious beliefs might have been, even to the extent of writing commentaries on Q! Since Matthew *and* Luke used the Q material, it must predate them both; so, according to the skeptics, Q represents the original Jesus as his earliest followers understood him. This is how the theory relates to this chapter's myth.

For the most part, Q doesn't include miracles of Jesus or exalted claims about his identity; there is no passion narrative or resurrection scene. All of the common sections in Matthew and Luke are sayings of Jesus, his ethical teaching. Here then (supposedly) is the real Jesus—the nice guy who teaches people to be kind but has no supernatural qualities whatsoever. In short, the Jesus found in Q never claimed to be the Messiah.

The only thing that can be said about Q with any certainty is that there are passages common to both Matthew and Luke that are not found elsewhere. The rest is speculation. It is one thing to notice the material, it is quite another to theorize that this was once a written source.

Really, this in itself shouldn't pose a problem. It is, however, a bit of a leap to reconstruct a supposedly pristine community of disciples who knew nothing of Jesus as the wonder-working Messiah who died and rose again. As addressed in chapter 3, there were too many eyewitnesses around for anyone in first-century Israel to beef up the story of Jesus. The claim that Jesus was the Messiah had to arise from somewhere very early on to gain the foothold that it did.

## BACKING UP THE CLAIM TO JESUS AS MESSIAH

What evidence is there that Jesus claimed to be the Christ? Let's work backward and see how far we can trace it. The second- and third-century critics of Christianity acknowledged the claim (though they didn't believe it). He was universally proclaimed as such by the early church fathers. Even the rival gospels and letters (see ch. 5) agreed Jesus was the Christ; they just sought to redefine what that meant. At an earlier point, from the time Paul's letters, the Gospels, and Acts were written, Jesus was never known as anything other than the Christ. This is impressive, but it still doesn't answer the question whether or not *Jesus* ever made the claim. That takes us to the cross.

### Of Kings and Messiahs

On the cross the Galilean was put on display as a warning to all would-be troublemakers. Fall afoul of the Romans, and they'll nail your hide to a tree. What hideous offense did he commit? We can see it on the charge affixed above his head: "THIS IS JESUS, THE KING OF THE JEWS" (Matthew 27:37). Why would anyone say such a thing, and what does being the king of the Jews have to do with being the Messiah?

As noted above, the words "Messiah" and "Christ" mean the same thing. Messiah comes from the Hebrew word for "Anointed One," and Christ is the Greek rendition of the same term. Great, you say, who (or what) is an Anointed One? I'm glad you asked. In the Old Testament, from time to time, God selected people for a special task. In a solemn ceremony oil would be poured over the person's head, the top-down saturation symbolizing the presence and empowering of the Holy Spirit. Some priests were anointed, as were some prophets. All of the kings were. It was for that reason that the term Anointed One, or Messiah, came to be so closely associated with Israel's king. Since there were many kings, there were many messiahs (so, in the Greek Old Testament, many christs).

Note how Jesus was accused of being the Christ before the Jewish ruling council (Mark 14:61). But when he was dragged before Pilate, the charge focused on Jesus being a rival king. " 'We have found this man subverting our nation. He opposes payment of taxes to Caesar and claims to be Christ, a king.' So Pilate asked Jesus, 'Are you the king of the Jews?' 'Yes, it is as you say,' Jesus replied" (Luke 23:2–3).

Just as *Messiah* and *Christ* are interchangeable because they mean the same thing—"Anointed One"—so *Christ* and *king* are also interchangeable because the title "Christ" has always had royal connotations. This little insight has a long history behind it.

## Is David the One?

One of the blessings promised to Abraham was that "kings will come from you" (Genesis 17:6). This promise was later focused on one of the twelve tribes of Israel. As Jacob lay on his deathbed giving a blessing to each son, one blessing clarified the kingly line: "The scepter will not depart from Judah, nor the ruler's staff from between his feet, until he comes to whom it belongs and the obedience of the nations is his" (49:10). These promises seemed to come to fulfillment in a lad from the tribe of Judah who was born in Bethlehem. No, not Jesus; it was his ancestor David. Anointed while still a young shepherd, he was destined to become Israel's greatest king.[26]

Saul was the first king, but his failures only caused David, his replacement, to shine that much brighter. David had his moments as well (Bathsheba and Uriah come to mind), but he was still a man after God's own heart. He served as the example for all the kings that followed him. A good king was like David (see 2 Kings 18:1–3; 22:1–2), and an evil king was not like David (see 1 Kings 14:8; 15:1–4).

God had taken a special interest in this king—so much so, that David's line was destined to continue forever. This is known as the Davidic Covenant: "Your house and your kingdom will endure forever before me; your throne will be established forever" (see 2 Samuel 7:11–16). So, as the nation began its slow slide into rebellion and exile, the prophets reminded the people of this promise.

Through the long series of failings, both in the nation and with her kings, Israel's longing for a king "like David" gave way to a longing for a "new David" (Isaiah 9:7; 11:1–5;[27] 16:5; Hosea 3:5; Amos 9:11–15). As such, the expectation came to focus on one specific individual—*the* Christ.

Through Jeremiah the Lord spoke of a day in the future when he would "raise up to David a righteous Branch, a King who will reign wisely and do what is just and right in the land" (Jeremiah 23:5; see also 30:9). In the same way God spoke through Ezekiel, saying, "My servant David will be king over them, and they will all have one shepherd" (Ezekiel 37:24), Notice that "king" and "shepherd" go hand in hand. Micah predicted a ruler of Israel who would come from Bethlehem (Micah 5:2), a promise sure to evoke the "new David" theme. The messianic overtones are hard to miss when we consider what else Micah said about him: "He will stand and shepherd his flock in the strength of the LORD, in the majesty of the name of the LORD his God" (5:4).

You need to remember that by the time these prophets spoke of "David" returning as the king, he had already been dead for centuries. These prophecies (and many more like them) refer to one of David's descendants, one of his sons.[28] This aspiration for the Son of David was inseparably tied to the longing for the promised king. From just such a connection, it was inevitable that the Messiah would be the Son of David. For that reason, the Messiah was also known as the Son of God.

## From Son to Son

"Son of God" is, first and foremost, a messianic title. Originally it applied to Israel as a whole. In the confrontation with Pharaoh, God declared, "Israel is my firstborn son" (Exodus 4:22). This sonship was later associated with the people's representative, the king. Psalm 2 is a fascinating glimpse of God's ideal for such a king. The rulers of the world kick up their heels "against the LORD and against his Anointed One" (2:2). In response he declares, "I have installed my King on Zion, my holy hill" (2:6). Then the divine decree is spoken to the new king as he ascends to the throne: "You are my Son; today I have become your Father" (2:7). David was installed as the "son of God," as were every one of his descendants who ascended to the throne (see 2 Samuel 7:14; Psalm 89:3–4, 26–27, 35–36; note the rebellion theme).

God had made a promise to David that he would always have an heir on the throne, but the exile seemed to put an end to the line. As the centuries progressed the nation longed for the son of David to arise. It wasn't the only idea of what a Christ should be, but it certainly was a popular one. The "ministry" of this kingly figure can be seen in a noncanonical book from a time after the Romans overran Israel, the *Psalms of Solomon*. After lamenting the disappearance of the Davidic line, the writer pleads:

See, Lord, and raise up for them their king, the Son of David, to rule over Israel, your servant, in the time which you chose, O God. Undergird him with the strength to destroy the unrighteous rulers, to cleanse Jerusalem from gentiles who trample her to destruction. (17:21–22)

The hope was for *this* Christ to dispatch the smelly Romans with all due haste, and Israel would once again enjoy the glory of her golden years. Such was the hope; it just didn't turn out that way.

## An Unexpected Expectation

All of this is the necessary background information for even beginning to grasp the importance to Israel of the Messiah's imminent coming. The Messiah's arrival was ingrained in the nation's DNA, and Jesus fit it to a T. Why, then, didn't the nation as a whole recognize him? That, too, was part of the plan. Jesus was destined to be rejected.

Once we pick up the rejection theme, another piece of the puzzle falls into place—Isaiah's Suffering Servant (Isaiah 53:3), who works miracles of mercy in the power of the Spirit (61:1–3), and who gives his life for his people (53:4–6; also see Psalm 22). He conquers death and is rewarded by God for his faithfulness (53:11–12; see Psalm 110). This facet of the Messiah's ministry was simply missed by all concerned until after the resurrection.

So what would the Messiah be like? He would be a king from the tribe of Judah, in David's line, born in Bethlehem, and a Spirit-empowered wonder-worker who was destined for rejection and death. He would conquer death and assume a position of power at God's right hand. This sure sounds suspiciously like a Galilean preacher I once read about, but this is reading the evidence after the fact. Since Jesus did not seem to fit the picture of the Messiah *as expected by Judaism*, it makes it all the more puzzling for anyone to claim that he was the one. Unless, of course, his words and deeds led his disciples to the conclusion that would form the basis of their message.

## THE FRAMEWORK OF THE GOSPEL

The fact that the Gospels were written within the lifetime of many eyewitnesses makes their portrait of Jesus all the more intriguing — incomprehensible, in fact, if indeed Jesus never claimed to be the Christ. Why? Because the confession that Jesus is the Christ forms the very framework of these written proclamations. The confession of Jesus as the Christ is the apex of the story, the dramatic turning point of the Synoptic Gospels (Matthew, Mark, and Luke).[29] The relationship of this confession to the rest of the narrative is clearest in Mark, so we'll use it as our representative sample.

In the first line of Mark, we are already told Jesus is the "Son of God,"[30] an identification made crystal clear at his baptism (Mark 1:11). Towards the end of the narrative, a Roman centurion sees the events surrounding Jesus' death and blurts out, "Surely this man was the Son of God!" (15:39). Being a Roman, and likely a polytheist, he probably didn't mean what a Christian would've understood. Instead, we have an instance in which the Roman spoke beyond his ability to comprehend. In any case, Mark made sure to mention it, and the Christian readers would be in hearty agreement. "Yes, he surely is the Son of God, whether or not you know what you're saying."

Mark's gospel is all about what it means for Jesus to be the messianic Son of God. For the first eight and a half chapters Mark highlights a question that drives many of the stories. Jesus performs miracles, forgives sins, and says astounding things, all of which lead people to ask "Who is this?" (Mark 2:7; 4:41; 6:2–3). Over and over the people respond to Jesus with wonder and amazement (1:22; 2:12; 5:20; 6:51; 7:37). The readers of Mark knew something the people within the narrative didn't at the time — he's the Son of God. Mark gives us insight into what a Son of God is supposed to be — a wonder-working marvel performing works of compassion for his people.

The story comes to a climactic peak in Mark 8. Jesus asks his disciples, "Who do people say I am?" (8:27). The buzz on the street was that he was either John the Baptist (risen from the dead!), Elijah, or one of the prophets (8:28). Never shy about pressing the issue, he continued, "But what about you [his disciples]? . . . Who do you say I am?" Peter spoke first: "You are the Christ" (8:29). Then "Jesus warned them not to tell anyone about him" (8:30). Jesus' understanding of the Messiah's role didn't jive with the popular version; he was no military conqueror.

## Say What?

Jesus' next statement didn't sit well with Peter. He told them he was about to suffer, be rejected, be killed, and then rise from the dead. No, that's just not right, thought Peter, who then proceeded to rebuke Jesus. The Messiah conquers! The Messiah rules gloriously! I'm sure Peter meant well, but Jesus saw the source of his objections. "Get behind me, Satan!" he said directly to Peter, "You do not have in mind the things of God, but the things of men" (Mark 8:33).

Satan's temptation was to get Jesus to go along with a *human* plan, a merely human, fallen-nature-inspired plan. "Jesus, knock off the suffering nonsense. Buck up and act like a Messiah!" Of course, Jesus *was* acting precisely as the Messiah; it's just that no one else knew that yet.

The next thing Jesus says is pretty hair-raising. "If anyone would come after me, he must deny himself and take up his cross and follow me" (Mark 8:34). Deny the human plan, like Jesus did, and follow God's way of dying to the self. Live for God. This is a lifelong calling, and I haven't yet found anyone who has fully mastered it except Jesus. And it cost him his life.

## Here's What It Means

So, the first eight and a half chapters show us what the Son of God is supposed to be like: a wonder-worker. The apex of the story is

Peter's confession, "You are the Christ." Jesus' idea of a Christ is the way of rejection, suffering, death, and lest we forget, resurrection. Did you notice the hint Jesus gave his disciples about the kind of death he would face? Any would-be follower of Jesus needs "to take up his *cross*." If you're new to Christianity, this section is probably a little unsettling; I know it flies in the face of some of the sugar-coated fluff that floods the airwaves. The sense of foreboding you may be experiencing is precisely where Mark wants to take us. The second half of his gospel fills in the rest of what it means to be the Christ, the Son of God.

From this climactic scene all the way to the end of Mark, there is a growing sense of fear and anxiety. "They were on their way up to Jerusalem, with Jesus leading the way, and the disciples were astonished, while those who followed were afraid" (Mark 10:32). He continued to reinforce the plan, which leads into what many regard as the key verse of Mark's gospel. Jesus will have none of the easy path because he "did not come to be served, but to serve, and to give his life as a ransom for many" (10:45).

This notion of impending doom hangs in the air all the way to his horrible death. Ah, but the story isn't over, because all along he'd been telling his disciples about the third day *after* his death (Mark 8:31; 9:31; 10:34). The resurrection vindicated his claim; he was exactly who he said he was. Allow me to sneak a little Luke into the mix, since he summarizes this so well: "Did not the Christ have to suffer these things and then enter his glory?" (Luke 24:26).

The answer is "yes," and from that time on historic Christianity has had no other explanation. From the early days in Jerusalem and as the church spread into the wider empire, there was but one basic message: this Jesus is the Christ (Acts 2:36; 5:42; 9:22; 17:3).

## SUMMING UP

That Jesus is the Christ, sent by the Father to usher in his kingdom, is at the center of Christian faith. Skeptics may assail such a claim, and are free to do so. They just can't overturn two thousand years of a proclamation that changes the lives of anyone who embraces it. From the very first Christian sermon, the church declared that the long-awaited expectation had been fulfilled. The Christ is Jesus, so Jesus is Lord. This core message is the essence of the gospel; the evidence of the gospel is a transformed life.

Sure, someone could respond to this by calling attention to hypocrites, flops, and failures, and they are indeed among us. For some reason, the faithful folks living out a real Christian life don't make it into the conversation. I'm talking about the peaceful souls who radiate God's love and genuinely care for people, those who selflessly serve the Lord. They are among us as well.

Some of you may have been put off by the darker aspects of this chapter—all that talk of foreboding, doom, and dying to the self. Don't forget the rest of the story. Christ died, but he didn't stay dead. We bury our own desires and experience the fullness of God's resurrection power. We come to realize that the nonsense we were clinging to does not compare to the sense of freedom and joy a fresh start brings. It's like being born all over again.

And one last thing. All along I've been assuming two key events as if they were historical: Jesus' death by crucifixion and his resurrection from the dead. If skeptics deny Jesus is the Christ, what do you suppose they think about those little items? That, my friends, is the topic of the next two chapters.

## GOING DEEPER

A good resource for this topic is Donald Guthrie, *Jesus the Messiah* (Grand Rapids: Zondervan, 1972). I found valuable insight in Nils A. Dahl, *The Crucified Messiah and Other Essays* (Minneapolis: Augsburg, 1974). The title essay is on pages 10–36. A penetrating look at the "messianic secret" can be found in Albert Schweitzer's classic, *The Quest for the Historical Jesus* (Minneapolis: Fortress, 2001 [repr.]), 296–314 (this is an English translation of his original work in 1906). Dahl and Schweitzer, you should know, are not writing from an evangelical perspective, but are very useful, nonetheless. An accessible summary of Q can be found in *DJG*, 644–650. Other helpful sources are listed in the Going Deeper section of chapter 3.

# Chapter 8

# JESUS DID NOT DIE ON THE CROSS

One way to get around the uncomfortable claims of Christianity is to go for its heart. If Jesus didn't die on the cross as our substitute, then his death has no bearing on anyone else, whenever and wherever it finally occurred. If he didn't die like this, we can forget about his dying *for our sins*. His resurrection doesn't do much for us either, if he didn't die as the Bible says he did. The more we can get Jesus tidily tucked away like a John Q. Anybody, the easier it becomes to discard the intrusive features of the gospel message, like sin, repentance, and living a holy life.

Let's be careful about the specifics of this myth. It's not that Jesus didn't die *at all*, but that he didn't *die on the cross*. That theory is yet another myth circulating in the popular culture, one that actually resurrects an old theory first made in the nineteenth century.

## SOME ALTERNATIVE THEORIES

One old assertion that denies Jesus' death on the cross is called the "swoon" theory. He didn't die; he just swooned, which means that he passed out from the beatings, flogging, and loss of blood (not to mention the lack of sleep from the all-night ordeal). Once they put him in the cool burial cave, he eventually revived and strolled back out to the land of the living. The story of a resurrection was a simple matter of those bumbling disciples mistaking the revived rabbi for a gloriously resurrected Lord. Silly disciples. While we're at it, shame on Jesus for not putting a quick stop to all this resurrection nonsense and all the bowing and scraping at his throbbing feet.

A variation of this theory appeared in the mid-1960s in *The Passover Plot* by Hugh Schonfield. Jesus was the mastermind of a plot to fake his death and resurrection, with the apostle John and Joseph of Arimathea in cahoots. Poison slipped to Jesus on the cross made it look like he died (though this theory fails to account for the soldier's spear). John and Joseph whisked the body away; the other disciples then mistook someone else for the risen Jesus. According to Schonfield, this is how Christianity started.

Why anyone who takes issue with Christianity would make such claims is obvious. Either scenario (or any further variation) totally undercuts the gospel. Jesus, then, was just a nice man who had a particularly bad day. No surprises there, assuming you've read earlier chapters in this book. What *is* surprising is how anyone with even a passing acquaintance with the evidence could make such a claim. Jesus' removal from the cross in any condition other than stone-cold dead is just not an historical option.

As we proceed, we are going down a well-traveled road. My goal is to tease out some key evidence, both biblical and extrabiblical, to help us decide the issue.

## A BROAD SKETCH

Let's begin with a brief survey of the extrabiblical sources concerning the crucifixion. Is there any evidence from the ancient world that advances an alternative to the gospel's description of death on a cross?

- From the Roman historian Tacitus we learn that the Christians trace their origin to one "Chrestus," who "suffered the extreme penalty during the reign of Tiberius at the hands of one of our procurators, Pontius Pilate" (*The Annals*, around AD 116). "Extreme penalty" is another way of saying "execution."
- Josephus likely informs us as well that "Pilate condemned [Jesus] to be crucified and to die" (*Antiquities of the Jews* 18:63–64, late first century AD). I say "likely" since this

section of Josephus is debated, but that particular statement is not in dispute.

- Lucian tells us: "Christians … worship a man to this day—the distinguished personage who introduced their novel rites, and was crucified" (*The Death of Peregrine,* around AD 170). A few lines later he refers to the leader as a "crucified sage." It appears safe to infer that the continual use of the term "Christian" indicates their leader was "Christ."[31]
- The Talmud, a later source, still maintains that "on the eve of the Passover Yeshu was hanged" (*Sanhedrin* 43a).[32]

In these sources Jesus is called a deceiver and a troublemaker, a usurper of honor due only to God (Jewish opponents) or to Caesar (pagan opponents), but all agree on his fate. Aside from the Gnostics, whose objections were philosophical and theological, not historical, nobody from the ancient world advanced any theory denying Jesus' death on the cross. No one advanced any theory that he survived the ordeal, or even that it was a trick. Even if you insist some of these sources don't say "cross," the main point is they all say that *he was executed and died.* It isn't until the rise of Islam *six hundred years later* that a forthright challenge was presented. The myth as it stands in this chapter didn't see the light of day until the 1800s. Beware of innovations.

You may complain the extrabiblical evidence is scanty, but its testimony is consistent. What we find is unbelievers corroborating our central premise. Tacitus and the gang all say what the Gospels do regarding the fate of Jesus. Every source that mentions it says he died. If it was a fact that Jesus didn't really die on the cross, why is it that no historian from the era even hints at such a conclusion? If he really didn't die in this manner and no one recorded the real reason, we actually would be dealing with an argument from silence. Arguments from silence are always tricky (you don't want to make too much of a conclusion based on what people do *not* say), but this silence would scream for an explanation.

All of these non-Christian sources square with the New Testament (with one discrepancy). In any event, our sketch yields the following: Jesus was considered a king (compare Matthew 2:2; John 1:49; Revelation 19:16), and received worship from his followers (Matthew 14:33; Revelation 5:12–14). He was crucified under Pilate (Matthew 27:2, 24) during Tiberius's reign (Luke 3:1–2).

The only discrepancy relates to an issue concerning the date of the crucifixion. Matthew, Mark, and Luke are all clear that it occurred on Passover, but by one interpretation of John's gospel, it appears to take place on the day before (agreeing with the Talmud). This is not a necessary reading of John, however. The details of this argument would take us too far afield from our main topic, but don't miss this point. We may have a discrepancy concerning which day, but our focus here is the biblical and extrabiblical agreement that Jesus of Nazareth indeed *died*. So far the record is clear; he did. Now, the New Testament writings add to the story, but can they be trusted?

## THOSE "OTHER" SOURCES

Why are the New Testament documents so quickly ruled out when examining historical sources? The anti-Christian books, blogs, and websites never tire of pointing out the relative scarcity of historical sources validating the story of Jesus *apart from the New Testament.* The New Testament writers, they claim, were believers and therefore biased. They couldn't possibly have been reporting real events, just their beliefs and spiritualized imaginations. The critics insist on verification from unbelievers, that is, from secular folks. While it is true that another set of eyes on the topic is useful, the blanket dismissal of the New Testament as valid evidence is itself *in*valid. It involves a cluster of misleading ideas, three of which we'll examine briefly.

### Are We Limited to Unbelievers?

The first problem is the notion that an unbeliever's report about Christianity is by definition unbiased. It certainly can be constructive when an unbeliever corroborates historical claims of the Bible, since there is no vested interest in validating Christianity. You can begin building a strong case for Christianity this way. The problem enters when one assumes an unbeliever is unbiased *by definition* and the only valid voice on the topic. It's as if only a non-Christian can tell the truth, and squirrelly Christians are only capable of uttering some garbled religious notions.

This is a fallacy because, while it acknowledges Christians have a vested interest in validating the New Testament, it assumes they have no interest in the facts. They do. It also assumes the non-Christian has no agenda other than searching out the objective facts. Not so. I have had countless discussions with non-Christians, read too many of their works, and seen too many Easter specials to draw such a conclusion. Some have an elitist air; others really do strive for a neutral tone (for which I am truly thankful); still others are just flat toxic. In any case, the whole point of the discussion, whether congenial or not, is to persuade people that Christianity is simply a belief system with no real bearing on reality.

Sometimes we're dealing with biblical scholars who started off as believers, but whose course of study converted them to agnosticism. Often, they remain in the field, if only to "enlighten" those of us backward enough to actually believe the Bible. In their minds they are truly doing a service, and I can't fault them for their desire to educate. Such presentations, however, are not neutral; they are striving to press a view. They are therefore biased presentations. Keep in mind; they are not for that reason alone invalid. This brings us to the next issue, bias itself.

### Unbiased Is Fine, but How Do You Do It?

It is often assumed that in order to address any issue fairly we have to do so without any bias. This is a fine goal, but the fact is we'll never make it, at least not completely. Anytime we come to a topic we bring ourselves to the task: who we are, what we already believe, and what we expect to find or accomplish. Progress is made when facts either verify or contradict our preconceived notions (leading us to new conclusions). Such is the process of learning. My Christian worldview is certainly a bias, but so is a non-Christian worldview. If we both share an underlying desire to see our views vindicated in the light of investigation, how is it that only the unbeliever can be fair-minded with the evidence?

The simple fact is that a purely unbiased approach is beyond our reach. When it comes to reconstructing the events of first-century Palestine, particularly the fate of Jesus of Nazareth, we have to sift through the sources, both secular and sacred. This brings us to a final problem in this little cluster of misconceptions—the claim that New Testament writers did not, even could not, relate the facts of history *because* they were Christians, and so were only relating their theology.

## They Believe; Therefore They Can't Be Trusted

The working assumption of many a skeptic concerning the New Testament is that it is solely a piece of religious literature. It was *by design* only loosely (very loosely) based on real events. The rest of the "history" recorded never really occurred or was vastly exaggerated. The writers had no interest in what happened, only in the spiritual lessons they could create out of whole cloth. If this is so, why did they take such pains to situate their story within a specific historical context and circulate their work in a time when eyewitnesses, pro and con, abounded and could easily expose the lies (Acts 26:26; 1 Corinthians 15:6)? Why is their central message grounded in history?

Now, if in fact Jesus was just an above-average guy, but his disciples blew everything else out of proportion, then we Christians need to have the rug pulled out from under us. Hopefully the fall will knock some sense into us. But if the claims about Jesus are true and a Christian strives to convince others about him, then the Christian is certainly biased *but is not for that reason untrustworthy.*

So, the Christian and non-Christian are in the same boat when it comes to bias, since both have an agenda to advance. The question is, whose story best fits the evidence? We have before us the claim that Jesus died on the cross (a claim that serves to *advance* the cause of the gospel) and the counterclaim that he didn't (a claim that serves to *nullify* the cause of the gospel). In which direction does the evidence point?

## NEW TESTAMENT EVIDENCE

The swoon theory (and any other version of a near-death experience) just could not have happened.[33] The theory maintains that people mistook Jesus as the risen Lord of glory, but that had to be after the following: He was beaten by the Jews (Matthew 26:67), and then by Roman soldiers (Mark 15:19); he was flogged (Matthew 27:26), a practice so brutal that prisoners often died from it. Finally, he was crucified (John 19:23), which entailed stretching the victim out and nailing him to a cross (20:25; Acts 2:23). The victim was affixed in such a way that the arms would spasm and pull out of joint. The position and body weight made breathing increasingly difficult, so much so that the victim had to push his body up (don't forget the nails in the feet) in order to exhale. This is why the Jewish leaders asked Pilate's permission to break Jesus' legs, as well as those of the other two with him as the Sabbath drew near, lest it desecrate the holy day (John 19:31–32). It sounds even more brutal, but this actually was an act of mercy. With their legs broken, they couldn't breathe and would quickly expire.

This practice of breaking the legs introduced another important event in the crucifixion scene—the piercing of Jesus' side. After the soldiers broke the other two victims' legs, they found Jesus had already died, so a soldier took his spear and made sure. The sudden flow of water (fluid from the sac surrounding the heart) and blood convinced a hardened Roman soldier that the king of the Jews' reign had come to an end (John 19:34). Don't miss the implication of the soldier's action; it was to ensure the victim was already dead and, therefore, didn't need to have his legs broken (as ordered).

So, we have a sleep-deprived, severally beaten, brutally flogged, crucified man whose chest had been freshly thrust with a Roman battle spear. He was wrapped in burial cloth and put in a tomb with a large stone rolled into place to seal it, not to mention a pair of Roman soldiers to guard it. Even if we grant, for the sake of argument, that he was alive, is it really credible to believe this severely wounded rabbi was able to even stand, let alone use his nail-pierced hands to push the stone back up its incline (at best a two-man job), while bracing himself on his nail-pierced feet? If he did manage to pull that off, why did the soldiers just let him waltz on down the trail without so much as a "Who goes there"?

Still, granting for the moment that he was able to muster the strength for repeated appearances, the only rational conclusion the disciples could have made was that Jesus escaped death by the skin of his teeth. They may have been amazed he was alive, or were inspired by his will to survive. But the sight of this severely traumatized person who merely revived could never have been mistaken for a glorious, resurrected Lord, nor could such a victim ever have convinced anyone that he had conquered death. This is the death-knell to the theory, since even the most ardent skeptics universally grant the point that the disciples *believed* he rose again.

Okay, let's grant the point. He's now making the rounds appearing to his disciples, showing up in locked rooms, and disappearing from sight. He even travels on foot with a couple of them to a little town about seven miles from Jerusalem, and later returns for more appearances. No one even suspects for a moment he oh-so-narrowly escaped death. No, they were all convinced that the one who died publicly stood before them very much alive again.

## NOT A SIDE ISSUE

The death and resurrection of Jesus form the centerpiece of the church's proclamation. Since the resurrection is the topic of the next chapter, I want to spend a little time demonstrating the importance of Jesus' death in the rest of the New Testament.

In Acts 2, Peter confronted the crowds of Jerusalem with the fact of Jesus' execution. It was God's plan, but Peter tells the crowd that they, "with the help of wicked men, put him to death by nailing him to the cross" (Acts 2:23). If Jesus didn't die, the whole argument loses its punch.

Paul also focused on preaching the gospel, "lest the cross of Christ be emptied of its power." This was so because the message of the cross "is the power of God" for salvation (1 Corinthians 1:17–18). No cross means no power, no salvation, and no message. It is through the cross, and Jesus' death on it, that God reconciled the world and brought lasting peace (Ephesians 2:16–17; Colossians 1:20). If Jesus didn't die, there is no such reconciliation or peace.

It was *the* demonstration of divine love, forever putting to rest any doubts about God's love for us (Romans 5:8; 1 John 4:9). Jesus' death on the cross was also *the* demonstration of his own humility and submission to the Father (Philippians 2:8). This was the means by which he learned obedience, and was perfected in it (Hebrews 5:8–9).

Jesus' death drives many New Testament themes. It is the reality behind baptism (Romans 6:3–4). It destroyed the Devil's work and set people free from the fear of death (Hebrews 2:14–15). It cancelled the accusations of sin held against sinful humanity and knocked demonic powers flat (Colossians 2:14–15). It's the reason elders, angels, and the crowds in heaven join in exuberant worship of Jesus: "Worthy is the Lamb, who was slain, to receive power and wealth and wisdom and strength and honor and glory and praise!" (Revelation 5:12). Don't miss "who was slain." As a matter of fact, he is worthy specifically "because" he was "slain" (5:9).

The concept of his death undergirds every single central doctrine of the New Testament. I've only stirred the surface of a deep ocean. Jesus is never regarded as having done anything less than dying a brutal death on our behalf, an event that gave the writers a rich source of imagery and metaphors for Christian living. All of this is meaningless unless the event really occurred.

Here's a question for you: if you're a first-century person and wanted to devise a new religion, why invent a tale specifically designed to elicit the ire of your countrymen and overlords alike? Ancient Christianity was the all-time equal-opportunity offender of all the religious, political, and cultural sensibilities then current. Its centerpiece is the death and resurrection of its hero. If *I* were going to float a new belief system, I'd make sure that, as the glory ship sails along, I wouldn't be making any waves.

## Why Worship an Oxymoron?

It is difficult for us to grasp the disgrace of the cross in the ancient world. We have roughly two thousand years of church history that has transformed it into a thing of beauty, whether adorning a breath-taking Renaissance painting or a delicate neck. In the first century, the cross represented nothing but brutality, a shameful death, and a truly cursed way to leave the land of the living. It was reserved for the worst offenders and was done as a public example of what lay ahead for any like-minded rabble rousers. That's why we read about people walking by shaking their heads at Jesus; note comments made by other witnesses as they watched Jesus' life ebb away (Matthew 27:38 – 50). He finally died with an anguished shout; the final punctuation on the scene was the thrust of a spear. The message was clear: Don't let this happen to you.

This event begged for an explanation. If Jesus was the Christ, what in the world was he doing on a *cross*? This was what lay behind Peter's rebuke when Jesus began to spell out the plan: he would be mocked, beaten, and then killed (Matthew 16:21 – 22). No, the Christ should conquer; he must prevail over the enemies of God and restore godly order to the chosen people (a common expectation). It's just not kosher to run around saying that the mighty Christ would be (or *was*) crucified.

Peter's comment in turn drew a sharp rebuke from Jesus (Matthew 16:23). Peter's understanding rose no further than the merely human and satanically inspired desire for an earthly victory (over the hated Romans). He had no room for the Suffering Servant. He failed to grasp the centrality of the cross.

## God's Hidden Wisdom

According to Paul, Peter was in good company. *No one* understood what was going on in the spiritual realm at the time. We see in 1 Corinthians that the church was divided over little factions lining up with their favorite preachers, but Paul redirected them to the power of the cross (1:17–18). The Jews wanted signs and the Greeks were enamored with wisdom, but Paul's message was a crucified Christ, a scandal for the Jews and utter nonsense for the Greeks (1:22–23). This was God's hidden wisdom, a plan to use folly and weakness (in the eyes of the world) to provide "righteousness, holiness and redemption," in other words, the power of God to transform lost lives (1:24–31).

Paul continues this focus in 1 Corinthians 2. He doesn't rely on a polished recital; his only focus is "Jesus Christ and him crucified" (2:2). Faith needs to rest on a worthy object, and human wisdom is just not up to the task (2:4–5). No one knew what God was up to; no one understood, "for if they had, they would not have crucified the Lord of glory" (2:6–8). This was God's plan, hidden for ages but finally revealed to the apostles by the Holy Spirit, who alone could provide this spiritual insight (2:10).

## The Curse of the Tree

Still, the cross had to be explained; it was a scandal to Jews and foolishness to the Gentiles. Let's focus on the scandal aspect from a Jewish perspective. The background for this reaction to crucifixion comes from the Old Testament: "Anyone who is hung on a tree is under God's curse" (Deuteronomy 21:23). Originally, the reference was to the practice of exposure, that is, of putting a corpse on a tree to allow nature to take its course in full view of all. Israel, rather, honored the body by anointing and wrapping it, and then laying it in a tomb so decomposition would discreetly take place out of sight (and other senses as they may be adversely affected). Only a wretch would be exposed by being affixed to a tree.

By the time Paul wrote Galatians, Jewish writers had already applied Deuteronomy 21:23 to crucifixion.[34] This was the implication for Jesus: he plainly could not have been God's Messiah since he died, as it were, on a tree. Only the worst of the worst were crucified; it therefore follows that Jesus was so obviously cursed by God that any attempts to honor him were beyond absurd.

Still, the curse was another inroad for explaining salvation. "Christ redeemed us from the curse of the law by becoming a curse for us, for it is written: 'Cursed is everyone who is hung on a tree'" (Galatians 3:13, citing Deuteronomy 21:23). Paul does not deny Jesus was cursed. To do so would be to deny the Scriptures. Jesus was cursed by God while hanging on the cross, since it was there that he took upon himself every shameful thing the human race is capable of doing. "He himself bore our sins in his body on the tree" (1 Peter 2:24). Sin was decisively dealt with, and then Jesus breathed his last.

## SUMMING UP

Let's lay this myth to rest. The death of Jesus in this fashion is a central tenet of the Christian message. It is carefully depicted, fully explored, and continually applied to various aspects of Christian life and thought. Christian teaching about redemption and forgiveness, even the metaphors for sacrificial living, are all meaningless apart from the historical reality to which they point. Why did the writers choose to focus so much of their attention on this event (not to mention mounting a defense of it)? Why didn't anyone interrupt Peter or Paul and say, "Hey, Jesus didn't die; he's living over there in Capernaum"? Why is it that no one from the ancient world ever advanced a theory that Jesus survived the cross (again, except for the

Gnostics)? As long as we're at it, why didn't anyone point to his survival on the cross as an explanation for the resurrection appearances? It's really pretty simple. Too many people saw him die.

This is so powerful an argument, by the way, that people who deny the resurrection point to the fact of his death as exhibit A! Dead people, as even a child can tell you, do not get up again. May I point out that the critics can't have it both ways? Either he died or he didn't, and you can't deny his death if you're going to turn around and deny his resurrection from it. I know; it would be difficult to find an *individual* trying to hold to both criticisms, but both mythical assertions originate from skeptical circles.

It is well established that he really died, and only someone with an agenda would deny it. Now, it's on to the other side of the coin, so to speak. Let's talk about the myth that he didn't rise from the dead.

## GOING DEEPER

You can read the sources cited in this chapter in their contexts by linking to: www.westarkchurchofchrist.org/library/extrabiblical.htm and www.provethebible.net/T2-Divin/D–0201.htm.

The full text of *The Death of Peregrine*, an ancient writing, mentioned in this chapter, is available at www.sacred-texts.com/cla/luc/wl4/wl420.htm.

For an explanation of the apparent discrepancy of the date of the crucifixion see D. A. Carson, *The Gospel according to John* (Downers Grove, IL: InterVarsity Press, 1991), 603–4. Gary Habermas deals more with *The Passover Plot* and the dismantling of the swoon theory (among other useful discussions) in *Ancient Evidence for the Life of Jesus* (Nashville: Nelson, 1984). Also, check out his article "Dr. Habermas Answers Important Questions" at www.garyhabermas.com/qa/qa_index.htm.

# Chapter 9

# JESUS NEVER ROSE FROM THE DEAD

In the previous chapter we dealt with the fact that Jesus died and was placed in a tomb. What difference does it make if he's still there? These affirmations, Jesus' death and resurrection, with their full theological significance, form the bedrock of Christianity. The real myth here is that a still-dead Jesus wouldn't have any effect on Christianity, but as Paul so aptly puts it, "if Christ has not been raised, your faith is futile; you are still in your sins" (1 Corinthians 15:17).

## IF HE DIDN'T RISE . . .

In February 2007 we were treated to the breathless claim that the bones of Jesus, and others in the family (including Jesus' alleged wife!) were found in Jerusalem. (I should say "again" because the initial "discovery" was in 1980.) Suffice to say it's been sufficiently debunked, but one statement really got my attention. John Dominic Crossan, a noted critic of evangelical Christianity, said that finding the bones of Jesus wouldn't destroy his Christianity or his faith.[35] I won't presume to discuss what his personal faith may be, but how a still-dead Jesus should affect Christianity is an issue of historical record. What Christianity actually is *by definition* concerns clear, nonnegotiable affirmations. Deny these affirmations and you simply cannot be a Christian.

I know, this sounds so intolerably narrow-minded, but bear with me for a little clarification. It's pretty clear Christianity as it is practiced today is capable of an incredible variety of expressions with all of the denominations, parachurch organizations, and renewal movements new and ancient. There are many issues we can wrangle over, and there are some significant gray areas.

That said, it doesn't rule out the fact there are some statements in Scripture that draw the lines clearly. We need to believe that Jesus is the Christ, the Son of God (1 John 2:22; 3:23; 5:5), and the sole means of salvation (John 14:12; Acts 4:12). All genuine believers of all denominations believe these things. These are defining doctrines of Christianity. The resurrection is another central belief. Paul declares: "If you confess with your mouth, 'Jesus is Lord,' and believe in your heart that God raised him from the dead, you will be saved" — a belief leading to justification and a confession yielding salvation (Romans 10:9 – 10).

Now, it might be tempting to say this verse doesn't say anything about what one *must* believe; it simply states the benefits of such a belief. But what if we take the opposite position of the verse? What if we deny that he's Lord and say he's still dead? It would follow, then, that we would *not* be justified and, as a result, *not* be saved.

## ALTERNATE THEORIES

Before returning to the specifics of Christian faith, we need to determine what happened to the body if Jesus did not rise from the dead. Do alternate theories hold up under scrutiny?

### Those Pesky Disciples

The oldest counterclaim to the resurrection can be found in Matthew 28:11 – 15. The soldiers guarding the tomb saw an angel descend and roll the stone away, and then they heard the report that Jesus had risen. At a loss what to do, they went and reported it to the chief priests, who paid the soldiers handsomely to say, "His disciples came during the night and stole him away while we were asleep" (28:13). This account apparently had some staying power, since "this story has been widely circulated among the Jews to this very day" (28:15), that is, when Matthew wrote, anywhere from the 60s to 80s.

Could this, in fact, be the real report and the *resurrection* be the fictional one? The claim stands that the disciples took the body while the guards slept. Since it was Pilate's order in the first place, Roman troops would have set a seal on the tomb (Matthew 27:65–66). Unauthorized entry would incur the penalty of death, as was falling asleep on duty, so it is unlikely they handled their duty with such a carefree attitude. Remember, the chief priests promised to intervene if the made-up-on-the-spot report ever made it to Pilate's ears (28:14). Still, this theory has a fatal flaw. Who can ever offer eyewitness testimony about what happens *while one is sleeping*?

Well, let's grant the point that the disciples are the culprits. If so, this only makes their unwavering and central testimony that Jesus in fact came back to life more puzzling. It is one thing to hold to a lie in the face of opposition; it is quite another to go willingly to one's death for it. All of the disciples (except for John) faced hideous deaths at the hands of their opponents.[36] Is it likely that not one of them "fessed up" while they were being flayed alive or nailed to a cross upside down?

## Those Crafty Leaders

Even if the disciples are off the hook, someone else could have taken the body, perhaps the Jewish leaders themselves. Once again, however, there's a problem. Given the leaders anticipated some shenanigans on the third day after the crucifixion (Matthew 27:63–64), why would they do something that fueled the very deception they went out of their way to squelch? Even if they had done such a thing, when the disciples started making a ruckus about the resurrection some weeks later, why didn't the Jewish leaders stop them by producing the body? Weeks of lying in a hidden tomb would tend to contradict the claim that Jesus was alive. No risen Christ, no Christianity.

Incidentally, it's a delicious irony that the Jewish leaders understood what Jesus said about the third day, but it was utterly lost on the disciples (Matthew 16:21–22; Luke 18:33–34). The irony is the leaders were compelled to lie about what had happened, and the disciples, who weren't even expecting it, came to believe in the resurrection only in the face of irrefutable evidence (Luke 24:36–43; Acts 1:3).

## Other Shady Characters

Who else could have taken Jesus' body? The Roman soldiers had no reason to do it, and every reason to do their best to ensure it stayed put. That was, after all, their assigned task; stealing what they were charged to guard would have gained them residency in their *own* tombs. What about Pilate? That would work, if we believe that he'd incite the very riot he was trying to avoid. How about the women? I suppose it's plausible if we can picture them overpowering trained soldiers. Maybe Mary knew some jujitsu.

Now, the women could've simply gone to the wrong tomb with Jesus' body lying in stately repose elsewhere, as some scholars have suggested. If so, then Joseph of Arimathea, who had personally hewn it out of solid rock (doubtless a memorable experience in itself), could've straightened things out (Matthew 27:59–60). Again, when the disciples started proclaiming the resurrection, a little stroll to the *right* tomb would've put an end to their folly.

## Let's Blame Fido

In the mid-1990s John Dominic Crossan made the novel assertion that since Jesus was executed as a criminal, his final resting place would've been a shallow pauper's grave, easy pickings for ravenous scavengers. Jesus' body was never produced because dogs had eaten it. It's worth mentioning that he doesn't offer any proof other than what he guesses might have happened, and that no other critic of Christianity has ever floated such a theory. I personally find it interesting, though. Remember, Crossan said in 2007 that finding Jesus' bones in a tomb wouldn't damage his Christianity or faith. What he didn't say was how it might affect his earlier bogus theory about the dogs.

## What Did They See?

Granting for the sake of argument that Jesus' body was whisked away, what accounts for the reports of his appearances? Keep in mind, no one—from the ancient enemies of the faith to the most current critic—*no one* denies the disciples *claimed* Jesus rose from the dead and claimed to have actually seen him. The question then becomes, "Why say such a thing?" If the answer to that question is "because they saw something," then we need to ask what it was they actually saw.

We touched on this in chapter 3, but we need to ask again: Was it wishful thinking, hallucinations, or maybe a bit of group hypnosis (or hysteria)? Perhaps it was really a ghost, the disembodied spirit of the terribly-wronged Jesus destined to roam the streets of Jerusalem ever seeking justice. All of these fail at a crucial point; they all present Jesus as intangible, and the appearances in the Gospels include the specific claim that he physically stood before his disciples. Some spontaneously reached for him (Matthew 28:9; John 20:17–18); on other occasions he showed them his nail-scarred body and insisted that they touch him (Luke 24:39–40; John 20:27). He even ate with them (Luke 24:42–43; John 21:12; Acts 1:4), which I guess would be a little difficult without a real mouth.

They could've all been lying, but this fails for the reasons listed above. It also fails to explain the empty tomb and reports of seeing Jesus alive again. What happened?

Pressing a little further, we need to look at a scoffer, a murderous persecutor, and a hothead that chickens out at the crucial moment, and ask what it would take to transform them into devoted followers of Jesus after his disgraceful death. I refer to James, Paul, and Peter.

## THE MOCKER, THE MURDERER, AND THE WIMP

### The Mocker

During the days of Jesus' earthly ministry he frequently met with opposition. Even his own family was worried about him, thinking he was maybe two candles shy of a menorah. On one occasion they tried to take charge of him (Mark 3:21); on another his brothers openly mocked him (John 7:3 – 5).[37]

These and other references to the family and to Jesus' brothers included James (see the list of family members in Matthew 13:55 – 56; Mark 6:3). The interesting thing here is that James later became known for his intense devotion to his brother. His knees were said to have developed thick calluses because of the long hours spent on them in prayer, and his godly lifestyle was a model for all, earning him the moniker "James the Just." Even more stunning, James became the leader of the Jerusalem church a few years after Jesus' death (see Acts 15).[38] James the mocker became James the leader. What could have caused such a change of heart?

In 1 Corinthians 15 Paul goes through a list of resurrection appearances. "Then he appeared to James" (v. 7) stands out. It doesn't take too much imagination to piece together a progression of events. His brother was brutally beaten, nailed to a cross, and then hastily buried when he'd breathed his last. Oops. Surprise! He's breathing again three days later. We can only imagine what went through James's mind as his "dead" brother walked up and said, "Hi." The aftermath we *do* know. The mocker became the camel-kneed disciple enthralled with the Lord, his brother, for whom he took the reins of the young church in Jerusalem, and to whom Peter, John, and Paul deferred. Let's not forget that James also gave his life for his brother.

### The Murderer

Speaking of Paul, his story is even more remarkable. Here was a man utterly dedicated to Judaism and the law. He was present at

Stephen's stoning (Acts 8:1) and even launched his own attack on Christians (9:1 – 2). Persecuting believers to their death (22:4), he set out to destroy the church (Galatians 1:13). Then, one day, he changed. What caused his famous change of heart? Perhaps he too had a little quality time with a "dead" man.

A confrontation with Jesus on the road to Damascus knocked Saul flat with the blinding flash of a stunning revelation. Jesus had a new plan for the little ruffian from Tarsus. When Jesus appeared and asked, "Saul, Saul, why are you persecuting me?" the blood had to have drained from his trembling face. Jesus commissioned him on the spot for the task of apostleship.[39] This appearance of the risen Jesus was the defining moment in Paul's life. The scene is repeated three times within Acts (9:1 – 18; 22:3 – 16; 26:11 – 18), and the implications of it surfaces again and again (Romans 1:4 – 5; 1 Corinthians 15:8 – 10; Galatians 1:15 – 16; Philippians 3:12). In all of Paul's letters the resurrection of God's Son has a central role.

## The Wimp

Our final example is Peter. Of course, it's a bit harsh, not to mention inaccurate, to sum up Peter's life as a shrinking violet; he was anything but. He was the one whose zeal and bravado often ran far ahead of any restraint he had tucked away. He proclaimed Jesus the "Christ" (Mark 8:29), walked on the water with him (Matthew 14:29), and stood up to the mob sent to arrest his Master, deftly slicing off someone's ear in the process (John 18:10, though I bet he was aiming for a forehead).

This same sort of "jump first and think about it later" attitude was likely in full swing as Jesus warned that his arrest and death were near. "I will lay down my life for you" was Peter's brave reply (John 13:37). Jesus knew, however, that a few folks were going to challenge him in a few hours and that Peter would crumble (13:38). The great apostle backed down from admitting he even *knew* Jesus, shrinking at the accusations of a young girl (Matthew 26:69 – 70).

A little over a month later Peter rocked Jerusalem with the fledgling church's first sermon (Acts 2:14–40). He refused to back down in the face of threats (4:8–12) and ventured out into uncharted territory, preaching to Gentiles (10:9–48). What caused such a change?

Of all the appearances, I'll just bet the little talk on the beach recorded in John 21 was the most memorable for Peter. Most commentators agree the threefold "Do you love me?" followed by the charge to watch over God's flock, was Peter's restoration. It was a reversal of the threefold denial.

Communing with the risen Jesus was nothing less, to Peter, than God's mercy opening up a new way. He called the relationship with Jesus a "new birth into a living hope through the resurrection of Jesus Christ from the dead" (1 Peter 1:3). His boldness now had a real focus—the reality of the living Lord. So the church's pastor told his people, "Prepare your minds for action; be self-controlled; set your hope fully on the grace to be given you when Jesus Christ is revealed" (1:13).

Jesus' resurrection was the historical fact that transformed these three, and countless others like them, throughout history. It is not easily brushed aside as irrelevant.

## "THE" MESSAGE

Recall that this is precisely what Crossan does with his offhand comment. Finding Jesus' bones may not be troubling to him personally, but it would be devastating to the Christian message. The resurrection, in the light of its prominence in the New Testament, is *the* defining event and central miracle of Christianity, *the* focus of the church's proclamation, from day one.

It is often pointed out that the first people to announce the resurrection were women. Though not so much of a big deal in our day, it is pretty stunning for the gospel writers (all four of them) to include this fact, because a woman's testimony was regarded as worthless in the ancient world. Stunning, that is, if the gospel writers were making up the story. Why include these culturally unreliable witnesses in such a prime position unless they were simply reporting the facts as they occurred?

It's also a bit gutsy to take that message for a test spin in the very town in which he was slain, proclaiming "Jesus is Lord" to the very ones who clamored for his death. It's unbelievably stupid to make the fact of Jesus' resurrection your focus a mere stone's throw away from the grave where he was laid. Stupid, that is, if he were still in it.

The apostles were threatened and mistreated, repeatedly forbidden to preach in the name of Jesus, but they refused to back down. The resurrected Lord was their message and reason for their courage; his Spirit was the empowering presence encouraging them to proclaim Jesus in the temple and the marketplace. Thousands came to faith, yet no one produced a body to stop them. Nobody said a word about a tomb still occupied with its Galilean guest.

Lacking the space to discuss all the ins and outs of this topic and the scores of verses that deal with the resurrection, we can still get a feel for how dominant the theme really is by doing a quick overview. After this sketch, we'll look a little more closely at a famous passage dealing with the topic. We have to keep a key question in mind as we review these passages: Can we dispense with the resurrection?

## Some Key Verses

Let's look first at the book of Acts. Peter's first sermon focused on the fact of the resurrection (Acts 2:14–40).[40] A few days later Peter affirmed Jesus' resurrection as the reason miracles were happening (3:16; 4:10). The resurrection was also Peter's main point before a Gentile audience (10:40–41). It was the same for Paul. Whether it was in a synagogue (13:29–31), before pagan philosophers (17:29–31), or before the Sanhedrin, a governor, or a king (23:6; 24:21; 26:7–8), Paul made the resurrection the centerpiece of his mission and message. Apart from it, according to the book of Acts, there was no message.

It's the same in Paul's letters. His call was from the God who raised Jesus from the dead (Galatians 1:1, 15 – 16). The desire to know Jesus, identifying with him in his resurrection (and in suffering), captivated his soul (Philippians 3:10 – 11). The resurrection powerfully demonstrated Jesus was the Son of God (Romans 1:4), the means by which God declares us righteous (4:23 – 25), and the content of our belief (10:9). The resurrection of Jesus is the power behind our renewed lives (6:4 – 5; 7:4; 2 Corinthians 5:15; Ephesians 1:19 – 20; Colossians 2:12; 3:1), and the hope of our future resurrections (Romans 8:11; 1 Corinthians 6:14; 2 Corinthians 4:14). It was, in short, the core of Paul's gospel (2 Timothy 2:8). What would Paul have said if one of his sermons were interrupted by a delivery of a certain carpenter's bones?

This only scratches the surface, but before moving on I want to focus on the classic passage on the topic of resurrection in the New Testament, 1 Corinthians 15.

## What If Jesus Is Still Dead? (1 Corinthians 15:12 – 19)

When preaching to the Corinthians, Paul had to deal with a clash of cultures. He was preaching the resurrection of Christ in a world that had no room for resurrection *at all* (1 Corinthians 15:12). If nobody ever rises from the dead, "then not even Christ has been raised" (15:13). This wouldn't matter much to scholars like Crossan, but for Paul it meant "our preaching is useless and so is your faith" (15:14). Let that one sink in a bit. All of Paul's travels, preaching, teaching, training, church planting—all of it would be a crock.

Some of the Corinthians had latched on to a worthless faith. Paul was a liar to them; but even worse, he was also making God out to be one, "for we have testified about God that he raised Christ from the dead" (1 Corinthians 15:15). The rest of this section takes another lap around the track, adding some stark conclusions along the way: if Jesus is dead, their faith is empty; they are still in their sins, and the dead are lost (15:17–18). Then comes the clincher: "If only for this life we have hope in Christ, we are to be pitied more than all men" (15:19).

That is, of course, precisely where Crossan's brand of Christianity would leave us. A still-dead Christ leaves us without any hope beyond the grave. If *he's* still dead, how could *we* ever hope to overcome our own deaths?

I've often heard it said that if Christianity turns out to be false after all, then at least we've lived a good life (living moral, loving lives with a sense of inner peace). That wasn't Paul's experience (Acts 14:19; 16:19–24; 23:12–15; 2 Corinthians 1:8–11; 11:24–29; Galatians 3:13–14; 2 Timothy 4:14–16). Just as the world hated Jesus, it hates all those who proclaim his message (John 15:18). Paul particularly took the full brunt of this satanically inspired fury—beatings, floggings, imprisonment, one stark-raving terror after another—precisely for stepping up to the plate for the cause of Christ (2 Corinthians 11:22–31; Ephesians 6:11–12; Colossians 1:24). Paul knew the glory to follow would make all the suffering far more than worth it (Romans 8:18). It would all be for nothing, however, if Jesus were still in a box. Paul just wasted his life getting the snot kicked out of him.

## He's Not Dead (1 Corinthians 15:20–28)

Paul didn't stand for any such possibility. "But Christ has indeed been raised from the dead, the firstfruits of those who have fallen asleep" (1 Corinthians 15:20). Unless you're familiar with farming practices of the ancient world, "firstfruits" may seem a bit strange. In Old Testament times Israel celebrated God's provision by offering him a portion of the first grains to appear, recognizing what God had done and appealing for a bountiful harvest. Calling Christ "the firstfruits of those who have fallen asleep" celebrates God's miracle of raising Jesus to life and the promise of a day to come when all his faithful ones will be raised to a new life.

Paul's argument here is not philosophical; it's biblical. Both in this section and again in 1 Corinthians 15:42–50, the resurrection is God's grand plan for the human race. Adam sinned, bestowing death and plunging the world into a long dark nightmare. Jesus came to fix what Adam had so totally messed up, but had to do so in his humanity. Only one who dies can have any chance of conquering death, for the only way to beat death is to come alive again.

### The "Others"

Before bringing this chapter to a close, I need to say something about the rest of the New Testament letters, Hebrews through Revelation. The references are not nearly as numerous as in Paul's writings, but they all share the same view. In Hebrews 13:20, God is invoked as the One who brought Jesus "back from the dead." James speaks of the "glorious Lord" (James 2:1, which evokes his resurrected body indirectly), whose return is near (5:7–8).

The resurrection was the focus of faith for Peter (1 Peter 1:3, 21) and the unseen power behind baptism (3:21). John affirmed that he physically touched the (risen?) Lord (1 John 1:1; see Luke 24:39), and shared the same kind of hope in transformation spoken of by Paul (1 John 3:2). Finally in Revelation, John refers to Jesus as "the firstborn from the dead" (1:5), quotes Jesus as declaring, "I was dead, and behold I am alive for ever and ever!" (1:18), and he has a vision of Jesus standing in the heavenly throne room, after he "had been slain" (5:6).

Even when the resurrection isn't directly mentioned, it is always in the background. Every teaching of the New Testament, particularly in the letters, takes as its starting point that Jesus is alive (again). That is how he is able to help us (Hebrews 2:18), how he can represent us in God's presence (6:19–20; 8:1–2), offer grace and mercy (2 John 3), intercede for us (Hebrews 7:25), return for us (1 Peter 5:4), and bestow eternal life on us (Hebrews 9:28; Jude 21).

I have risked presenting this detail in this compressed style for a simple reason. I want to impress upon you the fact that the resurrection is the focal point of the entire New Testament witness. Without it, there is no reason for Christianity. This just may be an occasion for Crossan to seriously rethink his position.

## SUMMING UP

Something happened about two thousand years ago that transformed a handful of assorted blue-collar workers, followers of an executed rabbi, into fearless apostles with a focused message: Jesus is alive. The resurrection proclamation formed the basis of everything the apostles wrote and did. It is the sole basis for the existence of the church. Counterclaims fall far short of explaining what happened. The body wasn't stolen; we need not look askance at some poor Palestinian pooch. No one erred by going to the wrong tomb; they examined the correct one, which was, incidentally, quite empty. Appearances can't be chalked up to hallucinations; there are just too many of them in such a variety of circumstances.

One could still deny that the resurrection happened, contrary to the evidence. There are many who do so, but one thing is for certain: no one can reasonably claim that a still-dead Jesus would have no effect on Christianity. If Jesus is dead, then so is our message.

## GOING DEEPER

It has been years since I've looked at them, but two books that influenced my thinking on this topic are Josh McDowell, *More Than a Carpenter* (Wheaton: Tyndale House, 1977; reprinted 2004), and *Evidence That Demands a Verdict* (San Bernardino, CA: Here's Life Publishers, 1972; reprinted 1979). He has since produced a series: *New Evidence, More Evidence*, etc. For a thorough scholarly study of Jesus' resurrection see N. T. Wright, *The Resurrection of the Son of God*, vol. 3 of *Christian Origins and the Question of God* (Minneapolis: Fortress, 2003). I am grateful to Arnie Gentile for his insight concerning James and Paul.

Another instance of breaking into a cold sweat (see the Going Deeper section from chapter 3) occurred while reading Gary Habermas and Michael Licona, *A Case for the Resurrection of Jesus* (Grand Rapids: Kregel, 2004). But once again, addressing this issue from an evangelical viewpoint leads inevitably to bringing up the same types of arguments. So, we have a similar approach, but there are also significant differences. In any case, I highly recommend this book as a resource for defending the fact of the resurrection.

# Chapter 10

# JESUS NEVER CLAIMED TO BE GOD

People today are willing to concede Jesus was a good man, a gifted teacher, and a sound moral example. But that's not the whole picture of Jesus presented in the New Testament. He is all of those things, but so much more. You cannot speak meaningfully about Jesus without immediately plunging into deep waters. That, my friends, is where the trouble starts, because Christians claim he is *God*. Others are convinced he's *not*. Some people take it further and, while acknowledging that the Bible may point in that direction, still insist Jesus *himself* never made such a claim. As you might have guessed, this last statement is simply a myth.

Before we deal directly with this topic, however, we must clarify some things. The moment we peer into Jesus' identity, we find that the Bible presents him as both divine and human. His humanity is pretty clear, but on the God side of the issue, we have to grapple with how he relates to the Father and the Spirit. If Jesus is God, was he really human? Who was he talking to when he prayed? How many Gods are there anyway?

These kinds of questions keep coming up, and you can't blame people for being confused. The New Testament looks us straight in the eye and insists there is only *one* God and in the next breath calls *three* persons "God." How this all pans out is the delightful topic of the next chapter (the Trinity). This chapter, however, focuses on the identity and person of Jesus, particularly, his deity and unity with the Father.

## WOULD *YOU* WORSHIP A CARPENTER?

Two key issues play into this particular myth. The first is whether the New Testament writers claimed Jesus was God, and the second is whether Jesus himself went along with such a claim (or, if he was the *source* of these claims). The second issue is the focus of this chapter, but we need to look at the first one to set the stage. It is one thing to refuse to believe Jesus is God (to be fair, it is a bit of a stretch to regard a Jewish carpenter as one's Creator); it is another thing to say the *Bible* never makes the claim. Too many verses clearly do just that. Allow me to give a quick overview.

John calls him God. "In the beginning was the Word, and the Word was with God, and the Word was God," and then John tells us that "the Word became flesh" (John 1:1, 14). Once you realize that the "Word" refers to Jesus (which no New Testament scholar, critical or otherwise, disputes), it's pretty hard to get around John's claim that the Word was in fact God.[41] It's also fairly easy to see we're already over our heads in some pretty deep theology, but we're just going to have to focus. Our only concern at this point is whether biblical writers call Jesus "God," which is clearly what John does.

Paul calls him God when he speaks of "the blessed hope — the glorious appearing of our great God and Savior, Jesus Christ" (Titus 2:13).[42] Peter also refers to him as "our God and Savior Jesus Christ" (2 Peter 1:1). Some say they are talking about two individuals (God, and Jesus the Savior), but the same kind of phrasing when referring to one person is routine. No one argues that "our God and Father" (1 Corinthians 1:3) refers to two beings, and no one says Paul is referring to two people when he calls his messenger Tychicus "the dear brother and faithful servant" (Ephesians 6:21). Even when New Testament writers call Jesus "our Lord and Savior" (2 Peter 3:18), no one bats an eye. The usual reason skeptics offer that "God and Savior" can't refer to Jesus is because they deny Jesus is God. In other words, it's a circular argument. Peter and Paul, however, couldn't have been clearer. For them, Jesus is their God; he is their Savior.

Not only did these writers call Jesus "God," but they also record the claims of others doing so. At first Thomas doubts Jesus rose from the dead (hence the nickname, "Doubting Thomas"), but when the risen Jesus suddenly appears in front of him his whole world is rocked. All wide-eyed and thunderstruck, he blurts out: "My Lord and my God!" (John 20:28). This is actually the first time a human being makes this astounding claim, a week after Jesus' resurrection. What he did *not* say was something like, "Oh my God, it's you!" He makes this statement *to* and *about* Jesus, and Jesus commends him for seeing and (finally) believing. (Why we still refer to him as Doubting Thomas is beyond me; he should be called "The-First-and-Most-Incredibly-Focused-Affirmation-of-Jesus'-Deity Thomas," but I guess that's a bit wordy.)

The writer to the Hebrews even says that God (the Father) calls Jesus (the Son) "God" when he explains the significance of some Old Testament passages. God calls his angels "servants," but when he refers to the Son he says, "Your throne, O God, will last for ever and ever" (Hebrews 1:8). Now someone could argue that the writer is misusing the Old Testament citation, but our only point at this stage of the game is whether or not New Testament writers call Jesus "God" or record others doing so. They clearly do.

## JUST WHO DOES HE THINK HE IS?

Beyond these types of clear affirmations, there are also several instances in which Jesus says or does something that in essence *depicts* himself as God, or ascribes to himself the attributes of God. Jesus' healing of a paralytic in Mark 2:1 – 12 is a fine example.

In the midst of the drama, Jesus tells the unfortunate lad, "your sins are forgiven." Was he just saying, "Cheer up, my friend; as a man of the cloth I can tell you that God forgives you," or was there more to it? We need look no further than the scribes' response. "He's blaspheming!" they grumble to each other. "Who can forgive sins but God alone?" For any God-fearing first-century Jew the expected answer to this question is, "No one." But there was Jesus, standing in a crowded Capernaum hovel declaring that he, Jesus, forgives the sin of a fellow townsman. If Jesus was *not* claiming the authority to do what only God can do, he had a good opportunity to straighten things out. He didn't. He pressed on and demonstrated his own authority "to forgive sins on earth" by declaring the paralyzed man healed *and forgiven*. (Incidentally, this may be a nice little allusion to God's actions in Psalm 103:2–4.)

It's true that he never says "I'm God" here; the point is that the episode *depicts* him as such. The scribes ask, "Who can forgive sins but God alone?" and Jesus answers, in essence, "I do." So what, you say? Well, it takes a little imagination to wrap our minds around the scribes' outrage, but it boils down to a simple observation. A carpenter turned preacher has no divine right to forgive *anyone's* sins (or more accurately, to do what only God can do). Because Jesus looked at the paralyzed man and did just that, the scene became one of several of those "Who do you think you are?" moments.

Another example of a depiction of Jesus as God is the image of Jesus as the ultimate judge, a role reserved for God alone in the Old Testament. Toward the end of the Sermon on the Mount Jesus told his disciples, "Not everyone who says to me, 'Lord, Lord,' will enter the kingdom of heaven, but only he who does the will of my Father who is in heaven" (Matthew 7:21). Notice they're calling him "Lord" in this judgment setting, with Jesus claiming the exclusive right to declare who does and does not do the will of the Father. This "will," of course, is how folks respond to *Jesus*. "Many will say to *me* on that day ... Then *I* will tell them plainly ..." (7:22–23; my emphasis). Not only is he the judge, but also the standard of judgment.

It's true that in nonbiblical Jewish writings of the era humans were pictured as having a role in the judgment. These individuals, however, were heroes and notables of the distant past (like Moses, Enoch, or some mysterious personage). It is one thing to use a literary convention in a book arguably never intended as Scripture; it would be another thing if Jesus employed such a familiar image in a fiery sermon. "Enoch will arise in the judgment and condemn you in the presence of God!" But no, this is very different. A formerly boring carpenter from hick Nazareth suddenly starts preaching that no one enters the heavenly kingdom apart from his say so. This is chutzpa on a grand scale.

## IS THE LORD THE "LORD"?

Pressing the issue still further, there are several passages in the Old Testament referring to Yahweh that are applied specifically to Jesus in the New Testament. This is what we should expect. When the first Christians sought to express the majesty of the risen Jesus, they pored over their ancient texts. Jesus himself had given them the pattern. "This is what I told you while I was still with you: Everything must be fulfilled that is written about me in the Law of Moses, the Prophets and the Psalms" (Luke 24:44). With illuminated minds they saw the Scriptures in a new light. Not only were they a record of God's dealing with his people, Israel, but they also became a rich resource for understanding the full significance of Jesus.

For the first time this tightly woven tapestry of the centuries-old plan of God became clear. The drama of the ages was being acted out before their very eyes in the life, death, resurrection, and glorification of Jesus of Nazareth. It was inevitable for them to see Jesus as, for instance, the one whose glorious arrival was proclaimed in the desert (Isaiah 40:3), the one who was pierced (Zechariah 12:10), and the one upon whom people should call for salvation (Joel 2:32). Inevitable on the one hand, but on the other hand, it was simply breathtaking for first-century monotheists to refer to Jesus in this way. Why? Because these Old Testament passages refer to Yahweh, the God of Israel.

### A Closer Look

Our English versions often use a substitute for God's name in the Old Testament. The Old Testament, you'll recall, was originally written in Hebrew (with a smattering of Aramaic). Through the course of time, God's name was considered so holy that a tradition developed of not pronouncing it. A rabbi would see the name "Yahweh" but say the word "*Adonai*," which means "Lord." English versions are influenced by this tradition and usually render Yahweh as "Lord," but here's a detail you don't want to miss: when translating "Yahweh" English versions use all capitals ("Lord"), but when translating "*Adonai*" only the first letter is capitalized ("Lord").

One more detail needs to be addressed before moving on. This "Lord" versus "Lord" issue only shows up in the Old Testament. The New Testament was originally written in Greek, which has only one word that can stand for either Yahweh or *Adonai* in quotations from the Old Testament. So when we examine some passages in a moment, you won't see the all-caps "Lord" used at all in the New Testament; it's always "Lord."

Don't get lost in the shuffle; the point of all of this is that several individuals in the Old Testament could be addressed as an *Adonai*, that is, as "Lord." God, of course, could be, but so could earthly kings and dignitaries, "masters" of every description, even the simple, polite "sir." But there is only one Yahweh. He is the Almighty, Maker of heaven and earth, the Holy One enthroned in glory and majesty, Redeemer of his people Israel, the One who rescued them with a mighty hand, gave them his law, and led them for millennia. Yep, Yahweh is the God of the Old Testament, the One and only.

Can you begin to sense why it was a little unsettling for the Jews of the early days of the young church? The carpenter's followers were running around referring to him as the Yahweh of their ancient Scriptures.

### What Were They Thinking?

Isaiah 40:3 predicted there would come a time when a herald would appear in the desert announcing the return of "the Lord" (Yahweh) to his people. This is fulfilled in Matthew 3, with John the Baptist using the Isaiah passage as his marching orders. His message was "Prepare the way for the Lord, make straight paths for him" (3:3). John warned the people that the Mighty One, who would baptize with the Holy Spirit and fire, was about to arrive (3:11). For those steeped in the Old Testament, the imagery and language would arouse an expectation of God's glorious return to save his people and judge her enemies, but all heads turn as the carpenter from Nazareth arrives (3:13). The one Isaiah called "LORD," Matthew identifies as Jesus.

About three years later the apostle John witnessed the death of Jesus on the cross. The guards were ordered to break the legs of the three victims crucified that day to hasten their death, but Jesus was already dead. A quick thrust of a spear satisfied the guard, but it intrigued John. He saw it as a fulfillment of prophecy: "They will look on the one they have pierced" (John 19:37).

"The one" John referred to is Jesus, and the quote is from Zechariah 12:10. The wording of Zechariah is slightly different, "They will look on me, the one they have pierced." Don't miss who "me" refers to. Zechariah 12 begins with: "This is the word of the LORD concerning Israel" (12:1). This message from "the LORD" is reinforced throughout the chapter; 12:10, the verse John applies to the crucifixion, is no different. The speaker is still "the LORD," as is obvious from the context. It is "the LORD" who says, "They will look on me, the one they have pierced," mourning for him as "for an only child," grieving bitterly as "for a firstborn son" (12:10). This being the case, "me," the one who is pierced, is "the LORD" (Yahweh). John calls him "Jesus."

The identity of the one who died leads directly to why all of this is so significant for us. The prophet Joel saw a day coming when "everyone who calls on the name of the LORD will be saved" (Joel 2:32). In Acts 2:21, Peter declares that the events on the Day of Pentecost fulfilled Joel's prophecy, only the "Lord" he tells us to call upon is Jesus.

Paul cites the same passage from Joel in Romans 10. This is right on the heels of the admonition, "if you confess with your mouth, 'Jesus is Lord,' and believe in your heart that God raised him from the dead, you will be saved" (10:9). The tongue confesses and the heart believes, says Paul, for "everyone who calls on the name of the Lord will be saved" (10:13). Joel urged people to call upon "the LORD" (Yahweh) and he would save them; Peter and Paul say "Amen. Call on Jesus."

## AS HE SEES IT

It is one thing for New Testament writers to call Jesus God, to depict him as such, or to apply the name Yahweh to him. The question remains: Did Jesus ever call *himself* God? If you mean by the question whether or not Jesus uttered the words "I am God," the short answer is no. Surprised? Don't be. What he *did do* was *describe himself* in such a way as to unmistakably claim *equality* with God, even *identity* as God.

Most of the time what Jesus said is lost on us, but his original audience picked up on it immediately. A good example is a story that unfolded in John 5. Jesus had just healed a man on the Sabbath, to the chagrin of the Jewish leaders. One should not work on the Sabbath, as he should have known, and healing someone was clearly doing work. Jesus is obviously evil! The rabbi from Nazareth defended himself by saying, "My Father is always at his work to this very day, and I, too, am working" (5:17). This *really* ticked them off. He wasn't just a Sabbath-breaker; he was "even calling God his own Father, making himself equal with God" (5:18).

### No Big Deal?

This accusation can easily sail right past us if we don't understand some basic principles of Judaism. The Sabbath was the day set apart for God's people to have a well-deserved rest and to reflect worshipfully on God's goodness. It was a holy day. It was ingrained in the very fabric of creation (Genesis 2:2 – 3) and enshrined in the law (Exodus 20:8 – 11). No one was allowed to work at all on the Sabbath, with two explicit exceptions. The first one was the priesthood (and later, synagogue leaders). Their very duties required them to present offerings and sacrifices; in other words, they worked on the Sabbath. But Jesus did not say, "My fellow priests and I are working." No, he said, "My Father is, and I am too." This brings us to the other exception for working on the Sabbath: God.

God, being God, is always on the job. The sun shines, clouds bring rain, flowers grow, and miracles occur. If he were to stop doing what he does (like sustaining the universe), everything would collapse in a resounding crash in the blink of an eye. "My Father works on the Sabbath; so do I." The Jewish leaders made the immediate connection that Jesus was talking about God, the Father. It was pretty rare for God to be called "Father" by the ancient Jews, but not unheard of (see Isaiah 63:16, for instance). For someone to claim God as "my Father" in the unique way Jesus did was indeed troubling, even scandalous. To claim *equal standing with him* was worthy of death. It was simply something nice men from out of town ought not do.

Maybe they misunderstood him; maybe Jesus did *not* make such a claim. Perhaps all he was saying was that he had a special relationship with God, so close that God seemed just like a Father to him. Here is a wonderful opportunity for Jesus to respond: "Wait a minute. You think I'm calling myself God's equal? Oh, come on, you guys; here's what I meant ..." followed by an explanation. But that's not what he said. Instead, Jesus gave a defense that actually got him deeper into trouble. Let's follow it verse by verse, beginning in John 5:19.

First, he only does what he sees the Father doing. In one sense, all of God's people are called to imitate him (Ephesians 5:1 – 2), but Jesus goes beyond this. He is not merely claiming to follow an ethical example; he claims an intimate, exclusive knowledge of the works of the Almighty, and he performs those very works. A little vague perhaps? Don't worry; it gets worse.

Jesus is the object of the Father's love, who works miracles through his ministry, even raising the dead (John 5:20–21). We need to look at this one a little closer. "For just as the Father raises the dead and gives them life, even so the Son gives life to whom he is pleased to give it." Notice what he does not say: "Just as God worked the miracle of resurrection through prophets in the past, he now does through me, just like a prophet." No, this runs much deeper. Jesus claims equality of power ("Just as God does, I do"), and equality of sovereignty ("Just as God freely chooses, so do I"). He claims to have the same power as God to raise the dead and to be able to do so to whomever he wants, just like God. This is pretty gutsy, but it gets worse.

Next he says the Father is *not* the judge (as the Jews had known him to be for millennia), but that he has delegated the task to the Son. We've already seen Jesus in the role of the end-time judge (Matthew 7:21). The real clincher in this passage is the *reason* he claims the Father has done this: "that all may honor the Son just as they honor the Father. He who does not honor the Son does not honor the Father, who sent him" (John 5:23).

We need to take a step back in time and hear this with first-century Jewish ears. Jesus, who was considered a backwater yokel by the cultured elite of Jerusalem, has just told them he is their ultimate judge. They owe him, Jesus, the same honor they owe God the Father, the exalted Yahweh of the Old Testament. What kind of honor did a first-century Jew owe to this God? We're talking about the God of Abraham, Isaac, and Jacob, the God of the promises and the covenants. He is the one who rescued Israel from slavery and brought them out with a mighty hand, gave them the law, established them in the Promised Land (twice, actually), revealed himself as holy, mighty, "the LORD of heaven and earth," and the one who commanded all devotion and love—heart, mind, soul, and strength. This all-encompassing heartfelt honor and worship they owed to God, was equally owed to Jesus.

Does he say "I'm God"? No, he simply claims equality with the One who sustains the universe, the sovereign One who alone gives life and raises the dead, the ultimate judge, who is worthy of all praise, worship, and unwavering obedience.

## They "Got" It, Do We?

There are several more examples that could be given, but space will permit only one more. This one is so clear we can afford to be brief, and it goes beyond the claim of equality—this is a claim of *identity*. Recall that God revealed his name to Moses from the burning bush as the great "I Am" (Exodus 3:14). At the end of a drawn-out controversy, Jesus told his opponents that Abraham rejoiced at seeing Jesus' day; in fact, "he saw it and was glad" (John 8:56).

The Jewish leaders were incredulous: "You are not yet fifty years old [stating the obvious] ... and you have seen Abraham!" (John 8:57). Everyone knew the great patriarch of the people of Israel lived about two thousand years before Jesus' day. What kind of nut would claim to have personally interacted with him?

Once again, the blue-collar worker from Nazareth plunges ahead: " 'I tell you the truth,' Jesus answered, 'before Abraham was born, I am' " (John 8:58).

If you'll recall the discussion of how English versions use "Lord" when representing Yahweh in the Old Testament, I need to tell you about a notable exception—the time Moses first encountered God. There he was, minding his own business as a muttering shepherd when he was surprised by a burning bush. It wasn't that it was on fire, but that it wasn't *burning up*. The "What the heck?" curiosity gave way to a divine encounter. Moses was witnessing a small sample of God's glory.

The details of this encounter need not detain us, except for one. When Moses asked God for his name, he replied: "I am who I am" and to tell Israel "I AM has sent me to you" (Exodus 3:14). "I AM," in this verse, is a translation of "Yahweh." (*Why* this is so concerns details of Hebrew grammar we'll just have to pass by.)

Now in John 8:58, there is no mistaking the allusion: Jesus claimed to be the great I Am, God Almighty, Israel's glorious King. His enemies got it: "At this, they picked up stones to stone him" (8:59). Why? Because claiming to be God was worthy of death.

## SUMMING UP

So, as a brief summary of the "this myth is busted" variety, the New Testament writers call Jesus "God" and depict him as such, doing what only God can do, applying Old Testament Scriptures about Yahweh directly to him without any attempt to justify the practice. They also record extended discourses in which Jesus himself makes the claim so unmistakably that he had to escape repeated attempts to kill him. The New Testament writers *called him* God because he so consistently presented himself to them *as* God.

Still, there is only one God. How that can be so and how Jesus relates to the Father and the Holy Spirit is the topic of the next chapter.

## GOING DEEPER

The deity of Jesus Christ is a fascinating and involved topic, concerning which this chapter merely scratches the surface. There are several short essays available online (search under "deity of Christ"). Some of them simply present the evidence, but others use groups that deny it as their springboard. For those of you who have studied Greek beyond the third semester I highly recommend Murray J. Harris, *Jesus as God: The New Testament Use of* Theos *in Reference to Jesus* (Grand Rapids: Baker, 1992), and Gordon Fee, *Pauline Christology: An Exegetical-Theological Study* (Peabody, MA: Hendrickson, 2007).

# MYTHS ABOUT GOD

# Chapter 11

# THE TRINITY WAS INVENTED BY FOURTH-CENTURY THEOLOGIANS

The previous chapter focused on the deity of Jesus. The Scriptures are clear he is God, but that still leaves some issues hanging. If Jesus is God, how does he relate to the Father and the Holy Spirit? Are there three Gods? If not, is the one God a three-headed monster? Some would have us believe so, or else insist that the whole concept was invented by enterprising souls in the fourth century. So, to kick things off, let's take a look at a famous church council and see how it helps us get a handle on the subject.

## WHAT'S THE DEAL WITH NICEA?

In the year 325, Emperor Constantine convened a church council to settle a theological controversy. One faction, the followers of a man named Arius, insisted Jesus was one of God's created beings. However exalted he was in comparison to mere humans, he was still inferior to God the Father. The other faction, led by Athanasius, insisted Jesus was of the same essence with the Father (and the Holy Spirit), even though he was a distinct person. Athanasius's views carried the day, becoming the official view of the empire. Now here's the question of the day: Was this doctrine a novelty?

We come now to a concept that has puzzled folks for centuries. My goal here is to clarify some of the issues involved that often get entangled. I want to shed enough light on the topic that you, friendly reader, come away with a greater understanding of who God is and how he reveals himself to us in the Scriptures. That said, God, being *infinite* (unlimited in his power, presence, knowledge, and majesty), can never be fully grasped by those of us who are *finite* (limited in all of the above). So don't be surprised if you get to the end of the chapter still scratching your head. Some things are just beyond our abilities. Let's just focus on the raw data of the Scriptures.

There are three main ways of dealing with this issue. First, for some, saying "Jesus is God" is the final word on the subject. In other words, when we talk about the Father and the Holy Spirit, we are just referring to *Jesus* but using different *names* (Jesus with different hats). This approach has ancient roots but is known today as "Oneness Theology," or, more informally, "Jesus Only."

Second, some people deal with the issue by denying the deity of Jesus altogether, relegating the Holy Spirit to an impersonal force, and affirming the Father alone is the one true God. Such approaches are called "unitarian." They all attempt to safeguard the unity of God but wind up denying any plurality in God's identity.

This brings us to a third expression, those who affirm the unity of God (that he is one) and his plurality as Father, Son, and Holy Spirit (he is three). How the three relate to each other and how we can still claim to worship one God has traditionally involved the term "Trinity."

## THREE IN ONE

When you hear the word "Trinity," what comes to mind? For some it refers to the God of the Bible. The classic expression is stated like this: God eternally exists in three distinct persons, Father, Son, and Holy Spirit, all of whom share one divine essence. Others (even sincere Christians) are confused about it and do their best to avoid the topic, unknowingly lapsing into a "Oneness" mentality. But for still others the term and the concept behind it are simply a sham, and therein lies the myth. It can take many forms, but the underlying idea is that the Trinity is not a New Testament doctrine. The word "Trinity," after all, is never used in the Bible, but was coined in a fourth-century church council. It bears no resemblance to what we find in Scripture; theologians just made it up and imposed it on the peasants with the help of a powerful hierarchy.

This in itself is a little hard to swallow, but proponents of this myth would have us believe the church was going along its merry way believing in God, but holding no higher view of Jesus than his being a good man. Then abruptly, three hundred years later, a cadre of shady characters in a smoke-filled room decided to say the simple rabbi from Nazareth is God! But so is the Father, and why not have a three-for-one sale and throw in the Spirit? So I guess the peasants, not wanting to make waves, just went along with it, and nobody else bothered to raise an objection.

As is often the case, this is one of those myths that does have an element of truth to it. It is true that the word "Trinity" never appears in the Bible. True, but completely irrelevant. The real issue is whether the *idea to which the word "Trinity" refers* can be found in the Bible; does it conform to the evidence of Scripture? It is also true that the term "Trinity" came from the conclusions about the nature of God that were hammered out by theologians, but the process began long before the council of Nicea in the fourth century (and continued for centuries afterward). *But why did anyone feel the need to do so in the first place and why come to such a baffling conclusion?* We'll look at these issues in a moment, but first, let's look at some of the usual ways people try to explain the Trinity.

## OF EGGS AND SPACE

Trying to clarify the Trinity can be a bit daunting. This doctrine is unique among all the world's religions, with no close second. (There are various "triads," like we find in Hinduism, but all of them consist of three distinct gods.) "Trinity" is a term that seeks to define in broad strokes the very nature of God — the fact that he eternally exists in three persons. No wonder people are baffled by it. Explanations are often met with a "How can this be?" response. This is because people rack their brains for a comparison — something, *anything*, that helps put the concept into plain words.

It is fairly common for folks to offer illustrations in the hopes of demonstrating a three-in-one concept, all beginning with "the Trinity is like ..." So we hear how the Trinity is like an egg, since an egg is a distinct unit, but consists of a shell, the white, and the yolk. Likewise, water exists in three distinct forms: solid, liquid, and gas, but all three are still that single entity — water. We are body, soul, and spirit; space has height, length and width, and on and on we go.

As helpful as these attempts may be on one level, they all finally fall flat. We just cannot wrap our minds around what the Trinity is precisely because we have nothing to compare it to. The Trinity is like nothing else in all of creation, our experience, or our imagination. We're talking about the very nature of God, who has no equal, no comparison, and not even an opposite. (Satan is merely a created being.)

## TO WHOM WILL YOU COMPARE GOD?

In my opinion, a good place to begin the discussion is Isaiah 40. Running throughout the chapter is a recurring theme that Yahweh alone is God. In verses 12 – 14, Isaiah asks a series of questions concerning who it was that made the earth, and who it is that can fathom his wisdom. They all have the same expected response: "only Yahweh." God's greatness is then compared to all of the nations, but their combined glory is but a drop in the bucket, a speck of dust. "To whom, then, will you compare God?"

- How about idols? No, they're just rickety figurines (40:18 – 20).
- What about all of the earth's inhabitants? Nope, they're just pesky bugs (40:21 – 22).
- What about royalty in all its splendor? *Yawn*, just wheat husks (40:23 – 24).

- "To whom will you compare me? Or who is my equal?" What about the vast universe? Nope. It's just his artwork, and if *it* is so incredible, how powerful do you think *he* must be (40:25–26)?
- No matter where we look, we have nothing to compare God to. He stands alone.

He has, however, revealed some things about himself we can piece together. If I may repeat myself from the previous chapter: the New Testament looks us straight in the eye, insists there is only *one* God, and in the next breath calls *three* persons "God." This is the nonnegotiable, bare-bones statement that drives the whole chapter, *whether or not we ever understand how it can be so.*

## WORSHIP AND DEVOTION IN THE EARLY CHURCH

Do the Scriptures back up what the term "Trinity" refers to? The word itself came about as a means of trying to describe a reality constantly borne out by the Scriptures: there is only one God, but the early Christians found themselves in a relationship with three persons equally worthy of that title. The apostles go out of their way to picture the reality of this tri-unity, without ever even attempting to define or describe it. They simply present it as a given, but why did it develop in the first place?

Once again, let's put ourselves in the ancient world. Consider the Jews in the first century, whose Scripture and experience tell them God speaks to his people by his Spirit. There are centuries of experience and tradition to this effect. Also, they know all too well the ancient creed: "Hear, O Israel: The Lord our God, the Lord is one" (Deuteronomy 6:4). They know this God has declared, "I am the first and I am the last; apart from me there is no God" (Isaiah 44:6). The interesting thing is what happens to those who came to believe a carpenter from Nazareth is the long-awaited Messiah.

From their perspective, Jesus comes along and says some incredible things, most of which did not make a lick of sense at the time.

They see him die; three days later they're eating with him (but it's a bit difficult with their mouths hanging open). About forty days later he goes up to heaven, and ten days after that the Holy Spirit shakes a room and rocks the world of a hundred and twenty Galileans.

A funny thing happens: as the story unfolds in the book of Acts, the familiar Spirit of God, who for all these years conveyed the very presence, power, and mind of Yahweh, suddenly brings the disciples into an encounter with Jesus. God's Holy Spirit connects people to *Jesus*. Jesus, you see, is perceived in an exalted status unequalled in all of their writings or experience. His name is invoked in prayer and worship; his authority is present for discipline and miracles. All this happens through the power of the Holy Spirit, who comes to the forefront in the affairs of the church.

The baby church goes about its task empowered by that Spirit, increasingly aware that he, the Spirit, makes the presence of the Lord Jesus Christ real to them. This divine presence is the reason their mission is so powerfully effective. The Holy Spirit reveals the reality of the message of Jesus, which all along was to make known the love of the Father (who sent him, and to whom he constantly prayed, and from whom he received his mission and message). All three persons of the Trinity actively engage in saving people.

The word is absent, but the concept is everywhere. Here's what I mean: there are pictures of the Trinity in action throughout the New Testament. When Jesus (the Son) is baptized, the (Holy) Spirit descends on him, and a voice from heaven (uttered by the Father) commends his beloved Son (Matthew 3:16–17). Christian baptism is to be carried out "in the name [not *names*] of the Father and of the Son and of the Holy Spirit" (28:19). Jesus (the Son) is exalted to the right hand of God (the Father) and sends forth the Holy Spirit (Acts 2:33). Paul prays for the grace of the Lord Jesus Christ, the love of God (the Father), and the fellowship of the Holy Spirit to be with his people (2 Corinthians 13:14). The author of Hebrews tells how the gospel was announced by the Lord (Jesus) and testified to by God's (the Father's) miracles and by the distribution of gifts of the (Holy) Spirit (Hebrews 2:3 – 4). Clearly, three persons are in view.

The New Testament writers, however, could not escape a few key facts. Their Scriptures declare there is only one God (Deuteronomy 4:35; Isaiah 43:10 – 11), a reality they gladly affirmed (Romans 3:30; 1 Timothy 2:5). They knew their heavenly Father was God. In fact, when "God" is mentioned in the New Testament without any other qualification, it is shorthand for "God the Father" ("For *God* so loved the world that he sent *his Son*"). Their experience with the risen, and then exalted Jesus impressed on them that he too was God (John 20:28; Titus 2:13; 2 Peter 1:1). All of their activities were empowered and directed by the Holy Spirit, himself God (Acts 5:3 – 4; 1 Corinthians 2:11 – 12). Yet, they are distinct persons — the Father is not the Son; the Father didn't die on the cross; the Spirit isn't seated at God's right hand nor did he rise from the dead. This is, however, where the Scriptures leave the discussion.

Incidentally, it's only three. It's never the Father, Son, Holy Spirit, and Bob. It's also only *these* three, never the Father, Son, and Mary; never Elijah, the Son, and the Holy Spirit. Always, solely and exclusively, we are presented with the Father, the Son, and the Holy Spirit. Here's a challenge for you — come up with an explanation without violating the two central affirmations: (1) there is one God, and (2) three distinct persons are called God. In light of the repeated drumbeat from both Testaments that there is only one God, and all three of these persons are called "God," we are forced to conclude that the one God exists in three persons, no matter what word we use to describe it.

## STILL, THERE ARE OBJECTIONS

The unity of essence *and* distinction of persons always need to be kept in mind. Many of the objections people raise against the Trinity ignore one part or other. So people say, "If Jesus is God, who is he talking to when he prays?" The answer is, "God, *the Father*."

The question doesn't acknowledge Jesus' real humanity and his distinction from the Father. Others object by saying, "If there are three persons, how can Jesus say 'I and the Father are one?'" The answer is, "Because they are." Here the question acknowledges Jesus' divinity, but again, not the distinction of persons.

I dealt with Jesus' unity with the Father in the previous chapter. What was said there, combined with the current chapter, should at least begin to address the unitarian objections (which all deny the Trinity by denying Christ's deity). Here I want to focus on those who hold to "Oneness Theology," which affirms his deity but denies the *distinction* of persons (and therefore the Trinity). For the sake of space I'm just going to focus on the Father and the Son, but the same could be done for all three members of the Trinity.

Simply put: Jesus is not the Father. If he is, then the New Testament writers have failed to grasp that fact. For instance, the dear mother of James and John asks Jesus to grant her boys prominent seats in his kingdom. Jesus replies that he is unable to grant the request because the positions "belong to those for whom they have been prepared by my Father" (Matthew 20:23). Jesus can't grant it, but the Father can. If this is one person we're talking about, could he or couldn't he grant the request? In another instance, Jesus told his disciples he didn't know the exact time of the second coming; but the Father did (24:36). If Jesus is the Father, did he or didn't he know?

This is the pattern borne out throughout the New Testament, with Jesus constantly distinguishing himself from the Father. The teaching of Jesus becomes nonsensical if we're really talking about one person (even if he's putting on different hats). In John 5:30–37 Jesus gives a defense of his actions. "By myself I can do nothing; I judge only as I hear, and my judgment is just, for I seek not to please myself but him who sent me" (5:30). Notice the "not this/but that" logic of the sentence:

Jesus seeks

not

to please himself

but

to please the Father who sent him.

If Jesus and the Father are just one person, then Jesus says, "I don't seek to please me, but I seek to please me." (He also then maintains that he sent himself.) He continues saying that if he testifies about himself, his testimony is not valid. But, "there is another who testifies in my favor, and I know that his testimony about me is valid" (John 5:31–32).

Again, the flow of thought is pretty compelling. His opponents are trying to back him into a corner along the lines of the principle of "two or three witnesses" (Deuteronomy 19:15). His statement runs like this: I don't testify about myself because that is insufficient. There is *another one* whose testimony, added to mine, validates my testimony (that is, the testimony of the Father, John 5:37). Jesus, being astute on issues pertaining to mathematics, knows well that 1+1=2. Now, if Jesus and the Father are really just one person, then Jesus has failed to wiggle out of the trap. "I don't testify about myself but another one does — he's, uh, he's *me!*" (He could have gone whole hog and invoked three witnesses: "me, myself, and I.")

One final example comes from a critical moment in the gospel story. Just before his arrest Jesus wrestles in prayer, pleading with God to be able to avoid the suffering looming before him. In his humanity he dreads the brutal death he's about to endure, as well as, doubtless, the burden of bearing all of our sin. In agony he cries out: "Father, if you are willing, take this cup from me; yet not my will, but yours be done" (Luke 22:42). Once again we have a "not this/but that" scenario. Here he says in effect *Not* 'my will,' which belongs to me, *but* 'your will,' which is different than mine, and which, in fact, I'd rather not submit to if it's all the same to you. *But* I'll demonstrate my perfect obedience and align my personal will with your distinctly different will."

How could any of this make sense if Jesus is the Father? (And should any of you be lapsing into the "Then how can they be one?" argument, allow me to direct you once again to the previous chapter. I told you this isn't going to be easy.)

This is just a small sampling. I could go on like this for days, but I think you get the picture (and the same could be done in terms of comparing the Spirit with the Son, or the Father). They all share one *essence*, but they are three distinct *persons*. If Jesus, the Holy Spirit, and the Father are really one *person*, then the New Testament writers have really bungled up the simplicity of it all and have actually been completely misleading.

## SOME PRACTICAL APPLICATIONS

A key theme here at The Chapel, my home church, is that living as if God is real leads to a transformed life. The message is a reaction against what is called "practical atheism." Many *say* they believe in God but do not *live* like it. So, practically speaking, they live as if there really is no God, and therefore, practically speaking, are atheists.

If I may, allow me to use this as an analogy for another problem in our churches today—"practical Oneness." Here's what I mean. Christians are quick to affirm the Trinity (in theory), but then deny it in practice. The result is an understanding of God that is essentially "Jesus Only." Many of our contemporary worship songs constantly collapse any distinction between the persons of the Godhead. We start singing praises to the Savior who died for us, and a line or two later we're calling him "Father." The Father didn't die for us. Now don't get me wrong, I am not saying that being centered on Jesus is a bad thing; it's not. It's a very biblical thing. We just miss the reason for it.

## Our Heavenly Father

God the Father rarely speaks in the New Testament. The first two times he does so, first at Jesus' baptism then again on the Mount of Transfiguration, he says much the same thing: "This is my Son, whom I love; with him I am well pleased" (Matthew 3:17; 17:5). In the second instance he adds, "Listen to him." Alright, what did Jesus say? Everything God wanted him to and nothing else besides. Jesus *never* spoke on his own accord, "but the Father who sent me commanded me what to say and how to say it" (John 12:49). He was pleased to do so, because he knew that God's "command leads to eternal life" (12:50). When we listen to Jesus, we are listening to the Father speaking *through* him.

When Jesus walked the earth, he told us of the Father's love and care for us and challenged us to love each other in divine perfection (Matthew 5:46–48). He constantly prayed to him (Mark 6:46; Luke 6:12) and taught us to do so as well (Matthew 6:9). Everything he said drew our attention to the Father's heart (Luke 6:36), or warned us to live up to his righteous standards (Matthew 18:35). He refocused us on the Father's kingdom (6:31–33), which the Father delighted in conferring on Jesus' "little flock" (Luke 12:32). Jesus' words and miracles showed us the Father was at work within him (John 14:10–11). Jesus knew the Father with unparalleled intimacy, and vice versa (Luke 10:22), and he revealed the Father to us with unparalleled clarity (John 1:18), so much so that he openly declared: "Anyone who has seen me has seen the Father" (14:9).

Jesus came from the Father and returned to the Father, longing to be clothed in his former glory (John 17:5). The avenue of his departure was the cross, upon which (and through Jesus) the Father performed the work of reconciling the planet to himself (2 Corinthians 5:18–21). When all is said and done, all the saints will be raised to new life, and all of God's enemies will be subdued, "then the Son himself will be made subject to him who put everything under him, so that God may be all in all" (1 Corinthians 15:28).

The writer of Hebrews tells us that God spoke through the prophets in various times and circumstances in the old days, but now "he has spoken to us by his Son." The finality of Jesus as the end-time messenger is due to his incredibly superior status. He was "appointed heir of all things" (by the Father) as the agent of creation. He radiates the glory of God (the Father), perfectly represents his very nature, and sustains everything "by his powerful word." With salvation accomplished, he took his seat "at the right hand of the Majesty [i.e., the Father] in heaven" (Hebrews 1:1–3). The Father has spoken decisively and finally through Jesus. Apart from Jesus, God has nothing else to say.

Once again, I have only provided a brief sample, but I've gone down this path for a reason. There really is a Trinity, and Jesus is enthralled with his Father and longs to reveal him to us. When we focus exclusively on Jesus, we ignore his entire focus of ministry, then and now. We have forgotten the Father. Our sanctuaries reverberate with boisterous worship of the Son while the Father waits in the lobby.

## Now That's the Spirit

Another thing Christians need to keep in mind is that the only presence of God we've ever known personally is the Holy Spirit. God is enthroned, his Son at his right hand, and we patiently await his return, but the Christian life on earth is carried on in the realm of the Spirit.

As a matter of fact, Jesus' whole ministry was in the Spirit's power: from his baptism (Luke 3:21–22), to his journeys (4:14), even the final commands before ascending to heaven (Acts 1:1–2). The Spirit filled the church and directed her ministry (all throughout Acts). He leads us to Jesus (John 16:13–15), indwells us (1 Corinthians 3:16), bestows gifts on us (12:7–11), plants and cultivates divine fruit within us (Galatians 5:22–23), prays through us (Romans 8:26–27), and testifies that we belong to the heavenly *Abba*, our dear Father (8:15; Galatians 4:6). And again, this is merely a sample.

## SUMMING UP

Was the Trinity invented? No. Rather, it was the inevitable response of the church's experience with God. He's the One who revealed himself to us in this mysterious manner, a fact borne out by the Scriptures. The *word* "Trinity" never appears, but the *reality* to which the term points is everywhere evident. Since it is a concept so deeply imbedded in the Scriptures, it is God himself who is responsible for it. This is the eternal, unchanging nature of this incredible God.

The New Testament writers expressed their experience with God in such a way that led later theologians to grapple with his identity and assign what they hoped was helpful terminology. The first-century Christians gave testimony to the *reality* of an experience; the church grappled with and argued about the *implications* of this experience for centuries, then merely put a *word* to it. In response to counterclaims being made, they settled on a definition for God that accounted for the data of the Scriptures: God's unified divine essence eternally existing in three distinct persons. One essence, three persons, hence a *tri*-unity, or "Trinity."

## GOING DEEPER

For a good overview of how the term developed in the midst of debates on the nature of Christ, see the article on "Trinity" in *Evangelical Dictionary of Theology*, edited by Walter Elwell (Grand Rapids: Baker, 1984). For a more in-depth look you should find Millard J. Erickson, *Making Sense of the Trinity: Three Crucial Questions* (Grand Rapids: Baker, 2000), and Kevin J. Vanhoozer, *The Trinity in a Pluralistic Age: Theological Essays on Culture and Religion* (Grand Rapids: Eerdmans, 1996). An essential study for those of you with a little Greek under your belt (again, past the third semester), check out Gordon Fee, *God's Empowering Presence: The Holy Spirit in the Letters of Paul* (Peabody, MA: Hendrickson, 1994). In addition, these sites may be helpful: www.piney.com/HsTheopTrinity.html; www.newadvent.org/cathen/15047a.htm.

# Chapter 12

# JEWS, CHRISTIANS, AND MUSLIMS ALL WORSHIP THE SAME GOD

In the dark days that followed the events of 9/11/2001, a well-worn belief received renewed prominence. As the nation geared up for war against radical Islam, the State Department made it clear terrorists were the target, not Islam itself. Not a bad move considering there are over a billion Muslims worldwide. Part of the rationale for focusing on the bad guys is the statement that, after all, Jews, Christians, and Muslims all worship the same God. While this statement is politically savvy, it is not an accurate reflection of any of the three religions mentioned. Those who assert the "same God" line do so out of a desire for people to get along. That in itself is not such a bad idea, and you may be enjoying the aroma of an olive branch. I smell a myth.

At first blush the statement seems reasonable. All three religions are resolutely monotheistic (the belief that there is but one God). All three trace their origins to the call of Abraham and esteem such figures as Noah, Moses, and David. They all acknowledge the human race is estranged from God, have Scriptures that serve as the guide back to him, and characteristically meet in houses of worship and are guided by spiritual leaders. There is a heaven to be gained and a hell to avoid. The list could go on, but far more instructive is how they *differ*, and do so irreconcilably.

## GOD OF WHICH COVENANT?

Before you accuse me of being a pinhead, as if *I'm* the one stirring up an otherwise tranquil unity, please understand this: these religions themselves do not present *themselves* as merely three ways of saying the same thing. Any one of the three, by definition, excludes the claims of the other two. It is, in part, an issue of origins.

Judaism traces its roots back to God's encounter with Abram (later renamed Abraham). He was promised a homeland and countless descendants to flourish within it. He would become great, be blessed, and become a blessing to the world. Oh yeah, he was promised a son. This was noteworthy since Abraham and his barren wife, Sarah, were well along in years. For them to have a child would be nothing short of a miracle. So, the promise of Genesis 12:1–3 is reinforced with a covenant ceremony in chapter 15. By chapter 21 the promised child is born, and in chapter 22 he's about to be offered as a sacrifice! Having passed the test, Abraham and his line is established throughout the rest of Genesis. The covenant promise given to Abraham is reaffirmed to his son (21:12) and grandson, and their descendants (28:13–14).

Thus, throughout the Old Testament, the Creator identifies himself in terms of this covenant. He is "the God of Abraham, Isaac and Jacob" (Deuteronomy 1:8; 2 Kings 13:23, etc.). *This* is the God who called and commissioned the great lawgiver and central human figure in Judaism, Moses (Exodus 3:16). God's covenant with Moses (the law), which was a direct application of the covenant with Abraham, becomes the guiding principle of Judaism.

So far Christianity agrees with the story wholeheartedly, so let's see how it squares with Islam. In the story about Abraham and Isaac, I failed to mention Abraham had a son prior to Isaac, whose name was Ishmael. Abraham was the father, but his mother was Hagar, Sarah's Egyptian maidservant. I leave the oddity of ancient childbearing practices to your further research, but I need to point out that according to Muslim commentators, it was *Ishmael* who was the object of God's test of Abraham's faith. Ishmael is also the one who inherited the blessing and became heir of the covenant. So Muslims worship the God of Abraham, Ishmael, and his descendants. By the way, this God is known as Allah.

Since Christianity embraces the Jewish Scriptures there is no problem with Judaism's description regarding Abraham, Isaac, and Jacob. But they are not content with discussions about the covenant until we account for the *new* covenant, of which Jesus is the mediator. The Father, then, continues to identify himself in terms of the covenant, but now it's the new one. God's full name in the New Testament is "the God and Father of our Lord Jesus Christ."

So, the Jews and Christians agree on the Abraham, Isaac, and Jacob connection, but Christians insist on the Jesus upgrade (which Jews and Muslims deny); Muslims hold the line at Ishmael. There is no middle ground here.

## WHAT'S IN A NAME?

I chose this route purposely to avoid an argument about God's *name*, whether Yahweh (for Jews and Christians) or Allah (Muslims). It would appear we're talking about the same God, just calling him by a different name, but this is not the real issue. The question is, rather, *which* God are we talking about and who is heir to the covenant? This is the heart of the matter. Who are God's people—Jews, Christians, or Muslims?

Quibbling, you say? Tell that to a Muslim imam. Tell him it makes no difference if he traces his roots to Abraham, *Isaac, and Jacob* or to Abraham, *Ishmael, and his sons*. Talk to a rabbi and say it doesn't matter if someone regards Isaac *or* Ishmael as the child of promise. While you're at it, tell any Christian that Jesus and the new covenant aren't necessary; Moses will do just fine. The issue here isn't whether *you* think this is splitting hairs; it's what Judaism, Christianity, and Islam think about themselves. This goes to the very heart of these religions. *They* don't think they're saying the same thing or worshiping the same God at all. It's a bit cheeky for an outsider to insist otherwise.

Now, let's push the topic a little further. If Jews, Christians, and Muslims all worship the same God, then they are *all* really his people. It would then follow that all that divides these three religions are superficial differences. No doubt some differences are surface level, but what about some of the key-defining convictions? Are these three religions just saying the same thing in three different ways?

## Whose Land Is It Anyway?

To whom did God give modern-day Israel? Jews claim it was promised to them (the implications of which are debated by Christians). Muslims say it should be exclusively theirs. I refer you to the nightly news to decide if this is an issue.

## Is Muhammad a Prophet?

The central creed of Islam is: there is no God but Allah, and Muhammad is his prophet. Reciting this meaningfully is the beginning of the process of converting to Islam. In the 600s, Muhammad believed Allah had commissioned him to rid Arabia of idolatry. So far, so good. Allah made everything, so attempting to worship any created thing instead of the Creator was obscene (also in Judaism and Christianity, just exchange *Yahweh* for *Allah*). He also held the deep-seated conviction that Allah had called him, Muhammad, to be the final prophet, superior to all who went before him. Since the list includes the likes of Moses and Jesus, the Jews and Christians of his day sent him packing. There has been some bad blood on all sides ever since.

So whether Muhammad is a prophet or not depends on whom you ask. Muslims say "Yes" as a tenet of faith; Jews and Christians say "No," also based on their tenants of faith. There's no middle ground here.

## What about Jesus?

Jews are a little divided on who Jesus was. Many acknowledge he was a good man, a lay preacher whose teaching and influence are admirable. Others are ambivalent, and it's probably fair to say many, if not most, modern Jews would just as soon not talk about him. For others he was misguided, even deceived. Still others take a dimmer view of the Nazarene and regard him as the illegitimate child of Mary and a Roman soldier. He was a liar, a charlatan, a demon, and fully deserving of his brutal death. One thing, though, does unite all Jews: the flat denial that Jesus is the Messiah, the divine Son of God, the Savior of the world. Jews regard the Christians' exaltation of Jesus as blasphemy, a violation of their central creed, "The LORD our God, the LORD is one" (Deuteronomy 6:4). When it all shakes out, Jesus is just not all that important in Judaism. He can be safely ignored.

How does he fare in Islam? Jesus is mentioned in the Koran mostly in complimentary terms. He was a holy man, a prophet, a miracle worker. He is called the Messiah, but no significance is given to the term. There is even a second coming scenario in which Jesus takes a role in the final judgment. He is *not*, however—adamantly *not*—the Son of God. Allah has no children, so it is blasphemy of the worst kind to suggest he does. Calling Jesus his "Son" is nothing short of idolatry (the sin and scourge of the planet). *Worshiping* Jesus is worthy of death.

Speaking of capital punishment, what about the cross? The Koran does depict the dramatic scene of a poor man's agonizing death, his blood soaking into the parched Jerusalem ground. It just wasn't Jesus. Muslim commentators are divided on the issue of what really happened. Some maintain that God slipped in a ringer at the last moment (Judas, in some versions of the story) while he whisked Jesus away to heaven. Whatever the case, it is clear Jesus didn't die on the cross. The rationale for this is that Jesus is regarded as a true prophet, and since God doesn't kill his prophets, according to Islam, the crucifixion simply didn't happen as the New Testament describes. We can also dispense with the resurrection; it just didn't happen so it's not an issue.

You cannot, of course, ignore Jesus as a Muslim, since he is mentioned in the Koran. Your time, however, is better served focusing on what Muhammad had to say about submitting to Allah.

This may come as a bit of a shock, but for Christianity, Jesus is God's Son, the expected Messiah, Savior and Lord of all. He was born of a virgin, lived a sinless life, and died for our sins on a brutal cross. He was hastily wrapped and placed in a borrowed tomb; three days later he strolled out of it, having neatly folded up his face wrap. For the next forty days he proceeded to present himself very much alive. He is worshiped and adored, the focus of prayer, our heavenly priest. He rules God's kingdom from his place of prominence in heaven, and he empowers his people by the Holy Spirit, all to the glory of his Father, God Almighty.

Ah, such detail, a recap is in order. For the Jews, Jesus is just a man — good, bad, or indifferent; to say otherwise (that he is God) is blasphemy. For the Muslims, he's a good man; to say otherwise is blasphemy. For Christians, he's the "the radiance of God's glory and the exact representation of his being, sustaining all things by his powerful word" and in whom dwells "all the fullness of the Deity ... in bodily form" (Hebrews 1:3; Colossians 2:9). Anything less is heresy, with no middle ground.

## HOW DOES GOD SAVE US?

As I said before, all three religions discussed in this chapter agree humankind has gone awry. God must step in and rescue us if there is any hope at all of gaining heaven, and he rewards those who turn to him. For the Jew, salvation revolves around keeping the commandments of Moses (as he is interpreted in the Mishnah and Talmud, later traditional Jewish writings). For the Muslim it is submitting to the will of Allah as revealed in the Koran. For the Christian, the New Testament declares it is by faith in Jesus, believing he died for our sins and that God raised him from the dead. So, Jesus is confessed as Lord, to the glory of God the Father.

Muslims maintain the Jews don't go far enough (stopping with Moses as the guide) and the Christians go too far (by their repulsive adoration of Jesus); both err by rejecting Muhammad. Christians will not consider any view on religion in which Jesus is not the central character, so the Jews and the Muslims shut themselves out by their refusal to bow to Jesus. The Jews think the other two are nuts. God spoke to Moses, the famous descendant of Abraham, Isaac, and Jacob. Period.

When the faithful die, where do they go? Judaism is a little vague, preferring to focus on how one lives in this life. Still, there are some indications in the Scriptures that conscious life continues after death, and the faithful live in the presence of God. Those who do affirm a physical resurrection view eternity in similar terms with Christianity, but there is no mention of Jesus. Christianity is much more detailed in its view of the afterlife, with Jesus occupying a central role. The dead in Christ go to be with him in heaven and worship the triune God. The day will come in which these righteous souls will be reunited with their bodies, freshly resurrected, and will live forever with God on a renewed earth, the eternal site of the heavenly Jerusalem.

The faithful Muslim really doesn't die; the soul is transported directly to paradise. Faithful Muslims will go either to the higher heaven, a beautiful realm that can only be represented allegorically as having flowing streams, abundant fruit, and blissful reunions with faithful spouses, or to a lower heaven, which pales in comparison to the higher heaven (but sure beats hell). Some descriptions go further and describe a very sensual existence, with flowing wine and lovely women at one's beck and call (seventy-two virgins by one reckoning—Islam can be a bit male-centered). A moment's reflection will reveal how different these views of heaven really are.

## ACCEPTANCE AT WHAT COST?

There *are* some ways that members of one of these religions can gain acceptance by another. All a Jew has to do is acknowledge Jesus is Lord, or that Muhammad is the final and greatest prophet. A Christian needs only to reject Jesus as the Messiah, or else submit to Allah. A Muslim could affirm that it was Isaac who was sacrificed and agree to follow Moses, or else call Jesus the Son of God. For any adherent of one of these three religions to be accepted by another one, he or she needs to affirm the central belief of one of them (but it can't be done for two of them). There is a word for this — "conversion" (frowned upon in some circles, a death sentence in others).

Are you beginning to sense that what we have here are three distinct religions, each having central beliefs that are unacceptable to the other two? If this is really not the case, then we have to come to some interesting conclusions.

If all three worship the same God, then Judaism, Christianity, and Islam are really the same religion. Judaism ultimately *is* Islam; Christianity *is* Judaism (also known as Islam). If I'm late for church but a mosque is closer, why not just go there? Why can't a Jew worship in a mosque? Who'd notice; who'd care?

I think Osama Bin Laden would be fascinated to learn that he's really a Jew (which is no different from being a Christian). As Billy Graham passes his baton to his son, it shouldn't make any difference if Franklin preaches Jesus or jihad. Why not staff some synagogues with Baptist or Presbyterian ministers? Does this sound like a workable plan?

## SUMMING UP

While it is certainly polite and a gesture of diplomacy, it is simply absurd to insist that three religions believe something that they do not. Not only do they *not* worship the same God, they also do *not* describe the means of making peace with him in the same way. Judaism, Christianity, and Islam make strident claims about themselves to the exclusion of all counterclaims. This being the case, may we safely put this myth to rest?

## GOING DEEPER

For a concise overview of major world religions a good start is Lewis Hopfe and Mark Woodward, *Religions of the World* (Englewood Cliffs, NJ: Prentice Hall, 2006). Each religion is examined in terms of its origin (or founder) and core beliefs. The presentations are sympathetic, allowing each religion to speak for itself. A different take on the topic is Ravi Zacharias, *Jesus among Other Gods: The Absolute Claims of the Christian Message* (Nashville: Word, 2000). The stated agenda here is to demonstrate the superiority of Christ.

I also found some websites helpful for ready reference. For Islam: www.letusreason.org/Islam7.htm; lexicorient.com/e.o/islam.htm; www.submission.org/hhd.html.

For Judaism, judaism.about.com/library/3_askrabbi_o/bl_simmons; www.religionfacts.com/judaism/beliefs; www.jewfaq.org/index.htm

For those of you who are seekers in terms of the Christian faith, a good place to start is John R. Stott, *Basic Christianity* (Grand Rapids: Eerdmans, 1986) or Gordon T. Smith, *Beginning Well: Christian Conversion and Authentic Transformation* (Downers Grove, IL: InterVarsity Press, 2001).

# Chapter 13

# ALL RELIGIONS BASICALLY TEACH THE SAME THING (ALL PATHS LEAD TO GOD)

What is God like? Isn't the concept far too complex for any one religion? Maybe the truth of God is distributed throughout all the world's religions. There is an ancient tale about some blind men coming across an elephant. Having never encountered one before, they examine it and then try to describe it. One of them got a hold of the tail and concludes that an elephant is like a rope. The one finding a leg said an elephant is like a tree; another one, finding a tusk, compares it to a spear, and so it went. Each one has a different impression based on their limited interaction, but every one of them is *right*, based on their limitations. So it is with God, as the story goes. All religions have a piece of the puzzle that conflicts with other beliefs, but ultimately, everyone is right.

Another story surfaces from time to time. This one is about a traveler approaching a mountain. From his perspective at the base it looks like a single peak, but as he nears the top, it turns out that there are actually two peaks, one in front of the other. Someone else traveling off to the side sees from the outset that there are in fact two peaks. So it is with God. We understand things one way, but someone else has another perspective and sees things differently, but ultimately, everyone is right.

These rather heart-warming stories illustrate one of the ways people regard the bewildering number of religions in the world. They all just teach the same thing—all paths ultimately lead to God.

Comments like this come up often enough. What usually gets the ball rolling is a Christian's claim that Jesus is the only way to heaven. This little head-turner is often met with an incredulous look. We live in the "let's just get along" age, so it's ill-mannered of Christians to insist Jesus is "it." Where *do* we get off saying such a thing? There are millions of religions, and no one has the right to say one is better than another.

It doesn't hurt to concede that the motive for this is a genuine desire for unity. As such, it does have the appearance of being big-hearted and broad-minded, especially in our pluralistic society. It is simply impolite to suggest otherwise. A tenuous truce ensues and all is well—until we actually examine it.

The blind men checking out the elephant all had their personal convictions, but they were all wrong. What they needed was someone who could explain things to them in a way they could understand but could never have reached on their own (in this instance, someone who could *see*). The mountain climber had an impression that there was one peak, but he was wrong; there were two. The hiker off to the side saw the *truth*. Too bad this was before the age of cell phones (or at least a bullhorn).

## THEY DON'T (SO THEY CAN'T)

We'll start the conversation with a tidy piece of reality. All religions do not teach the same thing; if that were so, there would not be so many *different* religions. Since they don't teach the same things, these religions can't be leading to the same destination. (If that makes perfect sense, you are free to go on to the next chapter.) The response usually offered is that the differences are only apparent. Peek beneath the surface and you'll see the underlying unity. Nevertheless, as they say in the Deep South, "That dog won't hunt." For instance, some of these religions believe in one God and others in many gods. Some actually say there is no God at all, while still others say *we* are gods. These are not descriptions of the same God in different terms; it's simply a different god (or gods, goddesses, or none of the above).

Some shoot for heaven, while others long to be absorbed into the divine; still others see the end as ceasing to exist altogether. Those are different places, attained by different paths. This is the problem with the "all paths lead to God" myth. We'll look at some of these issues in more detail in a moment, but we first need to wrestle with a little bit of logic. Then, after setting the stage, we'll see what the Bible has to say about it.

## A BASIC OBSERVATION

When it comes to all of the religions before us and which one(s) is (are) right, we only have two available options: *all* of them are wrong, or *one* of them is right. Two, some, or all can't be right because they *so fundamentally contradict each other.* Some religions thrive on the claim of being able to hold contradictory beliefs in mind and celebrate the unity, but the claims fail when subjected to examination. Here's why.

There is a fundamental principle of logic that cannot successfully be denied. I say "successfully" because anyone can *deny* anything. The issue at hand is whether the denial is plausible in this case. This principle is the law of noncontradiction. For us laypeople it goes like this: "Something cannot be both true and not true in the same way at the same time." Up cannot be both up and down in the same way at the same time. The object in the next room cannot be a table and a chair in the same way at the same time. There cannot be both one God (as an ultimate reality) and several gods (as an ultimate reality) in the same way at the same time.

Several challenges to this principle have surfaced from the time of Plato and Aristotle (who first articulated it) to the present—far too numerous and technical for even a cursory overview. Be thankful since most of them will have you reaching for the ibuprofen. My interest here concerns the person who hears of this basic principle of logic and says, "Nah, that isn't so." I've had this conversation a few times while sitting in a coffee shop, and a smile always finds its way to my java-sipping lips. The reason for my amusement is, for folks to deny it, they must *use* it. I say the law of noncontradiction is right; the other says it's wrong. The whole conversation would be utterly meaningless apart from the unstated perception that we both can't be right (in the same way at the same time). To say the law doesn't exist contradicts the opposing view that it does. In other words, the denial uses the law.

It really becomes interesting when you apply this law to all the diverse religions. They make truth claims to the exclusion of all competitors, contradicting the claims of others. All, some, or even two contradictory belief systems can't be reconciled. One stands out as true or they all go down in flames. It's one or none.

## RELATIVISM RULES

This is anything but a popular notion today. In fact, it is decidedly countercultural to be so unyielding. Our culture today is overrun by "relativism," the belief there is no ultimate truth, no objective reality. All is relative. One view is as valid as the next; this or that may be true for you but not for me. Relativism is taught (or simply assumed) in our public schools. It is the driving force in the media and is in the very air we breathe. When it comes to competing views, all one can reasonably affirm is that there are different opinions upon which we can hold a consensus. It is just rude to insist otherwise.

When you put this view to the test, the results can be anything from comical to frightening. A committed relativist would have to affirm there's no real difference between Mother Teresa and Hitler, Pol Pot and the pope, or, for that matter, Rush and Rosie. If it's all relative, then it's *all* relative. Collecting airplanes is no different from bombing airliners. Stamp collectors or child molesters are just pursuing choices. There is no real difference if I wring a rooster's neck in a solemn ritual or content myself with a bucket of the Colonel's finest after the Sunday service.

What relativists don't seem to understand is that their view is self-refuting—it contradicts itself. They say there is no such thing as truth in such a way that we're supposed to believe them; in other words, that they're telling the truth. In the same way, they say everything is relative but present their view as the only valid one. Relativism is the only way to go, period. I just have to accept it. There is no such thing as right or wrong until I disagree (in which case I'm just flat wrong). The irony is breath-taking.

Pointing these things out doesn't seem to get anywhere. I suspect the reason is that we're not on the same wave-length. I'm dealing with logic (or trying to), but the relativist is responding with emotion. Having exclusive beliefs doesn't *feel* right.

Now, to be fair, it wouldn't hurt Christians to concede the difficulty people have believing in one ultimate truth. The culture infuses relativism at every turn, so taking it slowly over the course of time, building friendships, and loving as Jesus showed us just may be the way to go. Still, true Christian love attempts to show people the narrow path.

## A VERY CLOSED "OPEN MIND"

The law of noncontradiction is just too narrow for a committed relativist, as is the notion of actual, objective truth. In such a climate, anyone maintaining there is one true religion is seen as hopelessly closed-minded. We are expected to follow the lead of the relativist—all beliefs are valid. Striving for harmony we need to see the good in all religions, as if they are all united into a big-tent, all-comers-welcome religion. But this is not the case. The "harmonious all" is just one other view in a growing inventory.

Let's say we have nine religions on a list. I insist that they're all different; my relativist friend Bob says they're all merely different paths to God. It isn't that my view of the nine is narrow and Bob's is broad. Bob has simply added a tenth. His view is every bit as narrow as the others because he insists it's *the only correct view* of things.

Unwittingly Bob joins a long list of people holding to an exclusivist belief. It isn't that Christians are singled out as the sole holdout in the get-along parade. All of the founders of the world religions presented their beliefs as the true path and looked askance at the claims of others. Moses had nothing good to say about the religions of Canaan (Deuteronomy 18:9 – 14). Gautama (the Buddha) renounced his ancestral Hinduism and launched a new movement. Jesus was unsympathetic toward competition (Matthew 24:23 – 26). Muhammad will brook no rival. Even the Dalai Lama, who insists all paths are valid, just doesn't have any room for a view that insists on only one.

## A RELATED MATTER

There are those among us who insist we should approach the topic of religion without any bias. We have to keep an open mind, we are told. Holding a particular view will skew the conversation, and we'll be unable to escape our preconceived notions. This all sounds pretty fair-minded, but there is a problem lurking. It's impossible.

We touched on this in chapter 8. Whenever there is something to observe, there is always an *observer*. When you come to a subject you bring *you*: your beliefs, your culture, your past, your hopes for the future, your present health, your current level of alertness, your education and expertise, the state of digestion relative to your last meal, the level of sleep deprivation, or how much you even care. Are the bills paid and the spouse happy? Are the kids a joy or a curse? If you're a Christian, we have to factor in whether you're "prayed up," whether you're "on fire" and morally strong, or "burned out" and a moral flop. Who we are, our state of mind and how we feel, has an effect on us. So right out of the gate we're already running a skewed race.

On a more practical level concerning the "approach without bias" notion, we can insist it be done, but what would it look like? How would we do it? If I am a staunch atheist approaching the topic of religion, I am not for that reason neutral. My bias is that there is no God, so all discussions about him (her, it, or them, for that matter), are merely academic. Anyone in this scientific age befuddled enough to actually *believe* these fairy tales is weak, out of touch, or worse. How could I reasonably be expected to keep an open mind when discussing the relative merits of Christianity and Buddhism if I think they're both a crock?

If you're a Buddhist, you can keep an unbiased and open mind all day, as long as at the end of it we wind up affirming Buddhism. The Hindu, with a sterling open mind, sees life on the planet as a multifaceted illusory expression of the one underlying reality. As long as we see it as well, the discussion can proceed unhindered by bias. A Christian will attempt to guide the conversation to Jesus.

If I think one religion is right, that's my bias; if I think all of them are wrong, that's my bias. If I am so incredibly open-minded as to say they are *all* right, that's just my narrowly imposed bias. Anything otherwise is really a charade, so we ought to just drop the pretense. It's okay to affirm a certain belief, and there is really no way not to.

Now, having said that, there is no reason to go to the other extreme and become an obnoxious bully. There is much to be gained from showing respect for others' deeply held beliefs. We need to keep in mind, especially as Christians, that we've long been pegged for being hateful and intolerant. If we really want to earn the right to be heard, we need to listen. Bias does not equal boorish.

## CAN THESE ALL BE TRUE?

We saw in the previous chapter that Judaism, Christianity, and Islam all hold core beliefs that cannot be reconciled. Let's press on a little bit further, compare a few more religious paths, and see where they take us. We'll do this by comparing their views of God, salvation, and the afterlife.

The big three of the last chapter all believe in one God (but conceive of him in irreconcilable ways). What happens if we take one of them, say Islam, and compare it to Buddhism? One branch of Buddhism, often referred to as Hinayana, is actually atheistic; there is no god (or even a soul). Another branch, Mahayana Buddhism, believes in heavenly beings, with the Buddha himself as a savior figure. So which is it: Allah alone, a host of heavenly guides, or zip? Are these all saying the same thing?

What about salvation and the afterlife? For the Muslim, submitting to Allah gains one an eternal paradise. For the Mahayana Buddhist it is gaining consciousness of being absolute (divine-like), thereby escaping the wheel of reincarnation. For the Hinayana it is ceasing from all consciousness (like the flame of a candle that's been blown out). Is this the same path? Are we in bliss, absorbed into the cosmos, or snuffed out of existence?

### He, She, They, or It?

What if we looked at Judaism and Hinduism? Judaism says there's one God, and philosophical Hinduism says there's one reality, Brahman. For the Jew, Yahweh is a personal God who made the universe, which has fallen into sin. He calls all humans to submit to him (rewarding those who do). For the Hindu, Brahman is not a person, but an impersonal force. "It" didn't create the universe; it *is* the universe. All that exists is Brahman. There is no physical world, no sin, no sickness, just the One. All is Brahman, and Brahman is all. The rest is illusion.

Popular Hinduism believes in the One as well, but Brahman is expressed through literally millions of gods (it's actually polytheism). The goal of the Hindu is to realize he or she is really Brahman! Once that is done, the Hindu escapes the endless cycle of death and rebirth and is absorbed into the One (like a little drop in a huge ocean). The Jew enters a covenant with God (and there is no other); the Hindu *is* a god (among many, that is, who are all One).

Speaking of reincarnation, both the Buddhist and the Hindu seek to escape it. The Jew is born once, and then meets his or her fate upon death (as do the Christian and Muslim). That's two against three but still no consensus.

I hate to be a stinker, but we do need to bring Jesus into the mix at some point. Folks scream there are many paths; Jesus says "I'm it." The Hindu says there's no such thing as sin; Jesus died on the cross because of it. The Hinayana Buddhist says there's no God; Jesus reveals God to us. They insist there's no soul; Jesus saves souls.

## What Was He/She/It/They (or None) Thinking?

Keep in mind, we're just looking at select beliefs. The more you explore the doctrines of these systems, the more profoundly they contradict each other. Sure, there are several points of contact as well, but they always need some qualification. Being generous is good and being selfish is bad in just about all religions (except for those who do not allow for the existence of good and bad). The human condition is not as it should be, and someone or something from the divine realm can help (or not, if there's nobody there). There is a path to follow that leads to the remedy, but every religion sketches out a different way to walk on it. Is one divine being responsible for all of this?

Taking the various views together, if this divine/thing/person/ whatever being(s) stands behind all of the world's religions and has told us how to get reconnected, and if there really is just one grand path, why is it so hopelessly muddled? Why did *he* (just for the sake of simplicity) tell the Christians to cling to Jesus, but tell the Muslims not to bother? Why did he inform the Jews "I'm one," but say to the polytheists "We're many," and not let the atheists in on the conversation? Why did he warn Christians not to deny the name of Jesus (even in the face of persecution), but tell Muslims he'd wipe them out if they dared to submit to Jesus? If this is really God, he's got issues.

## We Didn't Just Make This Up

Check out the Religion section in bookstores or go online and you'll find countless examples of the "all are really one" idea. Vague notions of spirituality and unity are everywhere; the New Age has left its mark. It's also pretty common to read descriptions about "Christ" as the one who will return and demonstrate the unity in all religions. Sometimes you find references to many "Christs." In other sources, "Christ" refers to a state of consciousness, not a person at all, that comes to rest periodically on religious leaders. Better still, "Christ consciousness" is something we *all* may attain. It's a concept, a higher plane, but certainly not the historical person, Jesus of Nazareth.

Christianity, however, grounds itself in history. That in itself is not unique, since Judaism and Islam do as well. It's the specific account of who Jesus is and what he did that makes Christianity stand out.

## THE PATH OR THE PERSON?

For many religions, embracing the beliefs about how to live are really all that matters. Whether the Buddha, Krishna, or Confucius actually lived, the important thing is the path of life, the *religious philosophy* if you will, presented in Buddhism, Hinduism, Confucianism, and the like. The story of Jesus, however, is not only set within history, it is set precisely within *Jewish* history. Also, it doesn't just present the teachings of a great guide; Christianity is focused on devotion to the *Person*, Jesus of Nazareth. Take Jesus out of the context of first-century Palestine and he (not to mention Christianity) becomes meaningless. All the attempts of other religions to enlist Jesus in their cause won't work for that very reason. Jesus was not a generic wise man whose teachings fit neatly into all of the world's belief systems. Jesus was a Jew who came to fulfill Jewish Scripture. He was born, lived, and died in ancient, Roman-occupied Israel.

### Breathing Jewish Air

The public ministry of Jesus began with his baptism. John the Baptist arrived in the Judean desert, an odd little man in funny clothes (with a bizarre diet) hollering that people needed to repent. There he was, like the prophets before him, telling Israel that she had become unclean (again). His message evoked other images from Israel's past: the exodus and wilderness wanderings, not to mention Israel's return from exile. Now God, who had been silent for nearly four centuries, was finally on the move again. His kingdom, which he promised to restore through a descendant of David, was at hand and judgment was just around the corner. The common people flocked to him for washing and spiritual renewal. In such a setting, we are inhaling the rich atmosphere of Jewish history.

John was causing such a stir that even the Jerusalem elite had to see what was going on. In a move surely designed to win friends and influence people, John looked at the power brokers of Israel and said, "You brood of vipers! Who warned you to flee from the coming wrath?" (Matthew 3:7). They too were in need of the cleansing rite. They too had to be the kind of people Abraham would affirm (John 8:39–41), but they were unwilling (Matthew 21:31–32).

When asked to give an account of himself, John replied, "I am the voice of one calling in the desert, 'Make straight the way for the Lord'" (John 1:22–23; citing Isaiah 40:3). With this, the Baptist aligned himself with a centuries-old promise that one day Yahweh would return to Israel, bringing salvation to those waiting for him, but a dreadful vengeance for those who were not (Isaiah 40:10–11; 23–24; 41:10–11).

This is not a depiction of a group of mystics seeking some form of enlightenment, Hindu, Buddhist, New Age, or otherwise. There is no chanting of mantras, no aligning of planets or harmonic convergence, no one discoursing about astro travel or alternate states. No one asked John if he'd been to India lately. What we *do* see is a gathering of common Jews who are freaked out because a prophet had returned announcing impending doom for rebels, but salvation for the ones willing to repent, just as their Scriptures describe. "Yahweh's about to show up; time to get ready for him." We also see the Jerusalem gang was unimpressed with the little nut on the river bank. They don't need to worry about him because their brand of Judaism is just fine, thank you.

There is one more thing you don't see — someone telling the crowd, the leaders, and John the Baptist that it doesn't really matter. All paths lead to God, so quit making such a fuss.

## The Stronger One

All of this is the preparation for Jesus' arrival. Anyone on the scene would have been expecting Yahweh himself, but Jesus shows up instead. He was baptized, the Holy Spirit descended on him, and the Father spoke audibly to the planet for the first time in centuries: "This is my Son [alluding to Psalm 2:6 – 7], whom I love [a possible allusion to the sacrifice of Isaac, Genesis 22:1]; with him I am well pleased [a likely allusion to Jesus' role as the Servant of Yahweh, Isaiah 42 – 53]" (Matthew 3:17).

This is how it starts. From that point on the beloved Son of God finds himself increasingly at odds with the powerful elite of Israel, all concerning disputes about the real meaning of Scripture and the faithful life that the Old Testament God accepts. The real sticking point is the carpenter's insistence that people believe exclusively in him.

The story of Jesus is only meaningful if he really walked the dusty streets of Galilee and met a cruel death in the nation's occupied capital about two thousand years ago. Jewish elites turned him over; a Roman governor ordered that Roman nails hold his brutally beaten body to a Roman cross. Jews and Gentiles, who didn't much agree on anything, were complicit in his murder. Someone else observing the scene had actually planned it — God. It had been God's will to crush him, regarding this death as a life-giving sacrifice (Isaiah 53:10). This is the path planned out from all eternity (Revelation 13:8), foreshadowed in every sacrifice throughout the Old Testament, and played out in the streets of Jerusalem. For centuries God had said, "Here it comes" and finally Jesus said, "Here it is."

**Only One Path**

Is it any wonder that the night before his death Jesus tells his disciples that belief in him is the only avenue to the Father? He is the only way (dare we say "path"?); he is the only truth; in him alone is life (John 14:6). There is no other way because only Jesus, the Beloved One whose obedient life pleased the Father, gave his life to pay for our sins (1 Timothy 1:15; 1 John 2:2). In his humanity he walked among us and perfectly represented us; he is the perfect and only go-between currently representing us to God the Father (1 Timothy 2:5–6).

This is why the simple fishermen and other rough-hewn characters dared to square off with the very ones who sent Jesus to his death: "Salvation is found in no one else, for there is no other name under heaven given to men by which we must be saved" (Acts 4:12). They experienced a one of a kind, life-changing reality.

## SUMMING UP

If another path was just as good (or if all of them were, for that matter), then Jesus *really* died for nothing, and his followers are worse than buffoons. What's more, *all of the world's scriptures* have failed to let us in on this little secret. Maybe you're not convinced Christianity is *the* path, but you should be able to recognize that *all* paths are not the same. This little myth is "Busted," as they say.

## SINCERELY YOURS, A POST SCRIPT

Hand in hand with the "all-paths" variety of myth is the notion that as long as you're sincere, God will let you into heaven. But, in fact, all paths emphatically do *not* lead to God. If I sincerely believe in a path that can't deliver, my sincerity may be admirable on some level, but ultimately it will fall short. That which we are sincere about must in fact exist.

When I was a teenager, I sincerely believed a certain young lady would eventually come to her senses and realize what a catch I was.

She didn't. I actually had this same deeply held conviction (delusion?) several times in my youth, but the little princesses persisted in their wrong-headed pursuits of other guys. My sincerity, you see, didn't square with the facts. Anyone can be sincere; it's just that, as is so often said, they can be so sincerely wrong.

## GOING DEEPER

As in the last chapter, you should be acquainted with the broad strokes of world religions; see Lewis M. Hopfe and Mark R. Woodward, *Religions of the World* (Englewood Cliffs, NJ: Prentice Hall, 2006). You may also want to familiarize yourself with the phenomena of modern cults, for which see Walter Martin, *The Kingdom of the Cults* (Bloomington, MN: Bethany, 2003). For a classic refutation of the supposed openness of relativism, check out Alan Bloom, *The Closing of the American Mind* (New York: Simon and Schuster, 1987).

My friend Chad Meister recently published a must-read for aspiring apologists entitled *Building Belief: Constructing Faith from the Ground Up* (Grand Rapids: Baker, 2006). On a different note allow me to suggest Don Richardson, *Eternity in Their Hearts: Startling Evidence of Belief in the One True God in Hundreds of Cultures throughout the World* (Ventura, CA: Regal, 1981). This is an engaging, though somewhat overstated, investigation on God's fingerprints in other religions. The thesis is that the God of the Bible has sown the seeds of the gospel in the hearts of the world's religions. It's not that all worship the same God, but that the one God has planted a seed in them. Finally, this site was useful preparing for this chapter: www.geocities.com/Athens/8916/index2.html.

# Chapter 14

# THE OLD TESTAMENT GOD IS A GOD OF WRATH, BUT THE NEW TESTAMENT GOD IS A GOD OF MERCY

This chapter explores a myth that is essentially built on a faulty impression. All of them are, in a sense, but this one is all the more difficult to overturn since it is so frequently reinforced *from the pulpit*. This is territory I'm trying to avoid — in-house debates (or if you prefer, "family squabbles"). The God of the Old Testament is endlessly pitted against the God of the New Testament, usually in terms of a fundamental change in the way he chooses to deal with people. And it doesn't stop there. The impression that there are two kinds of Gods filters into the popular culture. It is usually stated something like this: "The God of the Old Testament is so wrathful but the God of the New Testament is so merciful. How can this be the same God?"

The question is problematic because it winds up assuming a contradiction between the Testaments, and it raises the notion that there are actually two Gods whose ways are at odds with each other. Here's another difficulty: the question is correct in what it affirms, but incorrect in what it implies. It affirms the wrath of God in the Old Testament and his mercy in the New, but it implies God has *no* mercy (and is *utterly* wrathful) in the Old, and is *only* merciful (and has *no* wrath) in the New. These are the issues we will explore in this chapter.

## HOW MANY GODS ARE THERE ANYWAY?

How many Gods exist, biblically speaking, is pretty straightforward: one. The unified, uncompromised, repeated claim of both

Testaments is: "There is no other God" (Isaiah 45:14; Ephesians 4:6; James 2:19). We are commanded not only to believe the fact that there is one God, but also to respond in faith. However, not all have done so throughout history.

The notion of a difference between the Old and New Testament God goes back at least as far as a man named Marcion, whom we met briefly in chapter 5. He arrived in Rome around AD 140 insisting the God of the Old Testament was inferior (since he was so bloodthirsty and angry), but the God of the New Testament was vastly superior (focused, as he was, on love and grace).

This two-God notion surfaces from time to time and has gained a little recent traction with the publicity surrounding the discovery of the *Gospel of Judas*. This ancient piece of literature fits well with the so-called "Gnostic" texts of the second century (and later). Salvation is through *gnosis*, meaning "knowledge." Literary works like this were a reaction against the claims of the New Testament and set *evil* matter against *good and noble* spiritual realities. They had no room for a genuinely human, dying and rising Savior, and no room for a cross or a resurrection (the heart of Christianity). They also had no room for seeing the Old Testament as any reasonable background for the superior wisdom of the divine Jesus. *That* God can't be the New Testament God.

## HE SURE SEEMS ANGRY

The issues are a little different in our day, but the result is the same. Usually it's just an impression one gets from a cursory reading or vague acquaintance with the Old Testament (not to mention many a sermon). You cannot read it for long without running into a hair-raising story of God creaming some renegade or another. Anyone who stepped out of bounds with his law faced a barrage of efficiently thrown stones (Exodus 19:13; Leviticus 24:23). One day God ordered the faithful to grab swords and slay the rebels within Israel; three thousand men fell that day (Exodus 32:28). He often sent Israel's army to wipe out a whole town or even a nation: men, women, and children (Deuteronomy 13:12–15; Joshua 11:11; 1 Samuel 15:2–3). Who could blame someone for thinking this God might get a little testy from time to time?

Contrasted to that notion, the New Testament God is about forbearance and forgiveness. He's the "love your enemy," "turn the other cheek," "for God so loved the world" God. These have to be different Gods! But with the persistent monotheism of both Testaments, the only biblical answer is, "No, there's only one." How, then, do we account for this apparent disparity? Again the answer is an easy one. There isn't any. *Both notions of God are neglecting the other side of the coin in both Testaments.*

In the remainder of the chapter, then, we will demonstrate that grace abounds in the Old Testament and wrath is abundantly represented in the New. I am not downplaying God's wrath as seen in the Old Testament or attempting to sugarcoat it; neither am I denying the grace seen in the New. Since they are both assumed in the myth we're examining, we need to look closely at the other side in both instances.

## God's Wrath: Plan B

The wrathful nature of the Old Testament God raises the problem of evil, the topic of the next chapter. At this stage, however, we need to understand that wrath and punishment are not God's first choice. It's not even something he wants to do. God calls his acts of judgment his "strange work," his "alien task" (Isaiah 28:21). He truly wants the best for his world (1:18–20), but he calls the shots. After all, he *is* God.

The prophets are filled with God's pleadings for his people to return to him in faith and receive his blessings (Jeremiah 3:14, 22; Ezekiel 33:11; Hosea 14:1–2; Joel 2:12). The alternative was certain punishment. He didn't *have* to warn them, but he did, repeatedly (and for centuries). Why did he do this? Because he is by nature "gracious and compassionate, slow to anger and abounding in love, and he relents from sending calamity" (Joel 2:13).

## God's Mercy, the Heart of the Matter

After a long time of dealing with Israel in the desert after the exodus and after repeated instances of his people kicking up their heels against him, God was fed up. They could go on into the Promised Land, but God wasn't up for the journey. He was too angry with them (Exodus 33:3). But Moses had found favor with God, so he pleads with him to change his mind (which he graciously agreed to do). Moses then adds, "Teach me your ways so I may know you and continue to find favor with you. Remember that this nation is your people" (33:13). The whole conversation revolved around covenant faithfulness. Moses was pleading with God to show mercy to those who were undeserving of it, but who had received his promises and with whom he had entered a covenant. Then came the clincher: "Show me your glory" (33:18).

All Moses had known prior to this was God's scaled-down presence, his accommodation to what Moses' frail humanity could handle. In that way, Moses could talk to God "face to face" (Exodus 33:11), but in this crisis he needed more. It was as if he were asking, "God, who are you at the core of your being; what is your true nature?" Then he adds, "Can I see your awesome splendor as it really is?" God granted the first part, but to see his full glory would vaporize Moses on the spot. So God shielded him as his glory passed by, allowing him to see the afterglow (33:17 – 23). As that happened, Moses heard something no one had ever heard before. God's self-disclosure echoed through the canyon as he solemnly intoned:

> The Lord, the Lord, the compassionate and gracious God, slow to anger, abounding in love and faithfulness, maintaining love to thousands, and forgiving wickedness, rebellion and sin. (34:6 – 7)

This is who he is and what he is like. Here is a God with a heart that longs to show grace and mercy and who has a very long fuse. God reminds his people of this at key points throughout their history (2 Chronicles 30:9; Nehemiah 9:17; Psalm 86:15; 103:8; Joel 2:13; Jonah 4:2). This is so his people will take stock and worship him from a pure heart, or, in the case of straying, return to him for renewal and forgiveness.

## OLD-TIME RELIGION

I could have cast this chapter in terms of "the Old Testament is all about law, but the New Testament is all about love and grace." It reinforces the same misconception (Old Testament God: *mean*; New Testament God: *nice*), and I'm sure it works pretty well in sermons. It just isn't true. The gracious God of the New Testament is first revealed in the Old Testament. Serving this gracious and compassionate God has always been a matter of the heart rather than just following a dead formula.

God's loving heart forms the basis of the Old Testament law. When asked what the greatest commandment was, Jesus actually quoted an Old Testament summary of the law: "Love the Lord your God with all your heart and with all your soul and with all your mind" (Matthew 22:37 – 38; citing Deuteronomy 6:5). Then he threw in a second for no extra charge: "Love your neighbor as yourself" (Matthew 22:39; citing Leviticus 19:18).

This dual focus — God first, then people — is found in the very structure of the Ten Commandments. The first four all relate to a proper relationship with God, dare we say, with loving him. The rest all deal with the proper way to treat our fellow brothers and sisters; once again, all of them are love in action. Have you discerned a common element here?

No, I'm not cheating by sneaking in Jesus at this point. His testimony on this regard is crucial since he strove so valiantly to reveal to the people the heart of God behind the commands, the original spirit of the Old Testament law. Jesus, the very personification of God, looked at the law and summed it up as an expression of divine love, declaring that "all the Law and the Prophets hang on these two commandments" (Matthew 22:40).

## And So It Went

This heart focus was nothing new; it was just freshly emphasized by Jesus. Centuries earlier Moses had warned Israel she would be exiled for turning from God, but restored if she turned to him with all her heart and with all her soul (Deuteronomy 4:29). It was the only acceptable way to serve God (11:13; Joshua 22:5; 1 Samuel 12:24). Physical signs and actions represented the expected corresponding inner reality. So Moses wasn't impressed with the mere rite of circumcision if the heart remained callous (Deuteronomy 10:16). Likewise, Jeremiah implored the people to circumcise their hearts to avoid God's punishment (Jeremiah 4:4). Not content with the culturally appropriate display of expressing grief or horror, Joel told the people to rend their hearts, not their garments (Joel 2:13). This is a theme that continually resurfaces throughout the Old Testament. God's people needed the God of mercy and love to perform his loving acts of renewal on their behalf.

We see this heart-focus in such passages as 1 Samuel 15:22 – 23. Saul was raked over the coals for assuming that offering a hasty sacrifice would gloss over the fact that he had disobeyed God. Samuel let him know an empty ritual couldn't fit the bill, because the Lord doesn't "delight in burnt offerings and sacrifices as much as in obeying" what he commands. "To obey is better than sacrifice."

In another instance, when David was confronted with sins (murder and adultery), he knew in his heart that simply going through the motions of an offering wouldn't deliver the goods. "You do not delight in sacrifice, or I would bring it; you do not take pleasure in burnt offerings" (Psalm 51:16). It's not that these things were no longer necessary, they indeed were, and David delighted in giving them (27:6). It was just that David, perhaps for the first time, saw beyond the ritual to its intended purpose: "The sacrifices of God are a broken spirit; a broken and contrite heart, O God, you will not despise" (51:17). That's why he cried out, "Create in me a pure heart, O God, and renew a steadfast spirit within me" (51:10). He didn't need to check off a rule or two; he needed God to make him into a new person, a godly person from the inside out.

Maybe it was new to David, or at least he had a fresh appreciation of it, but it had always been the underlying reality. God wants our hearts to respond to him out of genuine love.

## A New Day Was Coming

There is another aspect of this topic that isn't often considered, namely, how the prophecies of the new covenant themselves reinforce God's merciful character within the old covenant. We see this clearly in God's vision for his people's future (of course, from the perspective of the Old Testament).

All was never hunky-dory under the old covenant, so God set the stage for the day when his new covenant would be enacted. The problem wasn't God or the fact that he gave the people a law. The problem was the people. Their hearts had become rock-hard, severely straining their relationship with God. What they needed was a reboot.

They would indeed be punished, exiled from the land (that's the wrath part), but God envisioned a time of incredible renewal and restoration. Through the prophet Jeremiah God spoke of a time when he would gather them again and rebuild the ancient towns. Not content with that, he promised to "make a new covenant" with the nation. It wouldn't be like the old one, " 'because they broke my covenant, though I was a husband to them,' declares the LORD." Instead, "I will put my law in their minds and write it on their hearts. I will be their God, and they will be my people." All will come to know him, and best of all, "I will forgive their wickedness and will remember their sins no more" (Jeremiah 31:31–34).

Don't miss this salient fact. The promise of a new covenant (a New *Testament*, if you will) is found within the pages of the Old Testament.

Ezekiel 36:24–28 gives us a glimpse of this as well. God will one day gather his people from exile and return them to their "own land" (36:24). He will deal with their sin in an incredible new way. He will "sprinkle clean water" on them to wash away their impurity and idolatry (36:25). What's more, he will give them "a new heart and put a new spirit" in them, removing their "heart of stone" in the process and giving them a new "heart of flesh" (36:26). Into that newly cleansed vessel God will put his own Spirit so that his people can follow his decrees and laws. And, as perceived by Jeremiah, Ezekiel sees the people reestablished in "the land I gave your forefathers," and then his heart's cry will be realized: "You will be my people, and I will be your God" (36:28).

These prophecies, which are fulfilled in the New Testament, are spoken within the pages of the Old. They reveal God's heart, his desire to restore, love, and forgive.

Notice the bestowal of the Spirit doesn't make his people into angry little rule-enforcers. It makes them new, purified, forgiven people who are at peace with their God. It is everything someone would long for, provided he or she knew God and desired to know him more. This longing forms the basis of the New Testament gospel, in which God's heart of love and forgiveness, mercy and grace are fully revealed.

## AS IN THE OLD, SO IN THE NEW

In the New Testament we find that *this* God sent his Son to our desperately needy world. The Son was, in fact, the "exact representation of his being" (Hebrews 1:3), clothed in flesh (John 1:14), and the very fullness of deity in bodily form (Colossians 2:9). Is it any wonder, then, that Jesus was so full of "grace and truth" (John 1:14, 17) and continually performed acts of mercy and compassion (Matthew

9:13; 20:34; Mark 1:41; 8:2)? This is what the Old Testament God is like, and this is precisely what we find personified in Jesus.

That the New Testament God is one of "mercy and grace" is assumed in our myth. What remains to be seen is the other side of the coin.

## The New Testament God of Wrath

Broaching this inherently negative topic is necessary, given the extent of the popular misconception. Most statements concerning God's wrath are on the lips of Jesus. This is so because Jesus speaks for God in the New Testament. He does so directly, authoritatively, and infallibly. What the other New Testament writers have to say on the topic originates in his teaching.

It must be noted, first of all, that God's wrath is reserved for those who reject the Son. Jesus reserves the harshest language for the religious leaders of his day because of their persistence in unbelief. He told them they would die in their sins (John 8:24) and utterly perish (Luke 13:5). *Anyone* who rejects the Son, in fact, "will not see life, for God's wrath remains on him" (John 3:36).

This notion of the persistent application of divine wrath on those who reject Jesus is known as the second death (Revelation 20:14). God's wrath, then, is most closely associated with hell, the place where unbelievers perish. The descriptions of it are grim indeed. Hell is a smoldering, worm-infested garbage heap (Mark 9:47–49), a dark place full of anger, sorrow, and regret (Matthew 8:12). It's an abyss, a bottomless pit (Luke 8:31), a lake of fire (Revelation 21:8), a place of eternal destruction devoid of the Lord's saving presence (2 Thessalonians 1:9). It is a fire prepared for "the devil and his angels," but becomes the eternal abode of anyone who foolishly follows their ways (Matthew 25:41). Hell is the fixed expression of God's wrath and the eternal absence of his mercy.

"It's all metaphorical," you say; "it's figures of speech." Yes, that's true, but what do the metaphors represent? Whatever hell is *really* like will be far worse than any of the attempts to describe it. Human language strains at making sense of an eternal black gulf that swallows up all hope and resounds with the anguished cries of regret and perishing souls. Whatever it is, it isn't recommended.

There is yet another aspect of wrath we need to consider. At the second coming of Jesus (and in the events leading up to it), the earth will witness an unprecedented outpouring of God's anger. The furious rage of the Creator will be fully and finally poured out on the planet. Those who refuse to turn to him and persist in rebellion will bear its full brunt (Revelation 14:9 – 10). It will be so horrifying people will rather be crushed under a mountain than face his wrath (6:16 – 17).

### The Stakes Are Raised

Not only does the New Testament reveal this wrathful side of God, but it should also be dawning on you at some point that this is far worse than anything depicted in the Old Testament. The punishments in the Old Testament pertained to this life (whether famine, pestilence, or exile), or resulted in an untimely death (whether by judicially sanctioned stones, or by an enemy's sword). Any notion of wrathful punishment after death is not directly addressed. Any talk of the afterlife at all spoke of the grave or the shadowy underworld (Psalm 6:5; Ecclesiastes 9:10). It's the New Testament that gives us the concept of eternal torment in a nasty flaming pit.

### Somebody's Gonna Get It

Did you ever break something when you were a kid? Maybe you were playing with a ball in the living room and knocked over a lamp. I don't know how it was in your house, but my beloved siblings and I instinctively knew that someone was going to be blamed. Somebody was going to get it. (I'll leave it to your imagination whose hide usually got tanned.)

That is precisely the situation we all find ourselves in. We've broken the lamp, God's way of truth, and his righteous character demands a reckoning. This is precisely where the mercy part comes in. We can either opt to take on the full fury of a holy God, incensed that we puny creatures dare oppose him to his face, or we can opt for his mercy. God's wrath was poured out on the cross. Jesus already took it. It is God's mercy that tells us to believe in his Son and trust him to pay the price for us.

How can he be merciful and send people to hell? He doesn't want to, so his mercy is extended to us through his Son Jesus, "who rescues us from the coming wrath" (1 Thessalonians 1:10). If we refuse his mercy, no mercy is left. One can't spurn the Savior and expect salvation.

## ON A BRIGHTER NOTE

Having made the case, I think it's a good idea to put this in perspective. I mentioned earlier that God's wrath is stepped up in the New Testament. A moment's reflection also makes clear that the blessings are as well. All the blessings of the Old Testament pertained to earthly life. It was peace, plenty, and safety in the Land of Promise. Families would thrive in the full bloom of health, enjoying the favor of the surrounding nations. Any blessing beyond this life was just a vague hint of immortality (as in Psalm 23:6).

In the New Testament, people have their sins completely wiped out and their lives remade. They are conformed more and more into the very image of Jesus, himself the image of God (Romans 8:29). As a result the Christian experiences peace with God and an intimate way of life in tune with the Spirit, who made all things and who indwells the believers. His Spirit resonates with the songs of heaven in our spirits.

Yes, we still struggle; we're not yet perfect. Sin reasserts itself, and the screech of Mother Earth sometimes reduces God's voice to a whisper. Christianity is tuning our ears to the whisper.

After a temporary separation of body and spirit after death, our spirits will be reunited with our newly resurrected and glorified bodies. God's heaven will come to a re-created earth, and we will spend all of eternity on a gorgeous planet infused with the warm glow of the glory of God (Revelation 21–22). That will be when God finally has his deepest desire fulfilled. "Now the dwelling of God is with men, and he will live with them. They will be his people, and God himself will be with them and be their God" (21:3). This is the grand fulfillment of the new covenant still to come, the eternal communion of a loving God and his adored children.

## SUMMING UP

As it was in the Old Testament, so in the New Testament, God doesn't want his people to suffer his wrath. His merciful character prompts him to have compassion on his creatures, expressed in concrete acts of salvation. Wrath is reserved for the ones who refuse it. *This* is the God of both Testaments. Myth "busted."

## GOING DEEPER

Two good overviews of Gnosticism are the articles on the subject in *Evangelical Dictionary of Theology*, edited by Walter Elwell; and in *DPL*. I am indebted to my friend Tad Trapp for the insights about God's heart of compassion as revealed in Exodus 34:6; his dissertation on the topic and a popular-level book are both forthcoming. I am also indebted to the interaction in a couple of doctoral seminars at Trinity: *Old Testament Quotations in the New Testament* and *Mystery in the New Testament*, both taught by D. A. Carson.

# Chapter 15

# WITH ALL THE EVIL IN THE WORLD, THERE CAN'T BE A GOD

She came here often, and if sheer repetition was any clue, this place was her favorite. The food was always good; the drinks flowed freely, and her youthful vitality always turned heads. It was such a beautiful day, clear and warm. Her heart swelled with the simple joy of a pleasant meal among friends. She just didn't know it would be her last.

He watched carefully just out of sight. He'd done this before and would do so again, but it was more than a compulsion; it was life itself. He felt no guilt, no remorse—just a controlled rush of adrenaline as all his senses focused on this carefully planned attack. He was ruthless, yet smart. He always chose his victim with the utmost care and waited for the right moment to make his move.

It came swift and brutal. No second thoughts, not even a hint of right or wrong: "Kill! Now!" was all that could possibly register. The crowd's panic was immediate as he rushed from the shadows; one glimpse and all scattered. All, that is, except for one. Her head was turned at just that moment. In the precious few seconds remaining of her young life she turned to see what had so frightened the others, rather than simply fleeing with them. Her last conscious thought was the hideous terror and searing pain of her throat being viciously torn open—a crimson death on a sunny afternoon.

There were scores of witnesses, but none would ever testify. There would be no call to the police and no investigation. No one would ever go to court or darken the door of a jail. In fact, there had been no crime. Cheetahs kill gazelles every day.

Nature shows are full of these beast-on-beast dramas. We may at times feel a tinge of remorse for the little critters biting the dust as the bigger critters devour them, but we know it's just nature. There is no evil involved. But what if we change the scene slightly, from a river bank on the edge of an African savannah to a trendy bistro in a college town? Our characters are now a lively group of college students blowing off steam on a beautiful afternoon. The victim is a lovely coed; her attacker is a serial killer psycho-brute.

Given the brazen nature of a broad-daylight assault, there would indeed be legal repercussions, but that's only because we as a society have decided to frown on such activities. He did nothing wrong; evil doesn't exist. We are all just animals doing what feels right for the moment. Should someone want to interject that anything goes *as long as no one gets hurt*, I would then feel inclined to point out that such a person is merely weak (and likely a victim as well in the not-too-distant future). Our tender coed was weak; her assailant was strong. It's survival of the fittest in a college-town café.

No crime, no foul. Nothing amiss at all, that is, if there is no God.

## YOU CAN'T HAVE IT BOTH WAYS

I find it a bit amusing when otherwise intelligent atheists complain God is AWOL when it comes to evil in the world. The fact that he doesn't do anything to stop it is a sure sign to them that he's not really there to begin with. This classic problem is usually posed something like the following:

- There is evil in the world.
- Christians believe God exists and is all-powerful and all-loving.
- But if God exists, either he really isn't all-powerful since evil triumphs.

- Or, he really could stop it all but doesn't; so he is not really loving.
- Therefore, given the evil, there can't be a God.

We are, of course, talking about the problem of evil and attempts to vindicate God in the midst of it. Classically, this is known as "theodicy."

You're probably waiting for the amusing part. Maybe "ironic" is a better term. The irony is the acknowledgment that there actually is undeniable evil in our world. Even those who attempt to deny it on philosophical grounds cannot help but carry on in this life as if it really exists. Even philosophers lock their doors and keep their wits about them on the mean streets. The irony is being appalled at evil and using its existence to argue that God does not exist. Yet, if God does not exist, there can be no such thing as evil. The only way there can be "evil" is if there is also something known as "good." You can't transgress what is right without an ultimate standard by which to gauge it.

Take God out of the picture and all we have left are the random meanderings of eons of mutations on increasingly complex amino acids. Nature is all there is. No one is horrified when army ants invade termite hills and crunch every obstinate termite in their path. No one bats an eye when egrets prey on pollywogs. The slowest zebra is the one meeting a slow death courtesy of a predator's claws and fangs. It's survival of the fittest on the grand stage of nature. So what if some thug whacks a pretty sophomore?

The moment you say something is evil, then you have implicitly acknowledged a real standard of right and wrong that transcends nature. You can't have it both ways. For God *and* evil to be a philosophical problem, they *both* must actually exist.

## ONE GRAND STORY LINE

Why, then, does God permit evil? When the skeptics attack Christianity with this issue, there are some scriptural claims that are granted for the sake of argument: God is all-powerful; God is all-loving; there is evil in the world. Why is it that the rest of the scriptural picture is ignored? The unstated assumption in the whole debate is that the world as it currently exists is the way God wants it. He likes it this way.

Years ago the late comedian George Carlin made the snide observation that everything God makes *dies*. The implication is that God is a loser. Does the Bible ever explain why there is death in the world? Does it ever attempt to explain why we automatically equate our humanity and our inherent shortcomings? "To err is human," as the saying goes, but has that always been the case (and will it ever change)? Why do the skeptics ignore Genesis 1–3 and Revelation 20–22? This is not a cop-out; it's the answer to the dilemma.

## No Problem

Think of those six chapters, the first three and the last three in the Bible, as bookends. The problem is introduced in the beginning of Genesis and resolved at the end of Revelation. We can even break it down a little further and compare the first two and last two chapters. The first two chapters of Genesis give us a glimpse of God's relationship with his creation at the very beginning. He creates a magnificent world, a garden paradise full of wonderful creatures. The crown of his creation are people made in his image. Adam and Eve are the caretakers of God's handiwork, living in unbroken fellowship with each other and with God. There is no sickness, fear, danger, sin, or death (not to mention taxes or politicians). All they have to do is tend the garden and eat from the bounty of the fruit-bearing trees—all of them, that is, except for one.

Turning to the end of the story, Revelation 21–22, we're back in paradise. It's a new creation with rivers and trees and people in unbroken fellowship with their God who has come to dwell with them. The Bible ends where it begins, but now there are countless people instead of two. They are redeemed and share in the endless breath of eternity. The test is over and the everlasting new day has dawned. There is no more mourning, pain, sickness, or death. The curse is removed and all is restored.

Curse? What curse?

That question brings us to the next set of bookends, the chapter after the creation of Paradise, Genesis 3, and the one right before its restoration, Revelation 20. These concern the fall and the final judgment.

## It All Springs from the Fall

Genesis 3 is the sorrowful tale of the birth of rebellion and the levying of a curse on the entire creation. This is known as "the fall," that is, the falling from grace of the human race, the entrance of sin and death into the universe. The world still retained much of its beauty, but the unpredictably dangerous quality of nature took on its ominous character from that day on. Nature, as Tennyson said, became "red in tooth and claw."[43] Worse still, all of the horrific failings of the human race stem from that one act of defiance. Adam and Eve chose to follow their own desires rather than God.

This rebellion is so deep-rooted that it is stamped on the hardwiring of every human being ever since. Every parent knows this. When it comes to selfishness, meanness, and obstinacy on the one hand, and sharing, kindness, and humble obedience on the other, which set of values needs to be taught, and which ones show up unbidden from the bassinet onward? This is the lot of us all. (If you know of a perfect and sinless person, aside from Jesus, please introduce the rest of us; we've never seen one.)

The history of humanity is an unbroken chain of misery, yet still punctuated with astounding feats of heroism and expressions of genuine love. Everyone is capable of goodness. It is simply the indelible imprint of God's image, even on the most ardent atheist. For the time being, that image is marred, but not removed. No one, however good and gifted they may be, can erase the stain of guilt or remove the sentence of death hanging over all of us. Only the One who imposed it has the power to deal with it.

At the end of the story, Revelation 20 is the perfect counterbalance to Genesis 3. The sequence of events and the exact participants are debated, but we are presented in this chapter with God's final judgment on the Devil and all who have foolishly chosen to follow him. Not only is sin dealt with, but death itself. The grand imposition of the unnatural state of the interruption of life is forever removed. Mr. Carlin, the day will come when everything God makes and everyone at peace with him will never die. Death will lose its reign of terror.

So, we see how the beginning chapters are resolved in the final chapters, but what about everything else in between? The consequences of human sin drive the Bible's story line and all of human history. Rays of light shine out, from time to time, in a dark narrative all the way to the final judgment. We are in the period of time in which evil reigns. So every example of injustice, horror, and abject misery, not to mention the elements gone awry (like a hurricane or tsunami), are directly addressed in the Bible's story of the planet's headlong plunge into rebellion.

## THE PLAN OF REDEMPTION

This standard biblical explanation is in no way meant to minimize the horrors we in fact see, nor is it offered as a pat answer delivered with dry theological detachment. And it still leaves a question hanging: Why doesn't God *do* something about it? That, apologies to Paul Harvey, "is the rest of the story." He has, and he will.

In the midst of this drama another story unfolds. If I may, allow me to use the analogy of bookends one last time. This next pair, though, doesn't neatly correspond to chapters. It begins in the middle of Genesis 3 and reaches its peak in Revelation 19, but repercussions continue to the end. This is the story of God's remedy to human folly—redemption through a unique man, God's own Son.

In Genesis 3 God first announces a plan to overthrow the Devil (in the guise of a serpent), the one responsible for instigating the whole kerfuffle. As we'll see in a moment, this is a promise of the first coming of Jesus. In Revelation 19 we see his second coming; the Son returns to earth in a glorious display of divine power. Those who didn't feel the need to include him in their lives meet with a frightful and inglorious end (1 Thessalonians 1:9–10). All those who were waiting for him and remained faithful are finally transformed, shining with God's glory (1 Corinthians 15:51–53; Philippians 3:20–21; Hebrews 9:28).

### The Son Takes Center Stage

Let's take a closer look at how the plan of redemption unfolds. Right at the heart of the problem with evil is God's plan for dealing with it. As a matter of fact, the remedy for the curse is announced in the midst of the curse itself! First, the battle lines are drawn. God says to the Devil: "I will put enmity between you and the woman, and between your offspring and hers" (Genesis 3:15). It appears that the reference is to those who follow his ways, but it gets more personal in the next line. The focus narrows, as the verse continues, to one of Eve's offspring in a contest with the Devil himself: "He will crush your head, and you will strike his heel." Christians see this as referring to Jesus.

The Christian interpretation of this passage isn't the only possible one, but it's uncanny how Jesus' crucifixion fits the bill. The stricken Jesus was affixed to the cross, nails through his feet ("you will strike his heel"). That was the Devil's best shot and all would have gone well were it not for the inconvenient fact that Jesus never sinned. The devil wanted to do away with this troublemaker, the only one he couldn't trip up. Maybe the Devil thought that at least Jesus would be out of the way so he could return to business as usual.

God had a different plan. He focused the penalty of all evil, sin, and rebellion—for all people for all time—on this one innocent victim. The moment Jesus died, the penalty was paid, and Satan's doom was ensured ("he will crush your head"). This is reflected in Jesus' words from the cross, "It is finished" (John 19:30). This is the triumph of God over all demonic power and entanglements of human sin (Colossians 2:13–15). God's own Son takes the stage and pulls the curtain on Satan's reign. The cross was the defeat of evil; the resurrection, then, defeated the stranglehold of death. If the Devil was wearing pants that day, I bet he had to change them.

### Meanwhile, Back in the Garden

Something else happened in the garden that revealed God's plan for fixing the problem of evil. The command to stay away from the forbidden tree came with the warning, "when you eat of it you will surely die" (Genesis 2:17), but it didn't exactly happen that way. They ate; they saw themselves in a new light; they tried to cover up as best they could, and beat feet for the bushes when they heard God coming. "Surely die" must've been ringing in their ears because God, for the first time, was someone they *feared*. The curse and its remedy came next, but after that we're told that God "made garments of skin for Adam and his wife and clothed them" (3:21). That was awfully magnanimous of him, giving them more durable threads than some hastily sewn leaves. Or was something else going on?

### There's a Carcass in Paradise

Where did he get the animal skins? The astute reader may safely guess they came from animals. What shouldn't be missed, though, is the fact that until this point there's no mention of anything having died. The threat of death was looming in the background as God confronted his rebels, but not only did he promise redemption, he also gave them a picture of it. Now, there is a lot of conjecture on my part in terms of the drama I'm about to describe, but the point of it all was crystal clear, as we'll see.

Picture Adam and Eve standing before God, their heads hanging low as they wait for their promised death sentence. Spiritually speaking, they *did* die, but they still would have been expecting physical death. Instead, God clothed them with animal skins. But what if they weren't nicely cured and brushed-out hides? What if God reached over and snatched the skin off of some sweet little deer standing nearby minding its own business? With a shriek little Bambi keeled over in convulsions as his blood-soaked hide was wrapped around Adam. Drip, drip. "When you eat of it you will surely die" was the sentence, but it fell upon an innocent animal instead. The first recorded death was one of atonement; God accepted a sacrifice on Adam's and Eve's behalf.

## An Ingrained Pattern

Did Adam and Eve know God required sacrifice as the means of drawing near to him? The very next story, Cain's murder of Abel, gives us a clue. God accepted Abel's sacrifice but rejected Cain's. We could debate the reason for God's response or note the effects of the fall (jealousy and murder), but I have an even more basic question. Why were they offering sacrifices in the first place? This is the first mention of people doing so. Where did they get such a notion? For that matter, why did Noah make an altar and offer animal sacrifices after leaving the ark (Genesis 8:20)? Why did Abram feel the need to make altars to God all throughout the land promised to him (12:6 – 8)? Why was Job making daily sacrifices for himself and his children (Job 1:5)? My guess is that it all goes back to the skins.

When God finally gave Israel detailed instructions about sacrifices, the practice had been in place for millennia. God was reinforcing the means of approaching him, always in reference to the spilling of blood. But this is not, as the critics allege, the ravings of a bloodthirsty deity. It is the solemn reminder that we deserve death, but God accepts a substitute on our behalf. Every bull, goat, and lamb slain on an Israelite altar pointed forward to the final sacrifice of Jesus, the Lamb of God.

Jesus' first coming defeated Satan by dealing directly with the Evil One's hold on the human heart. His second coming will rid the world of all remnants of his evil reign.

## A SNAPSHOT

This, then, is a snapshot of the Bible's story line, as well as the whole drama of human history:

> A Genesis 1–2: Paradise formed, God in fellowship with his creation
>> B Genesis 3: The devil prevails, paradise lost, sin and death reign
>>> C Genesis 3: Redemption promised
>>>> D Everything else: the story of redemption in the midst of evil
>>> C' Revelation 19: Redemption fulfilled
>> B' Revelation 20: God judges the Devil, sin, sinners, and death
> A' Revelation 21–22: Paradise restored, God comes to dwell with his creation

The basic upshot of all this is that the problem of evil, for all its horrors, is temporary. The end of the story is the defeat of all that is opposed to God and every wrong put right. Evil will be no more. Still, there are a couple of items that need to be cleared up.

**Just Who Is This Serpent?**

Beyond sin's grip on us and nature's bloody fang, something else went terribly wrong in the garden of Eden. The Enemy gained control of the planet. It's not that he wrested it out of God's hands or somehow tricked him. (Lest we forget: "The earth is the LORD's, and everything in it," Psalm 24:1.) No, God himself granted Satan a measure of control. When Adam and Eve listened to Satan rather than God, God allowed the Enemy to enter the picture—humanity found itself with another "god." He has limited, but very real power: "the whole world is under the control of the evil one" (1 John 5:19).

This is why Paul calls the Devil the "god of this age" who "has blinded the minds of unbelievers," preventing them from seeing "the light of the gospel" (2 Corinthians 4:4). He also points out that only through this gospel can people "come to their senses and escape from the trap of the devil" (2 Timothy 2:26). The enemy even tried to sidetrack Jesus with an attractive offer. Giving Jesus a vision of "all the kingdoms of the world," Satan offered to give him "all their authority and splendor, for it has been given to me, and I can give it to anyone I want to. So if you worship me, it will all be yours" (Luke 4:5–7). Pretty tempting, wouldn't you say? Of course, the temptation loses its punch if the Devil couldn't deliver on it. Jesus could've had, right then and there, wealth and power, supreme political and military control over all the (still-fallen) earth. All he had to do was leave God's path and follow Satan's.

This is exactly what has driven ancient conquerors and more recent despots throughout history—the desire for world conquest. Ever wonder why those who aspire to take over the world wind up being real pieces of work? Are they loving and caring, looking out for the underdog? Or are they more typically just deranged thugs whose reign brings terror and destruction? We see in Satan's offer to Jesus the reason this is so. Satan himself empowers the desire; we see his sneer in every Lenin, Hitler, and Mao.

## The Problem in the Problem of Evil

The *problem* of evil can be directly traced to the *author* of evil, the malevolent presence of the enemy—the Devil. So I first need to clarify something. All along I've been referring to the bad guy in Eden as the Devil or Satan, but those terms aren't ever used there. The enemy is called "the serpent" (Genesis 3:1). The actual identity of this mysterious being is only slowly revealed throughout the Old Testament until coming into sharp focus in the New Testament. Along the way God gives us pieces of the puzzle.

The story of Lucifer, a mighty angelic being falling to earth because of his rebellion against God, is a fairly familiar image in Christian circles. The most well-known example is in Isaiah. The mighty "morning star" was cast down to earth for wanting to "ascend to heaven" with his throne "above the stars of God," making himself "like the Most High" (Isaiah 14:12–14). The incredible pride that gripped his heart twisted his mind so out of whack he actually believed he could boot God off his throne. It just slipped his mind that he was a created being and no match for his Maker.

So far so good, but what Christians usually miss is that this is spoken against the (earthly) king of Babylon. It's as if God was saying through Isaiah, "Yep, I've seen *this* before." The evil spirit that animated the evil king mimicked the original sin. Isaiah, then, gives us a glimpse of a far more ancient drama—the *origin* of all evil.

Another example comes from Ezekiel. This time, the prophet is talking about the king of Tyre. "You were in Eden, the garden of God.... You were blameless in your ways from the day you were created till wickedness was found in you" (Ezekiel 28:13, 15). It's not that the earthly king was in fact in Eden, but God saw who was behind his terrifying reign. Once again, we are privy to God's perspective as he looks back on the fall of one of his mighty beings, who then proceeded to animate these kings.

Perceiving the Devil's presence in earthly evil is common in the Scriptures. This is why John, seeing the rising threat of the Roman Empire, referred to the seat of emperor worship in Asia Minor as the place "where Satan has his throne ... where Satan lives" (Revelation 2:13). Satan was behind this Roman puppet's murderous persecution. Whatever the precise identity of the beast in Revelation 13, John saw a system fully controlled by Satan, wreaking havoc with God's children. There have been, of course, many beasts. Every persecuting emperor, Attila, Stalin, and Hussein—every dictator or little hooligan with too much power who has trampled on the lives of God's people—is just one more example of the hideous and twisted spirit we know as Satan.

Why is there evil in the world? Because there's a devil who hates God and hates people—the greatest commandment put on its ear. But his reign will come to an end.

## NEW AND IMPROVED

In terms of the problem with evil, the question, "Why doesn't God do something?" has been answered. He has. The Devil pretty well jammed things up, so God sent his Son "to destroy the devil's work" (1 John 3:8). He'll one day finish the task. "Why doesn't he do it now?" reflects the deep-seated longing ingrained in us all for God to make it right. He will. The end of the story is the final outworking of God's plan of salvation (still future from our perspective). Meanwhile, "the creation waits in eager expectation for the sons of God to be revealed," the day in which "creation itself will be liberated from its bondage to decay and brought into the glorious freedom of the children of God" (Romans 8:19–21). The reason for the delay, as is often noted, is God's mercy.

There are people who oppose God but who will come to their senses someday. God withholds the final judgment because he's giving people an opportunity to do so. Folks can scoff and mock, but God "is patient with you, not wanting anyone to perish, but everyone to come to repentance" (2 Peter 3:9). Here is God's heart, yet again, on full display. His patience means salvation for those wise enough to turn to him.

Even God's patience, however, will one day wear thin; he'll suddenly pull the plug on the current creation. The universe, as it currently exists, will not endure, says Peter. "That day will bring about the destruction of the heavens by fire, and the elements will melt in the heat" (2 Peter 3:12). Fortunately, that's not the end of the story. "But in keeping with his promise we are looking forward to a new heaven and a new earth, the home of righteousness" (3:13).

This vision from 2 Peter (and many similar passages) gives us hope. We can endure this planet because we know we'll outlive it. A better one is on the way.

## SUMMING UP

With all the evil in the world can there really be a God? Yes. The presence of God is the only way we even can talk meaningfully about evil in the first place. Evil is here because we bought the lie and have been reaping a foul harvest ever since. God is about to torch the field and start again; he only delays because he's extending the day of mercy. One day evil will be a thing of the past, and no one will ever miss it. Evil just won't be a problem.

## GOING DEEPER

Three recommended books on the subject are C. S. Lewis, *The Problem of Pain* (New York: Macmillan, 1962); Peter Kreeft, *Making Sense Out of Suffering* (Ann Arbor, MI: Servant, 1986); and Norman L. Geisler, *The Roots of Evil* (Eugene, OR: Wipf and Stock, 2002).

An accessible treatment of this issue, featuring Alvin Plantinga's "Free Will Defense," can be found at www.xenos.org/essays/evilpo. htm. A little more in depth, but still written for the nonspecialist is www.allaboutgod.com/Problem-Of-Evil.htm. More in depth still is www.catholic.net/RCC/Periodicals/Faith/1112–96/philos1. html. Both sides are represented at plato.stanford.edu/entries/evil/. A scholarly treatment that includes selections from Christian and atheistic perspectives is *The Problem of Evil*, edited by Marilyn Adams and Robert Adams (Oxford, New York: Oxford Univ. Press, 1990). It never hurts to know what the other side is saying.

I first heard the take on the animal skins from Bill Stonebreaker, then pastor of the North Shore Christian Fellowship. I borrowed a couple of lines from one of Scott Chapman's sermons on the subject. I am grateful for Chad Meister's helpful comments on an earlier draft of this chapter.

# MYTHS ABOUT THE CHRISTIAN FAITH

# Chapter 16

# THERE WAS NO SUCH THING AS ORTHODOXY UNTIL THE FOURTH CENTURY

If we're going to talk about orthodoxy, perhaps a good place to begin is a clear definition. *Orthodox* can be used in different ways ("orthodox" is an adjective, "orthodoxy" is the noun). Basically the word means "right," or more technically, "correct thinking," but that's not always how the word is used. We often hear a colloquial expression using a negative form, like when someone's methods are *un*orthodox. In that case the idea is that someone *bends the rules*, or is even a bit *quirky*. Another more technical use is to refer to the Eastern Orthodox Church (whether Greek, Russian, etc.), which refers to an established branch of the church that arose in the ancient (Greek-speaking) Byzantine Empire and increasingly disassociated itself with the (Latin-speaking) Roman Catholic Church. In a similar way, Orthodox Judaism is a branch of that religion characterized by a strict observance of the Torah and Talmud. Other branches of Judaism, in their view, miss the mark.

For the purposes of this chapter, however, the term refers to the church's doctrine. Orthodox belief is the *correct* belief, the teachings of the church that can be traced back to the New Testament, the testimony of the first apostles. These are the kinds of doctrines affirmed by all Christians. Denying these doctrines places one automatically, and at best, on the fringe; more often than not, such denial brands one as a non-Christian.

This is where the myth really asserts itself—the blanket denial that there *was* such a thing as central, nonnegotiable Christian teaching prior to fourth-century thugs imposing it (as popularized, for instance, in *The Da Vinci Code*).

## HOW MANY "TRUTHS" ARE THERE?

Christianity is a multifaceted religion and has been so ever since a few decades after its humble beginnings. The New Testament is full of references to competing views about the identity and significance of Jesus and how to live for him. By the second century some of these views crystallized into religious movements with their own writings, leaders, and practices. A few of them were short-lived; some continued on for centuries; others resurfaced from time to time (some of which are experiencing a revival in our day).

Also, through the course of the centuries, the church experienced some significant splits. The Orthodox East and the Roman Catholic West split in the eleventh century, as did the Italian and French branches of the Roman Catholic Church in the fourteenth century. Both of these go by the name of "The Great Schism" (although the East/West split is the more usual reference). Another break occurred in the sixteenth century between the Roman Catholic and the Protestant churches, which is known as the Reformation. Numerous Protestant splinter movements resulted.

Today is no different. If anything it's even more diversified, as a glance at the yellow pages will demonstrate. Denominations are as plentiful as plastic surgeons in Hollywood or lawyers in D.C. You'll also find various "offshoots," shall we say, of historic Christianity, such as Jehovah Witnesses, Unitarians, and Mormons. Some consider them to be cults; they are quick to return the compliment, disdaining historic Christianity as sorely gone astray. In fact, these offshoots (or *sects*) deny that "mainstream Christianity" has any claim at all to being the historic Christian faith. A given sect presents itself as restoring the original Christian message, but so do the other sects. To the average observer it all looks like a hopeless mishmash. And that, my friends, is the snare.

It is not too difficult to imagine someone looking at this diversity (*tangled web* is more like it) and conclude that no one really has a clue. Every group thinks its teaching is the truth, and there's no way for anyone to know who's right (or even if there *is* such a thing as "right"). Casual observers throw up their hands and erect their walls; the conversation is nipped before the first tender bud can appear.

A more sophisticated approach, but no less skeptical, concedes the existence of a historic expression of Christianity stretching back into the fourth century. It has no claim to being *true*; it's just *old*. As a matter of fact, it was supposedly made up on the fly in an attempt to bring unity (and thus peace) to a troubled leadership in troubled times. Once again, the supposed villain is Emperor Constantine and a motley crew of shady church leaders carrying out their plots amid billows of bluish smoke. We've already seen their alleged role in arbitrarily picking which books to include in the New Testament (ch. 5) and in inventing a particularly confusing definition of God (ch. 11). Now in this myth, for myth it is, they are on the docket for inventing *all* central Christian doctrines.

## BEING THE EMPEROR HAS ITS PERKS

There can be no doubt the Christian world changed in the fourth century AD. After centuries of intermittent persecution of the church, sometimes severe, Emperor Constantine issued a decree in 313 that brought persecution to an end. Then, having consolidated power as the sole ruler of the empire, he issued an edict in 325 establishing Christianity as the state religion. A quick scan of any competent historical source should be enough to demonstrate the emperor's uncanny abilities and his ruthlessness, both as a military leader as well as a politician. Those who wield absolute power tend to get their way.

In the course of the events leading up to and following the Council of Nicea, Constantine had a direct hand in championing one interpretation of the New Testament, the so-called "orthodoxy" of Athanasius, to the exclusion of a contemporary competitor, Arius.

This is uncontested by church historians. My problem is with those skeptics who maintain there was no such thing as orthodoxy *prior* to the fourth century, or, if its existence is conceded, that it was simply one of several equal and competing religious notions with Athanasian orthodoxy ultimately winning out. It wasn't because of any inherent superiority or claim to be actually true; it just managed to gain the upper hand.

This implies that Christianity is only special in the sense that it has a long history and has many followers in our day. It's a popular system of belief; it has nothing to do with reality. Having neither the space, time, nor inclination to do so, I will leave further detailed discussions of the ins and outs of theology and church history to your personal study. My aim here is more modest. I want to show that the orthodoxy of the fourth century was founded on first-century writings, and that those writings display an awareness of other views that they vigorously opposed *because they didn't fit the facts.*

## EARLY OPTIONS

One way we could pursue this topic would be to cite the Nicene Creed and then demonstrate the theological origin of each statement within the New Testament. That may be fruitful, but I fear it would lapse into mere proof texting with several theological side trips. I want instead to demonstrate a broader reality within the pages of the New Testament: the awareness of and condemnation of counterclaims to the gospel message and the likely historical reason for it.

Skeptical scholars frequently point out that Christianity in the *second* century was very diverse. One could easily get the impression that several movements existed side-by-side *from the very beginning*, each having their own Scriptures and way of doing things. No one expression was able to legitimately claim to be "the truth" since there were so many valid competitors. What we know today as mainstream Christianity (Jesus is the Son of God, the risen Lord who died for our sins, etc.) managed to edge the others out by mere luck of the draw (or better press).

## A Unique Witness

This just won't hold water; on closer examination one little historical snippet stands out. Allow me to remind you of some items from chapters 3 and 5. The only Christian writings that can lay claim to originate from the *first* century are the New Testament documents (based on the preaching of the early church). There are no competing scriptures of the rival sects from that early; the writings with a radically different Jesus are from the second century and after, and they present themselves as *correcting* the Gospels. In other words, the message as we see it in our New Testament is *presupposed* in these later writings. What, then, was the basis for these unique first-century writings?

We need to keep in mind the gospel narrative unfolded in "real time," among numerous eyewitnesses, who provided valuable controls. The apostles and their associates *experienced* the events they wrote about. It is true that the second-century variations on the gospel certainly had their *roots* in the first century. These aberrations arose on the heels of the apostles' preaching. Much of the New Testament is focused on correcting these teachings, because they ran contrary to what the apostles knew to be true.

From the beginning the New Testament authors wrote from the conviction that God himself had entrusted them with the message. It was ingrained in them—first in their experiences with Jesus in his earthly ministry, and then through the direction of the Holy Spirit as the little church branched out into the wider Mediterranean world.[44] They were called by God to guard the gospel and pass it on intact. It was to become the sole basis of God's message to the world as his church gained ground throughout the Roman Empire. There was a right view of Christianity; the rest of them were false.

### Who Started It Anyway?

We don't have to look too terribly hard to find the first culprit to make such exclusive claims. It was the Galilean himself: "I am the way and the truth and the life. No one comes to the Father except through me" (John 14:6). When he sent his disciples to preach his message, he said, "If anyone will not welcome you or listen to your words, shake the dust off your feet when you leave that home or town" (Matthew 10:14). Come judgment day, Sodom and Gomorrah will look like a picnic in comparison.

It wasn't just his message; Jesus made *himself* the issue. "If anyone would come after me, he must deny himself and take up his cross and follow me," and "whoever loses his life for me and for the gospel will save it" (Mark 8:34–35). He spoke with such certainty and finality because he knew he had come from God and spoke his words. He would soon return to God and send the Holy Spirit to continue his work (John 16:4–11). He knew false teachers preceded (10:8) and would follow him (Matthew 7:15). Hostility awaited anyone who held on to his teaching (5:10; John 15:20), and he, as a matter of fact, made obedience the litmus test for demonstrating true love for him (John 14:15).

### Isn't One as Good as Another?

New Testament specialists often point out that the earliest testimony about the gospel is tucked away in 1 Corinthians 15. There Paul spells out some particulars that had been passed down to him. Since he wrote in the late AD 50s, and since he uses technical language for the passing on of an oral tradition, we must allow for some time for this to crystallize. The source is likely Peter and the Twelve (as suggested by the passage itself, but also from statements in Galatians 1:18–19 and 2:1–10). He presented this as a summary of the gospel he preached to the Corinthians, which they received and on which they stood. *This* gospel saves if held to firmly; otherwise, expressions of belief were "in vain" (1 Corinthians 15:1–2). Note the particulars:

For what I received I passed on to you as of first importance: that Christ died for our sins according to the Scriptures, that he was buried, that he was raised on the third day
according to the Scriptures, and that he appeared to Peter, and
then to the Twelve. After that, he appeared to more than five
hundred of the brothers at the same time, most of whom are
still living, though some have fallen asleep. Then he appeared
to James, then to all the apostles, and last of all he appeared to
me also, as to one abnormally born. (15:3 – 8)

Here's the deal: if someone claims Jesus has no relation to the
Old Testament, as was popular in the second century, he's wrong
(the key points were "according to the Scriptures"). If someone says
Jesus didn't really die, he's wrong ("Christ died" and "he was buried"). If someone says Jesus didn't rise from the dead, he's wrong
("he was raised"). If someone says Jesus was only raised symboli-
cally, he's wrong ("he appeared to" numerous named and unnamed
witnesses). There's a clear right and wrong. Anyone trying to offer
a different gospel did so in full view of the truth passed down for
apostolic safekeeping.

Paul's earliest letters show remarkable awareness of this trust.
He commends the church in Thessalonica, for instance, for the way
they received the preaching of the gospel "not as the word of men,
but as it actually is, the word of God, which is at work in you who
believe" (1 Thessalonians 2:13). This conviction, you should note,
pertained to the spoken word, the verbal proclamation of the gospel.
God spoke; the people listened, and that's the way it ought to be. He
had the same conviction of God's speaking through him "whether
by word of mouth or by letter" (2 Thessalonians 2:15). In fact, he
told the flock in Thessalonica: "If anyone does not obey our instruction in this letter, take special note of him. Do not associate with
him, in order that he may feel ashamed" (3:14).

If Paul could get a little irritable with people who thought his
instructions were optional, how agreeable do you think he was if

someone wanted to offer an alternate gospel or a different Jesus? Not very. This is what he had to say to a congregation that had previously accepted the teaching as he presented it, but lately were heading down an alternate path:

> I am astonished that you are so quickly deserting the one who called you by the grace of Christ and are turning to a different gospel—which is really no gospel at all.... But even if we or an angel from heaven should preach a gospel other than the one we preached to you, let him be eternally condemned! (Galatians 1:6–8)

Notice, a "different gospel" is *not* a gospel. It is a counterfeit that invokes some of Paul's harshest rebukes.

Perhaps you've heard somewhere along the way that the word "gospel" means "good news." In the New Testament, this particular "good news" concerns Jesus—specifically, his identity, ministry, death, resurrection, and exaltation. We are charged to place genuine faith in him, that is, to entrust our lives to him. God's response is to lavish grace on us, which is the undeserved outpouring of divine favor rendering us pure in God's eyes. Grace sets us apart for living an acceptable life in the ongoing process of our being transformed.

This is really pretty thrilling stuff, but what if someone wants to supplement the process with a couple of man-made rules to help God out? Paul was pretty clear. He didn't care if it was a preacher or an angelic vision; if they bring another Jesus they can ... Well, this is a family book, so let me just point out that the phrase "be eternally condemned" is a polite way of inviting someone to spend some considerable time in a very hot place.

Why the harsh language? Paul knew that the message he preached brought new life and forgiveness, peace with God, and deep inner healing. Other "gospels" were cheap and ineffective imitators that not only could not replace the real one, but wound up nullifying it. That's why he admonished Timothy to "command certain men not to teach false doctrines any longer nor to devote themselves to myths[!] and endless genealogies." Such doctrines "promote controversies rather than God's work—which is by faith" (1 Timothy 1:3–4).

If there is such a thing as *false* doctrine, there must be, at least in Paul's mind, something considered to be *true* doctrine. We don't have to look too far, for Paul warned Timothy that viewpoints and convictions abound that are "contrary to the sound doctrine." The safeguard is to cling to that which "conforms to the glorious gospel of the blessed God, which he entrusted to me" (1 Timothy 1:10–11). Anyone teaching otherwise "is conceited and understands nothing" (6:3–4). When it came to the gospel as the rule of faith, Paul didn't mince words.

This conviction was not something that slowly developed with many twists and turns, false starts and clarifications, finally coming to some theological closure in the fourth century. Nope. It was firmly in place midway through the first century (with clear roots all the way back into the 30s).

## But I Ate with Him

Here's another perspective. Counterclaims were certainly widespread in the first century, with most of the issues revolving around the person of Jesus. As we've seen in previous chapters; some groups saw Jesus as a good teacher but were unwilling to view him as anything other than human. A more common error, however, was the tendency to *downplay* his humanity (or deny it altogether). For these people the divine nature of Jesus was so obvious they couldn't fathom his being *really* human (the Docetists, mentioned in ch. 5). All four Gospels, however, go out of their way to show us both aspects of his nature (as is affirmed in the other New Testament writings). Keep in mind these are eyewitness testimonies of people who traveled with him from town to town and saw his wonders. They sat in stunned silence as he taught them; they gathered together around campfires for meals and fellowship. He got just as tired; his feet got just as dirty. When the time came, they saw his blood was just as red.

It is no doubt these experiences were in the back of John's mind as he wrote the little letter known as 1 John. He wrote it late in the first century to churches under his care in Asia Minor (modern-day Turkey). His message was based on that "which we have heard, which we have seen with our eyes, which we have looked at and our hands have touched" (1 John 1:1).

Apparently his churches were overrun with the type of people who denied Jesus' humanity. It really boils down to this: If Jesus was not really flesh and blood like the rest of us, then he didn't die for us on the cross, nor was he the sacrifice for the sin of the world. His blood did not wash away our sins. If he wasn't really human and didn't really die, then the resurrection wasn't physical either. If he wasn't completely human, then he cannot now fully identify with us or represent us in heaven, as the writer of Hebrews so carefully describes (especially Hebrews 2:14–18; 7:26–8:2). In other words, if Jesus was just a spirit, the entire gospel message falls apart.

We can picture John listening to the speculations of this supposed superspiritual Jesus as the "rival believers" continue to wax eloquent. I can just hear him respond, "Your theories are terribly interesting and all, but I walked with him; I touched him; I ate with him. I saw him die; I ate with him three days later." This simple appeal to his personal history formed the basis of what he insisted on as the correct (dare we say orthodox?) view about Jesus, and the means of discerning the source of teaching about him. "Every spirit that acknowledges that Jesus Christ has come in the flesh is from God, but every spirit that does not acknowledge Jesus is not from God" (1 John 4:2–3).

## "New" Isn't Always "Improved"

Throughout the New Testament the appeal is to remember the message as it was first preached, what they had "heard from the beginning" (1 John 2:24). Hebrews 2:1 – 4 warns the readers to "pay more careful attention" to the gospel so they don't "drift away." There is no escape for those who "ignore such a great salvation." Why? Because it "was first announced by the Lord" and was "confirmed to us by those who heard him." God himself even expressed his approval by enabling the apostles to perform "signs, wonders and various miracles" and by distributing "gifts of the Holy Spirit" (see also 2 John 1:9). According to Peter, believers were to be alert to avoid being "carried away by the error of lawless men" and wind up falling from their "secure position" (2 Peter 3:17). Jude told his people "to contend for the faith that was once for all entrusted to the saints" (Jude 3).

There was a core belief with a direct line of descent. God the Father told it to Jesus; Jesus told his disciples. The disciples, empowered by the Holy Spirit, preached it in the empire and left a written testimony of it. This is the witness of the first century, a faith "once for all entrusted" to his people. It's called the New Testament.

## UNITY IN DIVERSITY

Before closing this chapter out, I do want to acknowledge some of the diversity that exists in the New Testament, but put it in perspective. All of the writers have different approaches. It's not just that they have different styles, their theologies have different emphases. Skeptics seize on these tensions and cast the New Testament as a hodge-podge collection of beliefs with only the loosest connection, if any at all. The dreaded "contradiction" label gets bandied about rather freely.

This is really an issue of what theologians call "organic inspiration." God is the source of the teaching (that's the "inspiration" part), but he uses human authors (the "organic" part). Rather than dictating his message, he engaged the lives of these writers, using their experiences, personalities, and unique gifting. His Spirit infused them with power and wisdom to be sure, but they took this wisdom and addressed situations in the churches as they arose. We are given several snapshots of how God used people to address the issues of their day as they arose in real life.

For all the diversity, what you never find is any question about the identity or significance of Jesus. There are questions about the different genealogies (Matthew 1 and Luke 3), but he is never less than God in the flesh; neither his deity nor his humanity is ever compromised. There is a question as to the timing of his death (was it before Passover or on the Passover?), but he is always the Christ who died for our sins and rose again three days later. As for the second coming, *when* he's returning is completely up in the air (pun only partially intended); *that* he's coming is a core statement of faith. There is no other Savior named, no other path provided, no other God for us to worship.

## SUMMING UP

Once again, we need to open the doors and windows and clear out the conspiracy-laden air. Orthodoxy was not a fourth-century invention (or imposition). The early church always had a keen sense for truth and error. Their teaching came first from the lips of Jesus, then the Spirit-empowered preaching of his apostles, and finally the concrete expression in the New Testament. This is the core foundation of truth on which the church is built.

There were other groups, to be sure, each offering a rival Jesus and message. The church responded with their orthodox message, which they had from the very beginning. Don't be sidetracked; this little myth is "busted."

## GOING DEEPER

For a concise argument in favor of early orthodox teaching in Christianity (particularly, though not exclusively, debunking *The Da Vinci Code*), check out www.goarch.org/en/ourfaith/articles/article9567.asp. J. N. D. Kelly, *Early Christian Doctrines* (New York:

Harper Collins, 2003, rev. ed.) provides a thorough history of the development of early Christian thought, demonstrating that central doctrines (like the lordship of Jesus and his resurrection) can be traced to the apostles. See also Jaroslav Pelikan, *Credo: Historical and Theological Guide to Creeds and Confessions of Faith in the Christian Tradition* (New Haven, CT: Yale Univ. Press, 2005) and F. F. Bruce, "The History and Doctrine of the Apostolic Age," in *A Companion to the Bible,* H. H. Rowley, ed., (Edinburgh: T & T Clark, 1963).

# Chapter 17

# CHRISTIANITY IS HATEFUL, JUDGMENTAL, AND INTOLERANT

Everybody *knows* Christianity is hateful, judgmental, and intolerant. We've all seen countless people identifying themselves as Christians who are as mean as snakes, little zealots cramming the Bible down our throats. You can't tell them a thing because they *know* the truth, which includes the part that those who disagree "will fuel the fires of hell." This is delivered with a twinkle in the eye, as if they can't wait for it to happen.

Yes, *Christians* can be hateful, judgmental, and intolerant (not to mention hypocritical and lousy tippers), but the myth we're exploring here is whether or not *Christianity* is any of those things. Often it's really a case of confusing the *message* with flawed *messengers*. So let's take these topics one at a time, making a careful distinction between Christianity itself and the unfortunate adherents who give it a bad name.

## IS CHRISTIANITY HATEFUL?

The issue here is how Christianity presents itself. It's easy to get entangled in debates but the gospel message can be boiled down to a few brief statements. We are rebels by nature and are estranged from our Creator. Because of our sin we are deserving of hell (ouch). Yet, God loves us so much he sent Jesus to rescue us. Whoever turns to him in genuine faith and repentance is saved, transformed, and ultimately will live forever. (It's the explanations of all this that fill libraries.)

This is all prompted by the love of a just God. He is just—sin needs to be dealt with; *and* he is love—he offers a way of salvation. He is just—sin *dis*connects us; he is love—his mercy *re*connects us. God does this because, by his very nature, he is compassionate, gracious, slow to anger, and abounding in love (Exodus 34:6). Yet, he *will* punish those who refuse to budge (34:7). Here is a God so committed to reversing the effects of sin that he sent his Son Jesus—God with skin on—who perfectly embodied the compassion and mercy of his Father (John 1:14).

Whether it was lepers, the sick, a leaderless rabble, or a couple of blind men, compassion moved Jesus to perform acts of mercy (Matthew 14:14; Mark 1:41). He went out of his way to show the love of God to prostitutes, drunks, thieves, and corrupt people of every stripe (Luke 7:34; 15:1). He delighted in hanging out with riff-raff and probably wore his scornful nickname "friend of sinners" as a badge of honor.

It was the religious leaders who were the objects of his ire (Matthew 23). Their calloused hearts kept them from perceiving the compassion of God at work right before their very eyes. Jesus' life warmed cold hearts and healed bruised lives. This very love for the helpless drove him willingly to the cross. There he died a criminal's death, his life blood spilt for the rebellion of an undeserving world. We never need question his love for us. So then, how does Christianity get such a bad rap? Well, to put it delicately, that's because of the rest of us bozos.

## Misfires and Misfits

Before dealing with the failings of faltering Christians, we first need to talk about those who are Christian in name only. Jesus compared them to tares (weeds) among the wheat, which look like the real thing until harvest time; then their true nature as worthless weeds shows up (Matthew 13:24–31). There are many references to false apostles, prophets, and teachers, as well as antichrists, wolves, and hypocrites (7:15; Acts 20:29; 2 Corinthians 11:13; 1 Timothy

4:2; 1 Peter 2:1; 2 Peter 2:1; 1 John 2:18 – 19). They walk among us not always recognized, and I'm willing to bet that they do their share of giving the church a black eye.

That said, it still doesn't get the rest of us off the hook. There isn't a Christian among us who has always managed to radiate God's love. The extent to which we fail just reinforces the bad image we're trying to avoid. But having our lives infused with God's love is at the heart of our calling.

> Dear friends, let us love one another, for love comes from God. Everyone who loves has been born of God and knows God. Whoever does not love does not know God, because God is love.... Dear friends, since God so loved us, we also ought to love one another. No one has ever seen God; but if we love one another, God lives in us and his love is made complete in us. (1 John 4:7 – 8, 11 – 12)

It's as straightforward a statement as we could ever hope to see. God's loving presence is real in those who really love. *We* are the ones who make the love of God visible to unbelievers. This is the very embodiment of the greatest commandment. So, if I may, let me encourage my brothers and sisters to meditate on this before taking another breath.

## Command versus Conviction

Sometimes we Christians sully the message of love by forgetting a few simple distinctions. (By the way, if you're reading this before meditating on 1 John 4, you better be holding your breath.) We confuse God's commands and our personal convictions about them. God commands us to avoid sin; what actually constitutes sin, however, can be debatable. Murder, adultery, and stealing are all unquestionably sinful, but what about going to movies, smoking, or playing cards on Sunday?

For some people it's a personal conviction that these activities are just as sinful as murder. It's a matter of *personal conviction* on the *specifics* of living a God-pleasing life. The problem surfaces when we try to enforce a personal conviction on someone else. The result is legalism. So someone who just bought a pack of smokes and a deck of cards on the way to the movies on a Sunday (!) runs into a legalistic person and promptly gets an earful. People like this resemble the Pharisees of Jesus' day.

The Pharisees were zealous for God's law — so zealous, in fact, they came up with rules designed to keep people from breaking the law. It all sounded like a great idea until Jesus exposed their convictions as man-made rules that kept people from serving God (Matthew 23:13, 15). They were meticulous to the point of tithing a pinch of spice but missed the heart of God — "justice, mercy and faithfulness" (23:23). This was the error of the Pharisees; they shouted where God was silent and ignored what he required. They were shouting so loudly they couldn't hear God's whisper.

## An Open Hand

Paul weighed in on this issue. "Accept him whose faith is weak, without passing judgment on disputable matters" (Romans 14:1). Acceptance, even *tolerance*, is the key. We need to remember our ideas *about* God's Word do not *equal* God's Word. God commands keeping a Sabbath, so some Christians in Paul's day wanted to keep it on the traditional seventh day. Others chose the first day of the week in honor of Jesus' resurrection and repeated appearances; still others opted for regarding every day as sacred. Paul told them to decide and move on (14:5; Colossians 2:16 – 17). He goes into several other examples throughout the chapter but returns to one central theme: "Let us stop passing judgment on one another. Instead, make up your mind not to put any stumbling block or obstacle in your brother's way" (Romans 14:13). Rather than assuming the role of God's cop, we should make sure we're not the ones hindering someone else's walk.

The remedy is acceptance and love (Romans 14:1, 15), which also requires liberal doses of patience, forbearance, and gentleness — traits that don't often come naturally to us. Quite the opposite, actually, but these are the very things that God plants in our hearts and causes to grow. They are listed among other traits known as the "fruit of the Spirit" (Galatians 5:22–23; notice that "hatefulness" is suspiciously absent from the list). The more they grow in us, the more like Jesus we become.

**The Real Deal**

That's fine for debatable issues, but what about when Christians fall into real, industrial-strength sin? The same guidelines apply. "Brothers, if someone is caught in a sin, you who are spiritual should restore him gently" (Galatians 6:1). Peter charges his people: "Above all, love each other deeply, because love covers over a multitude of sins" (1 Peter 4:8; see James 5:19–20). When sheep wander from the flock, fellow sheep need to be the ones to go after them, not just the shepherd, but the issue here is the manner in which this is done. Wandering sheep need to be led back gently and lovingly. To change the metaphor a bit, we're all in the same life raft. Let's quit our bickering and toss the preserver to the drowning brother with the same concern that it was first tossed to us. Too often we've forgotten how we were drawn to faith.

**Remembering When**

Think about how the Holy Spirit brought us to faith. Somewhere along the line all of us were struck with God's goodness and the guilt of our souls. God's kindness leads us to repentance (Romans 2:4). With grateful hearts we start out as best we know how, but this pathway also includes plenty of correction as we learn what is, and what is not, acceptable Christian living. Sometimes we're stung by sermons exposing our shortcomings and downright sins, but being confronted with the truth assists our growth in Christ. The problem enters when we take that model, Christians correcting Christians, and apply it to *unbelievers*. We've forgotten how Jesus treated unbelievers, the pariahs of his day, and substituted how the New Testament writers wrote to wayward *believers*.

Have you ever heard a Christian get on somebody's case about taking the Lord's name in vain? I don't like to hear it anymore than you do, but God didn't call us to clean up everyone's language (or nitpick them to death about every flaw). First things first — clothed in mercy, lovingly share the gospel in the hopes that God grants repentance (2 Timothy 2:25; Jude 22 – 23); let the Holy Spirit do the work of cleaning them up. And, of course, once they're in *and* you've earned the right to be heard, *then* you can gently point out what the Scriptures say about living for God. You become a loving guide, not a Holy Spirit drill sergeant.

## IS CHRISTIANITY JUDGMENTAL?

Christians can be so judgmental, but is Christianity? Just about everyone knows John 3:16 by heart: "For God so loved the world that he gave his one and only Son, that whoever believes in him shall not perish but have eternal life." It's so popular not only because of its encouraging message, but also because it gives us a handy summary of the gospel.

Yet, there's a thorn on this flower. Those who so believe "shall not perish." Doesn't that mean that those who don't believe *will*? This aspect of Christianity just cannot be softened. It is the uncomfortable assertion that whoever *refuses* God's offer of salvation winds up in a world of hurt. Lake of fire, outer darkness, bottomless pit — whatever the image, it isn't very inviting.

There, you see? There's your judgmental God! He holds the threat of hell out like a club and condemns everyone who would rather politely choose some other path. Christianity brings judgment.

Well, that *is* one way to look at it, but consider this. If there were some other way that people could choose, then Jesus had a conniption just after he returned to heaven. Remember that he prayed earnestly for the cup (of suffering) to pass from him (Luke 22:42). If there were some other way to accomplish his task, he'd much rather take it (Matthew 26:39; Mark 14:35). He received no reply other than encouragement to face the cross, knowing that a joyful reception awaited him afterward (Hebrews 12:2).

Jesus, strengthened in his resolve to do the Father's will, went to the cross and took the condemnation of the world on himself. If we acknowledge that fact (in worshipful surrender, not just mental assent), an amazing exchange takes place. "God made him who had no sin to be sin for us, so that in him we might become the righteousness of God" (2 Corinthians 5:21). God initiated it and Jesus willingly followed it through. This is how God *so loved* the world. It's not judgment he offers; it's salvation.

Although John 3:16 is well known, the next two verses are not. They set the topic of judgment (condemnation) in perspective: "For God did not send his Son into the world to condemn the world, but to save the world through him." We have our part: "Whoever believes in him is not condemned, but whoever does not believe stands condemned already because he has not believed in the name of God's one and only Son" (3:17–18). God wants to save us from a judgment *already* hanging over our heads. Yes, God imposed it, but before you get twisted in a knot saying he's unfair (blaming you for what Adam did), remember he provides the remedy (forgiving you through what Jesus did). Creators sort of have the right to do things as they wish.

The real problem isn't intellectual; it's moral. We chafe at being told what to do and really don't like having a spotlight shining on our faults. "This is the verdict: Light has come into the world, but men loved darkness instead of light because their deeds were evil" (John 3:19). We're bugs in the kitchen caught off guard when someone throws the lights on for a midnight snack.

Sometimes Christians get tagged with the charge of being judgmental just for pointing out the truth. It doesn't matter how gentle or loving you are; the response from the unbeliever is like surprising a porcupine. People feel like they're being judged precisely because they are, but not by the Christian. It's by God himself. They sense accurately that their lives are out of sync with the Lord. But rather than turning to him for his gracious remedy (and a life that far outshines the brief pleasures of this life), they respond with hostility. Hearing God's Word can be like nails on a chalkboard. It cuts across the grain; it's heading into a stiff wind. No, some knees just will not bow. This is a moral issue, not an intellectual one.

God takes no pleasure in judgment. He wants to save. The entire thrust of the New Testament is for people to realize their guilt, confess their sins, forsake a sinful life, and turn to the One who longs to lavish grace on them (Ephesians 1:7 – 8). When we do so, we can't take any credit for it. We have simply responded to God's gift and have entered his work. "But whoever lives by the truth comes into the light, so that it may be seen plainly that what he has done has been done through God" (John 3:21). Christianity is not judgmental; it freely offers salvation. Those who refuse it have only themselves to blame for the unpleasant consequences.

## IS CHRISTIANITY INTOLERANT?

Yes, *Christians* certainly can be intolerant. There are so many denominations and spin-offs. All it takes is for someone to voice a line of thought different from what we now hold near and dear and out come the daggers. But, as you are primed to expect by now, the question at hand is whether *Christianity itself* is intolerant. This time the answer is a firm "Well, yes and no." It's "no," in terms of who can become a follower of Jesus. The invitation goes out to all (unbridled tolerance). But it's "yes" in terms of Christianity's acceptance of a competing path to God (Christ takes a dim view of competition). Let's look at each of these in turn.

### All Are Welcome

Jesus' final commands launched a revolution that has been spreading for two thousand years. Simply put, his offer of salvation extends to everyone (Matthew 28:18 – 20; Acts 1:8). Is he selective?

No. God "wants all men to be saved and to come to a knowledge of the truth" (1 Timothy 2:3–4); it's the church's call to "see to it that no one misses the grace of God" (Hebrews 12:15). This is to continue until the return of Jesus, whose delay is due solely to God's mercy and patience (2 Peter 3:9).

All of these passages reflect the ancient Old Testament promise: "Turn to me and be saved, all you ends of the earth; for I am God, and there is no other" (Isaiah 45:22). It has always been the cry of God's heart to reach the world (Genesis 12:3; Galatians 3:8). This is the eternal love of the Creator for his estranged creation.

## Roll 'Em

It is amazing how this message of love is transformed into an ugly caricature. All we have to do is ask folks on the street and keep track of their responses. Christianity doesn't fare well in popular culture. Just look at the way high-profile evangelicals are usually accosted on TV. Regardless of who is being interviewed or who is doing the interviewing, one of the first interchanges runs something like this:

HOST: So, do you believe that Christianity is the only way and all others are going to hell?

GUEST: Well, er, yes. But ...

HOST [*interrupting*]: Are Jews going to hell, what about Hindus, how about good people, what about people who have never heard?

GUEST: Well, you see, the Bible says ...

HOST [*again interrupting*]: Isn't the Bible just one of many holy books? It's just written by men; what makes you think it alone is right, or that *your* religion is the only way?

GUEST: Uh, Jesus said ...

HOST: Jesus said, Buddha said, Krishna said, Muhammad said; a lot of religious leaders said a lot of things and it's pretty arrogant for *you* to think that *you* alone are correct. How can you be so intolerant and judgmental?

GUEST: Well, I ...

HOST: That's all the time we have today. We'll be back after these important messages from our sponsor. [*Cut to a commercial*]

Yes, this is a little contrived, but not much. (It's actually pretty tame compared to some recent displays.) The conversation gets repeated in countless variations and has been for centuries. The gospel is cast as a message of condemnation that sends people on their way to the flames with narrow-minded zealots cheering them on. Once the conversation goes down this track, it is a bit difficult to get it back. It's as if the gospel is excluding people *by design*, as if the *goal* of Christianity is to make sure most people don't make it. It is just so hard for people to focus on the fact that all are welcome, indeed, strongly encouraged to join the family of God.

This scenario does point out an aspect of the gospel that is, in fact, intolerant with the potential for looming judgment. The gospel self-consciously presents itself as the *only way*, and people just don't like having their options narrowed to one choice.

### Any Contenders?

We are taught from the cradle that life is full of options and we need to be open-minded. All opinions are worthy of a fair hearing and there's more than one way to skin a cat. Any hint that Christianity is *the* way is met with sneers and caterwauls. What could possibly possess someone to suggest such a thing in this era of tolerance? This is how the charge of arrogance enters the discussion. There are many roads to heaven; it is arrogant to suggest otherwise and (horrors) claim to have found the only true one.

The charge of arrogance would be undeniable if there *were* several equally valid religions but someone decided to go with a particular one. Exalting a personal opinion to the level of absolute truth would be a little audacious. But Christians don't claim they like this one better than any other; it's not a matter of personal opinion but a deep-seated conviction on the nature of reality. It's an issue of *revelation*. This is still pegged as arrogance, but it's worth pointing out that it's only arrogant if it isn't true.

I've already dealt with Christianity's exclusive claims in chapters 12 and 13, so I want to focus on God's authority to call the shots. It really is pretty simple, as long as you grant a few premises (at least for the sake of argument). These premises reflect the way the Bible presents God and the nature of reality. So taking things at face value, I want to sketch out why the gospel message is the only one God endorses.

Let's start with God before he created anything. We can't picture poor God all alone in some expanse of empty space. Space, even empty space, is a "thing" and is just part of his creation. So before there was *anything* else, *all* that there was — was God! (Try to wrap your mind around an omnipresent Being whose presence infinitely comprised the sole being of all reality.)

Now, before he cut loose with the first "Let there be . . ." there were already several things on his mind. From *before* the beginning (a turn of phrase sure to earn the scorn of any competent philosopher), God's plan was firmly in his mind, but remained a mystery to all until the coming of Jesus (Matthew 13:35). He had already prepared the place for his people in his coming kingdom (25:34). He chose the path of holiness for those he would adopt through Jesus (Ephesians 1:4; Acts 13:48), knowing as well who would refuse him (Revelation 17:8). Although he wasn't known by that name, Jesus was there (John 1:1) sharing in the glory of the Father (17:24) and already chosen for the task of crucifixion (1 Peter 1:20; Revelation 13:8). It's not that it suddenly popped into his mind; it was the eternal purpose of God to be performed by the willing Son (Ephesians 3:11), offered through the eternal Spirit (Hebrews 9:14). This was the plan from all eternity.

Shortly thereafter, he stretched forth the heavens and pitched a tent for the sun. He formed the earth, gathered some dirt, and infused a little mud pie with life. It wasn't long before the first man (at the suggestion of his lovely bride, herself prompted by a mysterious being) put his own desires ahead of God's and promptly plunged the world into misery. The plan was off and running. From that time on there is a dichotomy: a fallen, cursed creation (which included thinking, feeling beings) and the Creator who saw it coming. He knows everything and has all power, and his presence fills the whole universe. His creatures have only what they are given, and more often than not mess it up. Having conceived of the plan of salvation from all eternity he launched it on the heels of creating the world, all for the purpose of revealing his very nature as a loving Savior to bring these estranged people back to himself.

Genuinely knowing *this* God and the Son he sent is eternal life (John 17:3), so we need to respond by taking hold of the eternal life to which we were called (1 Timothy 6:12). How would *you* feel if one of these little rebels thumbed his nose at *your* eternal plan and said, "Nah, I've got a better one"?

God doesn't put up with other plans of salvation because he knows there really aren't any. They're just inventions of fertile imaginations, the prompting of malevolent spirits, or a little bit of both. None of them can come through for us; they can only wow us with slick advertising. Since God alone has the power to save and has so dramatically demonstrated his love through the cross, people who get snookered by these counterfeits cut *themselves* off from God and his salvation. God is intolerant of other religions because he knows them to be empty promises based on false hopes. He knew it from the start.

## SUMMING UP

So is Christianity hateful? No. It's a message of supreme love, proven by the cross. Is it judgmental? No. It is accepting of all, but it does insist on life change. (Come as you are, but don't expect to stay that way.) Judgment is reserved for those who reject the generous offer of forgiveness and a new life. Is it intolerant? Yes and no. No, because it's tolerant of everyone, offered to everyone, and excludes no one. Yes, because it's intolerant of any other way; it cost Jesus a brutal death. This is the path God chose. He can do that. He's God.

Incidentally, I wonder why no one is concerned when Christianity isn't tolerated. It won't do to say that it's because Christianity itself is intolerant. That would indicate we should only tolerate those whom we already tolerate.

## GOING DEEPER

For further reading on this topic, refer to the Going Deeper sections for chapters 8, 9, 12, 13, and 16.

# Chapter 18

# CHRISTIANITY IS ANTI-SEMITIC

This is definitely an area in which I need to tread carefully. Just broaching the topic of anti-Semitism is enough to cause folks to duck and cover. It is a deeply emotional and troubling subject, so, for the record, let's be clear on what we're talking about. The terms "anti-Semitic" and "anti-Semitism" refer to the specialized bigotry whose focus of animosity is the Jewish people. I certainly want to acknowledge the effects of centuries of hurt, mistrust, even bloodshed between church and synagogue. My focus, however, is the way the New Testament is misunderstood on this topic and therefore misused.

## THE NATURE OF ANTI-SEMITISM

That anti-Semitism exists among us is beyond dispute. I am assuming you read the previous chapter, so you can rightly anticipate my laying the blame on *Christians* (whether genuine or not), not on Christianity itself. We cannot, however, so easily breeze over the church's receiving some blame. This is precisely because there are people who name Christ as Savior and hate Jews (in the same breath), not to mention the too-long history of this horrid legacy of hatred. From church fathers (like Tertullian or Augustine), through the Reformation (Luther comes to mind), and into our own day, this ugly notion has hung around like a bad odor in a room. What we need to do is clear the air, so to speak.

### Others in the Conversation

Many modern Christians are shocked to learn that some church fathers were so venomous toward Jews in their writings. The surprise comes with such force precisely because hatred toward the Jewish people is so foreign to them. I'm referring to people brought up loving the Old Testament and seeing the Jews as a special people singled out by God to be a light to the nations, first by giving the world God's law, then by giving us God's Messiah. There are some, in fact, so enamored with all things Jewish that they incorporate elements of Jewish culture and worship into their church life (preferring to be called *messianic congregations*).

Let's not forget the Christians during the Holocaust. The mere mention of the era conjures up the horrible spectacle of Christians ignoring the plight of their Jewish neighbors. That was inexcusable, but we need to remember the heroic Christians who hid Jews from the Nazis and resisted Hitler at every turn. Excellent examples are found in Corrie ten Boom's *The Hiding Place*. Dietrich Bonhoeffer's ordeal in a Nazi prison is also well known, but there were many others. In fact, millions of Christians perished in the camps alongside their Jewish neighbors. We just don't hear much about them.

### Some Things Are Mislabeled

Some of what is labeled as anti-Semitism is actually simply affirming the gospel message. Salvation is found in Jesus Christ and no longer in following Moses. It's not a hateful comment; it's a religious conviction. It wishes no ill will upon Jews (or anyone else, for that matter). It's exactly the opposite, since it offers salvation to the Jews (and anyone else interested). People may be offended at the suggestion that what they currently believe can't deliver the goods, but no offense is intended.

As was discussed previously, the exclusivity of the gospel is only horrendous and rude if it isn't true (or just a matter of personal preference). Just look at it from the opposite perspective. It is not necessarily hateful for modern Jews to regard Christianity as simply wrong. I never hear of people charging Jews with being anti-Christian and hateful for refusing to believe in Jesus, nor should they. Those who *do* respond in hate (and they too are among us) actually engage in the very practice they oppose.

If the New Testament is true and salvation is found only in Jesus, wouldn't it be hateful *not* to tell Jews? It would indeed, but not simply because we would be withholding this gift from them. It would be so hateful because this is *their* story, which God was gracious enough to extend to us Gentiles.

## JUDAISM, THE PROPHETS, AND JESUS
### Kith and Kin

A point that keeps coming up in this book is the fact that Christianity arose from Judaism, a useful insight that gets the conversation rolling in the right direction. The New Testament writers go out of their way to present their beliefs as nothing less than Judaism having come to full flower. Long before they wrote, when people first started following Jesus, there was no such thing as Christianity. It wasn't even a dim concept in anyone's mind in Israel. For the Jews of the first century there were two main groups of people: Jews and Gentiles (that is, God's people and outsiders). That means the followers of Jesus were all Jews, perhaps considered nothing more than a band of rabble-rousers (going increasingly off kilter), but Jews nonetheless.

Jews and Gentiles, that was it. Even so, Judaism was a diverse blend of competing versions. In Jesus' day there were several groups vying for the claim of being the true heirs of the Law and the Prophets, the true people of God. They were all expressing various expectations, beliefs, and manners of day-to-day living. It was pretty common for folks to align themselves with one or another of them. (Those who didn't were just the "people of the land," scorned as the unwashed masses.)

The most prominent groups were the Sadducees, Pharisees, Zealots, Herodians, and Essenes. The Sadducees and Pharisees were at loggerheads; the Zealots wanted to drive out the Romans and their sniveling little sympathizers, the Herodians. The Essenes just said, "A pox on all your houses," and kept pretty much to themselves, many of whom went off to live in a commune in the desert. They considered themselves to be the "sons of light," the people of the "new covenant," the end-time faithful remnant waiting for the day of the Lord and the defeat of all evil. We can add to this list a group similar to the Essenes in several respects. They were the followers of the Way (Acts 9:2; 22:4), also known as the Nazarene sect (24:5), the group known for raising a ruckus all over the empire (17:6; 28:22). These were disciples of Jesus.

Jesus had his disciples, but so did John the Baptist and the Pharisees (Mark 2:18). The Jewish leaders in Jerusalem considered themselves "disciples of Moses" (John 9:28). The scribes and rabbis gathered disciples around themselves as well (as indicated in the writings from the era, such as those of Philo, Josephus, and [later] the rabbis). This was just standard Judaism, but it did give rise to a bit of tension.

### Match, Anyone?

Keep in mind that Israel was an occupied country; the tension between Rome and the Jews was a volatile powder keg. The Romans were getting tired of the protests and occasional hotshot messianic pretenders. All someone needed to do was spark a revolt at the wrong time, and the whole thing would blow. For this reason the Passover season was always a concern, as people from far and wide filled tiny Jerusalem to the brim. Year by year the ancient traditions and promises of the Scriptures were celebrated under the watchful eye of an increasingly nervous overlord.

All of this was not lost on the Sanhedrin, the governing body of Israel (that is, as puppets of Rome). They were charged with keeping the people in order; a precarious peace was the rule of the day. Everybody just needed to get along. Troublemakers were dispatched with all due haste. It was such a touchy situation because the Jewish leaders knew if they lost control, Rome would swoop in and take over, stripping them of all power (John 11:48). The threat of being wiped out by a legion or two hovered over their heads like a rotating Kansas thunderhead. Just ask Dorothy; that's *real* bad.

This was the smoldering cauldron Jesus entered to begin his peaceful revolution. The nation was already on the brink of upheaval as the former carpenter gathered a small following and announced that the long-awaited kingdom of God had arrived. Overlords don't like to hear about rival kings. The Jerusalem elite didn't like to have their comfy way of life threatened or hear that their way of life was off base, especially from a Galilean hill-country yahoo. Trouble was, the Galilean was fearless. Worse, he performed astounding miracles. Still worse, he exposed all the hypocrisy, sin, and compromise of the small and great alike. The small, that is, the offscourings of Jewish culture (drunks, whores, and tax collectors, to name a few), came to him in droves. The great, the Pharisees and Sadducees (not to mention the high priests), withered under his unflinching gaze and despised him. Exceptions were noteworthy, but far too few.

## Fulfill, Not Abolish

So when you thumb through the Gospels, you see a story unfold in purely Jewish territory expressing purely Jewish hopes in purely Jewish categories. Lest we misunderstand each other, Matthew, Mark, and the gang tell a *Jewish* story. It is the story of one Jewish sect with its vision about the expectations and aspirations of the ancient covenant people, and their Scriptures, coming to fulfillment before their very eyes.

Jesus did not preach a new God, introduce new Scriptures, or suggest the old ones were faulty; nor did he ever suggest the heroes of the past were inferior in any way. Instead, he said they all looked forward to and welcomed his coming (Matthew 13:17; John 5:46; 8:56). He wasn't telling them a new religion; he was bringing an ancient one to its fulfillment.

At the beginning of his ministry Jesus confirmed his continuity with the Scriptures. "Do not think that I have come to abolish the Law or the Prophets; I have not come to abolish them but to fulfill them" (Matthew 5:17). After his resurrection a few years later, he explained the events leading up to it:

> "Did not the Christ have to suffer these things and then enter his glory?" And beginning with Moses and all the Prophets, he explained to them what was said in all the Scriptures concerning himself. (Luke 24:26–27)

This is the broad sketch, if you will, of his earthly ministry set within the ancient tapestry of God's dealing with his people Israel. It was within this grand scheme of the Old Testament that Jesus interpreted specific details of his ministry: the merciful nature of his message (Luke 4:18–21; cf. Isaiah 61:1–2) and the people's refusal to listen to him (Matthew 13:14; cf. Isaiah 6:9–10), as well as their hatred of him (John 15:25; cf. Psalm 35:19). He interpreted the details of the passion narrative in the same way: his betrayal (Matthew 26:24, 54, 56; *general reference to the Old Testament*), arrest (Luke 22:37; cf. Isaiah 53:12), desertion (Mark 14:27; cf. Zechariah 13:7), and the beating, crucifixion, and resurrection (Luke 18:31–33; *general reference*). This was the Jewish Messiah dying on a Roman cross fulfilling Jewish Scripture. There is nothing specifically Christian here, nor was it specifically anti-Jewish. It is simply what later developed into Christian teaching.

### A Time-Honored Tradition

When Jesus announced the coming of the kingdom, he did so in Jewish terms, and when he was snubbed, he rebuked them in Jewish terms. In his scathing confrontations with the leadership, Jesus was in line with a long tradition—the prophets. Israel was *always* going astray. From the time of Moses through the time of Israel's kings, the nation frequently lapsed into idolatry and copied the vile practices of the nations around her. The powerful elite forsook God and his law, treated the weak with contempt, and indulged themselves in the fat of the land. They frequently compromised their Jewish convictions as they rubbed shoulders with powerful Gentile nations, opting for the security of alliances with earthly kingdoms rather than looking first to God. Any attention paid to Yahweh and his covenant was a polite nod, a little lip service, perhaps a little burning of incense or an offering of a lame goat. They had become what God loathed, so he raised up prophets to call them to repentance. More often than not, however, the prophets stuck their accusing fingers in Israel's brazen face and called her evil, no better than the rank pagans around her (speaking, of course, from the perspective of an ancient Israelite).

Israel's affront against God was deeply personal and required harsh corrective measures. God had entered into a covenant with his people, comparing it to a divine marriage, but his wife turned out to be a whore (Hosea 2:4–6). Israel's rebellion and idolatry, therefore, were seen as adultery, even prostitution (Ezekiel 16:30–34). Over and over the prophets warned her about exile and destruction, but the leaders mistreated or killed the prophets and went on their merry way for centuries. God continued to call her to return right up to the day he had finally *had it* and divorced her — meaning of course, the exile (Isaiah 50:1; Jeremiah 3:8).

The prophets were famous for confronting this rebellious nation. Israel was dumber than a donkey, just a "sinful nation, a people loaded with guilt, a brood of evildoers" (Isaiah 1:3–4). They were corrupt (Hosea 5:3), arrogant (Jeremiah 50:31), and incurably sinful (Micah 1:9), a people who loved evil and hated good (3:2). Horrific punishment was their lot (Isaiah 5:13, 25; Jeremiah 7:20; Lamentations 2:1–5). All of these threats had one central purpose — to wake Israel up and bring her back to God (Isaiah 1:18; 31:6; Jeremiah 3:14; Joel 2:13–14). Were the prophets anti-Semitic?

## Same Tune, Different Singer

When it comes to nailing Israel for being sinful, Jesus spoke to the Jewish leaders just as the prophets of old had done. He gave them the same sort of rebukes for the same kind of reasons (except for idolatry, which was pretty much under control). He wasn't being anti-Jewish; he was being pro-God and pro-Scripture, and thus completely pro-Jewish. The only problem was that he insisted on *his* version of things.

We also need to keep in mind the rest of the story. Israel's refusal to repent moved Jesus to tears; he wanted to gather the people, but *they* were unwilling (Luke 13:34). He had been sent specifically to the Jewish people, to the lost sheep of Israel (Matthew 10:5–6; 15:24). All of his disciples were Jews; the outcasts that flocked to him were primarily Jews (he did have sporadic dealings with Gentiles and Samaritans, but they weren't his focus). His quarrel was with the leadership; the common, very Jewish "people of the land" welcomed him gladly. Why, then, would anyone take Jesus' teaching as anti-Semitic?

## Fightin' Words

It's actually pretty easy. All we have to do is take Jesus out of his Jewish context and we can make him sound like a Grand Wizard of the Ku Klux Klan. He called Jewish leaders such endearing things as blind fools (Matthew 23:17), snakes (23:33), and members of a demon-possessed, wicked generation (12:43–45). They were incapable of hearing the truth even though it (he) stood right in front of them (John 8:43). They were lying children of the Devil (8:44, 55) who, in the banquet of the end time, will find themselves tossed out on their ears (Luke 13:28). The Jewish leaders were loveless, clueless, and, in a word—godless.

Reading such verses as if this were an Archie Bunker talking to a rabbi and the charge of anti-Semitism is not too much of a stretch. Put Jesus back in his Jewish world, however, and he sounds like the last in a long line of prophets confronting Israel with her evil and calling her to repent.

## No Accident

You can easily get the impression from reading anti-Semitic rants that the "Christ killers," those villainous Jews, took poor ole' Jesus and put a premature end to his promising career. This is sheer nonsense. Remember from the previous chapter that the crucifixion was all God's eternal plan. Nobody took Jesus' life from him; he gave it willingly (Matthew 16:21; John 10:17–18). This was no accident or afterthought; God hadn't lost control.

The Old Testament prophesied his rejection by his people (Isaiah 53:1–3), his death (53:4–10; Zechariah 12:10), and his resurrection (Isaiah 53:11–12). Jesus repeatedly warned his disciples that suffering and death lay before him, but he would rise again in three days (Matthew 16:21; 20:18–19). Jesus willingly and specifically died *for* his people (John 11:51–52). On the Day of Pentecost, Peter referred to Jesus' arrest and death at the hands of the Jews as a direct result of "God's set purpose and foreknowledge" (Acts 2:23). If the Jews *hadn't* killed him, we'd all be in a heap o' trouble.

## A Missed Opportunity

Speaking of the Day of Pentecost (as recorded in Acts 2), if ever there was an opportunity for the followers of Jesus to condemn the Jews, this was it. The scene was the ancient feast of Pentecost, about a month and a half after the crucifixion. The crowds that witnessed the events of that fateful Passover were still there. The disciples of Jesus were as well, waiting for the Holy Spirit to empower them for their ministry (Acts 1:4–5). When the Spirit arrived, Peter was filled with power and boldness and quickly found himself facing the mob that clamored for Jesus' death mere weeks earlier. Here was his chance to really lay on the guilt, but Peter didn't take it. Instead, he preached the church's first-ever sermon, a Spirit-led Jew talking about the Jewish Messiah to his "fellow Jews" (2:14).

Peter explained that the Spirit's presence heralded the arrival of the last days according to the prophet Joel (Acts 2:16–21; citing Joel 2:28–32). This was so because the Messiah had come. In Acts 2:22–23 Peter makes repeated reference to "you," the Jewish people. God accredited Jesus "to you" by his miracles done "among you" just as "you yourselves know." God's predetermined plan arranged for him to be handed over "to you," and "you," with the help of wicked men (that is, the Romans), murdered him. The story doesn't end there, for God raised him to life, as he had promised through David centuries before (2:24–28). Jesus was exalted to God's right hand and sent the Holy Spirit, who was responsible for the commotion among them.

The clincher came when Peter said: "Therefore let all Israel be assured of this: God has made this Jesus, whom you crucified, both Lord and Christ." Hearing this, the murderers of Jesus were "cut to the heart" and cried out, "What shall we do?" Peter led them to repent and be baptized in Jesus' name, so that they too would receive his Spirit and forgiveness for sins, chief of which was the crucifixion itself. Those who had cried out "Crucify him!" weeks earlier realized his death was for them. The ones who shouted, "Let his blood be on us and on our children!" (Matthew 27:25) had their sins washed away by that very blood. Three thousand people became disciples of the Messiah that day—all Jews, every single one of them. The Christ killers became Christ followers.

### And So It Goes

The rest of the New Testament is no different. The band of Christ followers continued to grow, eventually becoming known as Christians (Acts 11:26), but they never lost sight of their Jewish roots. Peter continued to preach Jesus as the fulfillment of Jewish hopes (10:42–43; 1 Peter 1:10–12; 2 Peter 1:19). Paul's ministry was specifically "first for the Jew" (Romans 1:16), so he went first to the synagogues and proclaimed the Christ as the fulfillment of

Jewish Scriptures (Acts 13:27; 17:2–3). His testimony and ministry, as well as his defense before his Jewish and Roman accusers, had the same focus (26:22–23; Romans 1:1–2; 3:21; 15:8–12; Galatians 3:13–14).

Even the letter to the Hebrews, which more than any other New Testament letter expresses the superiority of Jesus and the new covenant, is at pains to do so in the language of fulfillment. The same God who spoke through prophets and circumstances in the old covenant spoke through Jesus in the new (Hebrews 1:1–2). New covenant realities are expressed in specific comparison to the old covenant (2:2–3; 9:13–14; 10:28–29). The new covenant itself is nothing more than the fulfillment of the old covenant promise of Jeremiah 31:31–34 (Hebrews 8:8–12).

James and Jude frequently allude to the Old Testament (James 1:1, 25–27; 2:11, 21–25, etc.; Jude 5–7, 11). The book of Revelation does as well. The unfolding visions in Revelation are simply incomprehensible apart from recognizing the detailed interweaving of Old Testament imagery and language. (Crack the book; pick a verse.)

## WHY, THEN, DID ANTI-SEMITISM ARISE?

As to why anti-Semitism arose in the first place, I would venture three guesses. First, the Jewish people looked on the Jesus movement as an increasingly dangerous sect. From the standpoint of safeguarding the traditions of their law and heritage, they sought to put a stop to it and its audacious claims. They killed the leader (Mark 3:6; John 11:50), then harassed his followers (Acts 4:5–22; 5:17–42). This having failed, they killed a powerful witness, Stephen, and then burst forth in open persecution (6:8–10; 7:57–8:1). When Paul began his missionary ministry, the Jews were jealous and stirred up trouble everywhere he went (13:50; 14:2, 19, etc.), culminating in his arrest (21:27–28). Persecution at the hands of the Jews became the norm of Christian existence.

However, the scriptural response to persecution is clear: flee it (Matthew 10:23) or endure it (1 Corinthians 4:12), but never, *ever*, retaliate (Matthew 5:39; Romans 12:14; 1 Peter 2:21–23; Revelation 2:9–10). My guess is Christians in the early centuries missed that little point and lashed out.

Second, for all their brilliance, the church fathers (some of them anyway) at times failed to sufficiently meditate on the Jewish origins of Christianity. Focused more on disputes about doctrine and a developing system for expressing theology, Christianity became increasingly divorced from its Jewish roots and, at least in some quarters, became philosophical and speculative. In such a climate, combined with the persecution mentioned above, what Paul had so strenuously warned against became all too common. The graft boasted against the root (Romans 11:17–22).

Third, let's not forget about the enemy. All the hatred is the personification of a spiritual battle (Ephesians 6:12). Satan relishes the thought of Jews hating Christians and Christians hating Jews. He delights in the watching world concluding religion is altogether hateful or just a bunch of hooey—anything to keep our eyes off of the crucified Jew who rose in triumph, God's personification of love.

## SUMMING UP

So then, is Christianity itself anti-Semitic? That would be the case only if Moses and the Prophets were, only if we can successfully divorce Jesus from Judaism and expunge all references to the Old Testament from the New Testament, and only if we can say that God the Father himself is anti-Semitic.

## GOING DEEPER

You can find the subject addressed from a modern Jewish perspective at www.jewishvirtuallibrary.org/jsource/antisem.html. John Chrysostom's alleged anti-Semitism is challenged in www.chrysostom.org/jews.html; according to the author, "Anti-Semites who wish to justify their hate will have to look elsewhere." A suggested book from the same site, presenting Jewish and Christian perspectives, is *Interwoven Destinies: Jews and Christians through the Ages*, edited by Eugene J. Fisher (Mahwah, NJ: Paulist, 1993). A concise history of the rise of anti-Semitism by Heiko Obermann (Princeton Dept. of Jewish Affairs/Relations) can be found at motlc.wiesenthal.com/site/pp.asp?c=gvKVLcMVIuG&b=394713.

Check out www.jcrelations.net/en/?item=813 for a speech by Winston Churchill in support of the Jews during the Holocaust, the Christians who sought to help them, and Hitler's slaughter of millions of such Christians. Bonhoeffer's books have become classic expressions of Christian faith in the midst of trial: see his *Letters from Prison* and *The Cost of Discipleship*, as well as *The Wisdom and Witness of Dietrich Bonhoeffer*, meditations by Wayne Whitson Floyd on texts from Dietrich Bonhoeffer (Minneapolis: Augsburg, 2000).

Chapter 19

# I CAN WORSHIP GOD UNDER A TREE; I DON'T NEED THE CHURCH

The United States was built on rugged individualism. "Go west, young man" is ingrained in our national psyche as indelibly as black ink on a white cotton shirt. After all, we trace the birth of our nation to the Declaration of *Independence* and the fierce war it spawned. A ragtag band of farmers squared off with Britain's finest, eventually sending the Redcoats back across the deep blue sea. From that time on, *freedom* and *independence* became the watchwords of the fledgling country, fueling the pioneering spirit that eventually stretched its boundaries "from sea to shining sea." However idealized this sketch may be, it enshrines self-reliance and intestinal fortitude. Stand up for yourself no matter the odds; you can accomplish anything you set your mind to. You are the master of your destiny—your own best ally or your own worst enemy.

Self-reliance lies behind the familiar objection to Christianity, that it's a crutch for the weak. While atheists and agnostics are fond of saying this, I want to illustrate in this chapter how the self-reliant attitude affects people who profess belief in God. Our culture breeds the attitude that we *as individuals* can worship him on our own and as such don't need the church, or, as it is often stated, we don't need "organized religion."

Once again, we have here a mixture of truth and error. The first part of the statement is true: we can worship God anywhere, all by ourselves. As a matter of fact, my personal best times with God are just that—a country trail and a battered pocket Bible, just me and God (and my feisty pup Rascal tagging along). So I can identify with enjoying God's company in solitude, but a private time with God is not the sum total of our lives with him. God designed Christianity to be a family of like-minded believers; as such, the second part of the statement is the problem. We really *do* need the church, even if we can come up with fine-sounding reasons to avoid it.

## REASONS WHY PEOPLE AVOID CHURCH

### One Bad Apple ...

An underlying, unstated assumption is that the church is a human invention. When people say, "I believe in God but I don't need organized religion," they usually have an idea of the ones who organized it. At best they picture well-meaning, though misguided and befuddled folks putting together a spiritually flavored social club. At worst they are power-hungry hypocrites, shady characters bent on separating you from your money and loading you down with guilt in return. In the middle are the faithful fogies — benign, but completely out of touch. What is the church? Just empty-brained bleeding hearts, yesteryear's dinosaurs, or malevolent backstabbers? Those seem to be the only choices offered.

Where do such notions come from? It just may be the case that there are enough examples to lead the casual observer to draw such a conclusion. You know as well as I do that we could draw up a long list of both the infamous and the obscure. It seems like we've got bad apples by the bushel. With such a track record, who could blame anyone for giving the church a hearty "No thank you"?

### Too Much of a Bother

This jaded perspective is not the only thing that hinders people from joining the church. Some people are just too busy (or claim to be). They work all week and need the weekend to catch up with yard work, the kids, or various errands. Sometimes it's as simple as a desire to sleep in, or it's just other priorities (all the big games are on Sunday). Whatever the issue, people don't want to be bothered with trivial things, like going to church.

## Jesus 'n' Me

One other category I'll mention here will be the focus of the remainder of the chapter. These are the people who desire to have, or already have, a relationship with the Lord Jesus, but see no need for his church. It is simply irrelevant. "Jesus and I are just fine, thank you very much," is the underlying attitude. Given that the church is a mess, it is still not a valid excuse to avoid joining one. It's a simple matter of obedience.

## JESUS AND THE COMMUNITY

The biblical view of the community can be traced to Jesus. He saw the community relationship as that of a vine and its branches (John 15:1 – 8). All the branches (the disciples) need to be connected to the vine (Jesus) in order to accomplish anything. It's a beautiful image of a corporate entity, with the Father overseeing it all as a wise gardener. The branches must remain on the vine; otherwise they wither and die, good only for kindling. The author of Hebrews warns his readers: "Let us not give up meeting together, as some are in the habit of doing." Instead, they are to "encourage one another" in light of the final day (Hebrews 10:25).

### It's a Family Affair

You should know the New Testament was almost exclusively addressed to churches. Paul wrote to churches in Galatia, Thessalonica, Rome, and the like. Likewise, James, Peter, John, Hebrews, Jude, and the author of Revelation all addressed their comments to specific church congregations. The New Testament writers teach the family of God to treat each other in a way that honors him — a godly influence in a godless world.

### A Glorious Vision

We may have our doubts about the value of the church, but the New Testament writers did not. The more you dig into the ideal as God sees it, the more glorious it becomes. Jesus himself envisioned his church as a victorious gathering of his people, against which all the council of wickedness and death itself would not be able to prevail (Matthew 16:18). Paul tells us Jesus is the "head over everything for the church, which is his body, the fullness of him who fills everything in every way" (Ephesians 1:22–23). In the midst of comparing the marriage bond to the relationship of Christ to his church, Paul tells husbands to love their wives,

> just as Christ loved the church and gave himself up for her to make her holy, cleansing her by the washing with water through the word, and to present her to himself as a radiant church, without stain or wrinkle or any other blemish, but holy and blameless. (Ephesians 5:25–27)

This is "God's household … the church of the living God, the pillar and foundation of the truth" (1 Timothy 3:15). It is nothing less than the revelation of the "glorious riches of [God's] mystery," which is further identified as "Christ in you, the hope of glory" (Colossians 1:27). By the way, the "you" is plural, but more on that in a moment.

In the same way, Peter points out believers are "like living stones" that are "being built into a spiritual house to be a holy priesthood." Together these new covenant priests offer "spiritual sacrifices acceptable to God through Jesus Christ" (1 Peter 2:5; see Hebrews 13:15 for a similar theme). John pictures the church as a gathering of children who are faithful followers of Jesus, anointed with God's Spirit and walking in his light (1 John 1:7; 2:20, 27). All of humanity is succinctly divided into two categories: the fellowship of the children of God and the children of the Devil (1:7; 3:10). Leaving this fellowship shows one's true colors (2:19).

## A PRISTINE SNAPSHOT

Christians often express a nostalgic yearning for the good old days of the early church. So pure, so pristine. One might get such an impression from reading about the brand new church in the heady days following Pentecost (Acts 2:42–47).

Perhaps things would have continued in this wonderful vein had there not been one glaring problem with this and all subsequent church gatherings: people!

## Not Always So Pristine

The sobering offset to God's great vision for a glorious church is the reality of how frequently we mess it up. Much, if not most of the New Testament, is concerned with correcting the problems that so quickly crept in. The next time you hear someone pining for the early church, you need to ask, "Which one?" You'll probably be met with a puzzled look because people are not always used to thinking about the several local churches referred to in the New Testament. Usually the reference will be to the early Jerusalem church of Acts 2, but even *that* church didn't stay that way. It wasn't long before some greedy little liars tried their hand at putting on a good show, but God found a way to indicate his displeasure (Acts 5:1 – 11).

Bickering arose between the Greek-speaking Christians and the locals, which required the intervention of the Twelve (Acts 6:1 – 6). As the church began to go across cultural barriers and meet with great success, the charlatans and counterfeits were right there with them (8:18 – 20; 16:16 – 18). They were a generous church, but circumstances soon outstripped their resources landing them in dire straits, which prompted Paul to gather an offering for them.

## The Church in Corinth

I could go on and on, but space doesn't permit it. Instead, I want to focus on a good example of an early church by doing an overview of 1 Corinthians. This letter is helpful for our purposes in two ways. First, Paul describes the church using several memorable metaphors (a field, a building, and a body) and continually wraps his discussion around them.

Second, if ever there was a messed up church, if ever there was a church that deserved to be completely shut down, it was Corinth. If we needed an example of a collection of baby Christians, hypocrites, and out-and-out sinners, it was Corinth. If ever Paul had occasion to tell people to leave the congregation and go worship God in purity and simplicity under yon sturdy oak (or whatever grew in ancient Corinth), this was it. He didn't. What we do have is a letter written to a struggling congregation in which Paul seeks to correct several specific problems, always with the ideal of the unity of God's family in view. It's called 1 Corinthians, but its subtitle should've been "A Letter to a Messed-Up Church."

Corinth was a prosperous city with both a lively land route and a livelier seafaring commerce. The worst of its reputation lay in the past (as the city had existed over a century before Paul visited in the mid-50s AD). Much of the city's notorious promiscuity was related to the practice of "worshiping" Aphrodite by engaging with temple prostitutes. (I guess that's one way to bolster your weekly attendance.) That problem may have persisted in the rebuilt city of Paul's day, but the reputation as a party town with a lively sexual appetite was simply what you would expect in a sailor town.

Aphrodite's temple and the other shrines dedicated to pagan gods were their pride and joy. For Paul, they were an insult to the Father of the Lord Jesus Christ. God had his temple there too, but it wasn't a structure. Instead, it was a group of people who identified themselves with him by turning from pagan gods to become disciples of Jesus, his Son. What's more, God had filled this small community with his Holy Spirit and given them various spiritual gifts. *They* were his temple.

Yet, they were a messed-up church. Its members were the equivalent of spoiled little brats, spiritually speaking. Rather than being the spiritual cream of the crop, as they saw themselves, they were worldly and fleshy. A recurring theme throughout the letter is that of a church divided—little minds forming little groups in a vain attempt to gain the upper hand. This, and other problems, not to mention a plea for help (1 Corinthians 1:11; 7:1), convinced Paul he needed to clarify some issues.

Much of the letter is taken up with specific sins and their immature responses to them, but it really comes down to *why* most of these sins were singled out. Besides being bad form for an individual Christian, engaging in these sinful practices posed a real threat to the church as a whole. Divisions threatened the unity and thus the health of the corporate body, God's temple (1 Corinthians 3:17). So Paul was prepared, if need be, to show up with a whip (4:21; surely an exaggeration, but it reminds me of Jesus in John 2:14–15). The debacle of the young man and his new (step?) mama threatened to work through the whole congregation like yeast through a loaf (5:6–7). Suing each other was shameful precisely because of the nasty spectacle of Christians at each other's throats in full view of a watching world (6:6). While one "liberated" Christian may feel emboldened to continue eating meat sacrificed to a pagan idol, the real problem is the harm done to the young believers (8:4–13). Their nonsense at the supposed Lord's Supper was so hurtful God actually allowed them to succumb to sickness and early deaths (11:29–30).

What's the point of all this? Again, we're looking closely at a church loaded with sick puppies. Yet, it is precisely to this rancid gathering that Paul writes some of his clearest expressions of what the church is and how to function within it. He doesn't tell them to convert to Christ; they had (1 Corinthians 1:2). He doesn't tell them they need the Holy Spirit; they were exceptionally gifted (1:5; 12:7–12). He doesn't even tell them to stop meeting together in light of their destructive nonsense; instead, he gives guidelines for right behavior (11:27, 33–34). At every turn Paul tells them to live up to who they are in Christ. They are God's field, his building, indeed, his temple. They are God's church, individuals together comprising the body of Christ, with Jesus as the head.

*Field.* Both metaphors of the church as a field and a building are mentioned in 1 Corinthians 3:9. As a field, the idea is a cultivated plot of land, not a wild one (3:5–8). Paul has in mind his own ministry of "planting" (he led the Corinthians to faith) and Apollos's ministry of "watering" (teaching the young Christians how to grow in their faith). God gives the actual miracle of growth, and the individual "plants" together will produce a harvest. The idea of a plant in its own pot is simply not in view.

*Building.* The church as a building initially focuses on its foundation, Jesus Christ, upon whom each individual part must build carefully. There are many parts, but one edifice. Paul is concerned that no one person exalts another, or one's self, which would in fact hinder the unity he is so desperately trying to promote. This leads into the passage concerning the church as a temple (1 Corinthians 3:16–17; see also Ephesians 2:21; 1 Peter 2:5).

*Temple.* When it comes to spiritual matters, we're just not used to thinking in terms of belonging to a group. Religion is a private matter, we are frequently told. So, we read familiar passages as if they are talking to an individual and then apply them accordingly. But when we do that, we actually wind up missing the point. The image of the church as a temple is a case in point.

> Don't you know that you yourselves are God's temple and
> that God's Spirit lives in you? If anyone destroys God's temple,
> God will destroy him; for God's temple is sacred, and you are
> that temple. (1 Corinthians 3:16–17)

Many versions make it so easy to miss the point by rendering the first few words: "Do you not know that you are a temple of God" (NASB, see also ESV, NEV, NKJV, etc.). It's easy to conclude Paul is talking about you (or me) as individual Christians. *I* am a temple of God and the Holy Spirit lives in *me*. Likewise, *you*, as a special individual, are a temple as well, and God lives in *you*. While that is true, it's hardly the point.

Even more mischief is done when it's applied to issues of health. *You* are a temple of God so *you* better not smoke (or eat junk food). If you do, you'll destroy God's temple, so he'll destroy you! While keeping healthy is certainly wise, it has nothing to do with this passage. And do we really want to equate cheeseburgers with eternal damnation? The problem has to do with the little word "you." New Testament Greek, like many modern languages, distinguished between a plural and singular "you." Standard contemporary English does not. I say "standard" because we use slang for the plural all the time (y'all, y'uns, youse). I say "contemporary" because the KJV handles it quite well; the English of that era still had a singular ("thou") and a plural ("ye"). "Know ye not that ye are the temple of God?" Not knowing any better, it's easy to read "ye" and think it refers to "me." It doesn't.

All instances of "you" in this passage are plural. This is why the NIV uses the expression "you yourselves." The NLT makes it even clearer: "Don't you realize that all of you together are the temple of God?" That covers the first instances, but the rest of the passage needs a little tweaking as well.

Since the issue of divisions is the main theme of the first four chapters, it's best to read 1 Corinthians 3:16–17 in this light. And since Paul uses a plural form that contemporary standard English doesn't reflect, I've taken the liberty of expanding it a bit to bring out the full flavor of the original (with my interpretive additions in italics):

> Don't you *folks* know that you yourselves *together* are God's temple and that God's Spirit lives in you *folks corporately*? If any *individual among you* destroys God's temple, *like some of you scoundrels are in the process of doing*, God will destroy *any such individual*; for God's temple is sacred, and you *folks, all of you together*, are that temple, *God's visible manifestation of his redeemed community*.

The remedy for their plight is to think about who and what they are as a gathering of believers and who is in their midst (namely, God himself, by his Spirit).

Once that's cleared up, the next step concerns acting accordingly by living up to this new identity. Rather than depending on their earthly wisdom, they needed to rely on the Spirit's wisdom. Rather than living like freshman frat boys (and the appropriate female equivalent), they needed to live like a people indwelt by a holy God. There is no hint that the plan is for any one individual to do it alone. Going it alone, by the way, is the unfortunate sentence reserved for the unrepentant youngin' who was carrying on with "mama" (1 Corinthians 5:13).

*Gifts and parts.* While the Corinthians equated spiritual giftedness with maturity, Paul certainly does not. The issue is addressed in 1 Corinthians 12. The problem was that some of the Corinthians thought their particular gifts elevated them above others, who in turn were likely feeling a bit intimidated by these supposed spiritual giants. Just as likely, they were looked down upon by the self-anointed select few.

In 1 Corinthians 12, attention is often focused on the list of the spiritual gifts, what they are, how they differ from each other, as if that were the sole point.[45] But the chapter is not about the gifts; it's about their *misuse* and how they are intended to operate. Paul's purpose here is to demonstrate God's response to their immature misunderstanding.

"There are different kinds of gifts," to be sure, but Paul repeatedly stresses that they're all from "the same" source, the triune God (1 Corinthians 12:4–6). Verse 7 is the heart of their purpose: not for any one person to stand out (to the detriment of those not so spectacularly gifted) but "for the common good." God's desire is that these gifts serve the entire church. The same focus continues in verses 8–10; the different gifts derive from "the same Spirit" (or "that one Spirit"). So in case we didn't get it, Paul reiterates, "All these are the work of one and the same Spirit" who parcels them out "just as he determines" (12:11). *How* they should be used flew past the Corinthians, so Paul launches right into verse 12, "the body is a unit." Their church wasn't operating like one.

*Body.* No one person can possibly be so fully gifted as to handle all the church's ministry needs. We really do need each other. Also, no part of this collective unit need wallow in self-pity because of some supposed lack or spiritual inferiority complex. No, "the body is a unit, though it is made up of many parts.... So it is with Christ" (1 Corinthians 12:12). Paul goes on to say how "we were all baptized by one Spirit into one body," regardless of our station in life, "and we were all given the one Spirit to drink" (12:13). Again, Paul is hammering the point— "we," "all," "one Spirit," "one body." I emphasize this because these are often the throwaway lines that are ignored on the way to the good stuff.

Next comes the illustration concerning the body's various parts making the case for their independence, or lamenting that they're not up to speed with the rest (1 Corinthians 12:14–26). Such protests are absurd, since "God has arranged the parts in the body, every one of them, just as he wanted them to be" (12:18). The human body needs to function as an integrated unit "so that there should be no division in the body, but that its parts should have equal concern for each other" (12:24–26). What happens if you cut off your finger? How healthy will it be in a few days if we leave it on the kitchen table? It may make for an interesting conversation piece, but I'll bet it won't survive very long on its own.

The punch line comes in 1 Corinthians 12:27–31: "Now you [*all*] are the body of Christ, and each one of you is a part of it." God has arranged *this* body for the gifts to work in concert to promote the cause of Christ. An individual cut off from the others is not God's plan; a Christian needs other Christians to grow and mature.

## A CHURCH BY ANY OTHER NAME

When people mention "the church," what do they mean? The image that comes readily to mind is the building with the tall steeple (or any other design we've come to associate with the term). "Where is your church?" is a question seeking an address, not a mystical reality about the exalted Christ among his people as they gather for worship. That description, however, brings us to another part of the answer. It's really not the building; it's the gathering within it. "Where does your church meet?" is a question that receives a variety of responses, whether it's a traditional "church building," a school, theater, warehouse, or office building.

This too fits the New Testament pattern. While it is true that the early church met in homes (Acts 8:3; Romans 16:5; 1 Corinthians 16:19; 2 John 10), that wasn't the only place they met. Initially, the early Christians gathered in the temple (Acts 2:46; 3:1; 5:42) and commandeered synagogue services whenever they could get away with it (13:14–16; 14:1; 17:1, etc.). Failing that tactic, Paul wasn't stymied when he needed another venue, like a lecture hall (19:9) or a riverside (16:13). In our day, it is simply convenient to have buildings set aside for worshiping the Lord and for fellowship. Calling a building a church doesn't make it so; that depends on the nature of the members' regular gatherings.

Ideally, the church is always pictured as a group of like-minded people, united under the banner of Christ, gathered to worship, learn, and share lives with like-minded souls. So if I may conclude, the entity of the church is what's important. It is made up of people committed to God and to each other. Where they meet is irrelevant.

## SUMMING UP

It is a comforting reality that we can encounter God anywhere, even under a tree. Fellowshiping with God like that is strongly encouraged, but don't confuse it with the church. If you want to meet with other like-minded souls under a stately maple as an expression of the church—a gathering in Jesus' name for the express purpose of worshiping, learning, and growing in Christ—have at it. Where the church meets isn't really important; *that* we meet is imperative. If we want to grow as he intends, we need to join with his people and live the Christian life within the Christian family. This is his plan; he's given us no alternative.

## GROWING DEEPER

A good defense of the necessity of the church can be found at www.
apologeticspress.org/articles/2463. An interesting interchange is "In
Defense of the Church: A Response to Chad Hall" at www.christi-
anitytoday.com/leaders/newsletter/2004/cln41101.html. (There is a
link to Hall's article.) Kenneth Myers provides a chilling assessment
of the effects of pop culture on the church in *All God's Children
and Blue Suede Shoes: Christians and Popular Culture* (Wheaton,
IL: Crossway, 1989). See also Gordon Fee, *The First Epistle to the
Corinthians* (Grand Rapids: Eerdmans, 1987) for further comments
concerning 1 Corinthians 3:16.

# Chapter 20

# DOES ANY OF THIS REALLY MATTER?

We come at last to the end of a long conversation, having wrestled with many, sometimes difficult, topics. Concerning the Bible, we've seen that it is trustworthy, at the very least, as a record of the beliefs of the ancient Jews and the apostles' teachings about Jesus. There are many ways to account for these beliefs. I hope you can see the best explanation is this: these people experienced the things they wrote about.

Throughout this book I've attempted to paint a picture, the repetition of which is hard to miss. A core reality lies at the heart of addressing so many of the myths discussed—the straight line from the Old Testament, through the yearnings of Israel, to the teaching of Jesus, which comes to us through his apostles, all of which is recorded in first-century documents. We know it as the New Testament.

Speaking of which, the New Testament has stood the test of centuries of attack. As more discoveries surface and as we come to a greater understanding of the first-century world, the better and more clearly we are able to see the gospel message. It hasn't been lost in translation; it wasn't made up on the fly. It's a message that changes lives and rocks the world of any generation brave enough to embrace it.

We looked at Jesus, the very center of the Bible's message. His coming was promised from the beginning and was fulfilled on dusty streets, a sandal-clad visitor with a lasting legacy of eternal life. The source of his power, love, and wisdom, not to mention the miracles he performed, was God, his Father. It was God's Holy Spirit that empowered Jesus' ministry, rather than the dark arts of mysterious gurus. The claims about him reflect his own words and deeds. Jesus is the One he claimed to be: God's Messiah, the sacrifice for the world, brutally killed, and resurrected in triumph. That particular feat is not often done.

Next we sampled some views about God. That he exists as a Trinity is no fourth-century invention; it is his ancient self-revelation. Inventions abound, of course, like saying all religions have the same basic message. Not only is it the case that they *do not*, they simply *cannot*. It's funny how people insist on God's conforming to all sorts of religious paths but cannot wrap their minds around the fact that the Old Testament God and the New Testament God are one and the same. He is the One who endures the present evil in light of the certainty of its final demise.

Finally we looked at the Christian faith itself. It didn't have to wait until the fourth century to sort things out. The message has always been the same; several centuries of challenges merely served to sharpen its message. That message, incidentally, concerns the intense love God has for us and the gift of life available through faith in his Son. It's unfortunate that this message is so often garbled, filtered as it is through leaky earthen vessels (Paul's "jars of clay," 2 Corinthians 4:7). It's tragic when *our* prejudices and failures are confused with *his* gospel. Yet, as imperfect as we are, we will wind up gathered at his feet, a motley crew with flaws and baggage, united only in our devotion to God's dear Son — the habitation of God's Holy Spirit.

## LAPS AROUND THE TRACK

Something you may have noticed throughout this book is the way certain events and key passages kept coming up. Things like the creation and fall (and aftermath), the call of Abraham (and the patriarchs), Moses, and David, the Promised Land (entry, exile, and return) are tucked away in different chapters. This is the main storyline of the Old Testament. Each pass provides a little more information and the stories are told from slightly different perspectives. A hope develops—an expectation of the coming of a King who will one day rule all kings. In broad strokes I've tried to keep one central theme before your eyes—God is faithful. He will fulfill his promises.

I've done the same with the New Testament. We run into John the Baptist's testimony (from him as well as about him), Jesus' incredible ministry, his horrible death, his glorious resurrection, and his ascension to the right hand of heaven's Majesty. *This* Jesus is Christ, the Lord. He was the heart of the church's teaching and preaching as it spread throughout the Roman Empire. It will continue to do so no matter what until the day God says "Enough," and sends his Son to put an end to the age-old rebellion. As God created this world, he will create a new one. This is the main theme of the New Testament, and once again, we see the overall message—God is faithful. He will fulfill his promises.

## HAVE WE SILENCED THE SKEPTICS?

I don't want to leave you with the impression that all that can be said *has* been said. No, this is just a modest beginning. You will quickly find the skeptics aren't likely to yield ground easily, especially if the alternative to their views entails anything that smacks of surrendering to Jesus. I hope you won't waste a moment arguing. Share your beliefs; defend the gospel. If the response is receptive, proceed cautiously and prayerfully. If not, just stop. Jesus focused his time on those most ready to receive him and knew when tossing pearls was a waste of time. Should we try to do things any differently?

## A LAST NOTE CONCERNING SOURCES

It has occurred to me throughout the writing of this book how often I'm passing along the thoughts of other authors (or sermons, or classes, perhaps gospel tracts—things picked up along the way).

These have become ingrained in my thinking and are authentic expressions of my faith; I just don't have a clue from whom I first heard them. Perhaps we need a category of public domain items: "Generic Christian Stuff." In the event that you recognize a source for something I've said that really should receive due credit, I will be happy to add the citation to any reprinted version of this book.

## A FINAL OBSERVATION

Now what remains to be seen is the grand "So what?" Or to put it a little more politely, "Does any of this really matter?" It doesn't, of course, if the skeptics are right. Christianity is just an invention, a merely human, outdated attempt at gaining power over others, a misguided venture which should just quietly slink away. None of this matters if the relativists are right (which if they are, there's no right or wrong to begin with). Beliefs are just opinions and everyone has at least one, no better, no worse than any other (unless the relativist doesn't like it). None of this matters if indeed all paths lead to God, assuming his/her/its/their existence, regardless of how impossibly untraceable the paths turn out to be. The topics in this book only matter, my friend, if Christianity is true.

My sincere hope is that you have picked up some valuable insights along the way, and even more importantly, have drawn closer to God in the process. His promises are worth looking into; his Word can withstand all scrutiny. His gospel is a message worth defending.

1. The early church fathers were the leaders from the late first century through the fourth century. Their writings are a valuable window into the early centuries of Christianity, but were never intended to be Scripture. For more information see http://www.spurgeon.org/~phil/fathers.htm and http://www.earlychristianwritings.com/churchfathers.html.

2. From personal correspondence with Klyne Snodgrass, a former colleague of mine at North Park University.

3. The fathers affirm Peter as the source with Mark as the person writing down his preaching, but they also posit Matthew as the first written gospel. This view has been challenged by much of current scholarship, which argues for the priority of Mark. See Robert Stein's *Synoptic Gospels: Origin and Interpretation*, 2nd edition (Grand Rapids: Baker Academic, 2001) for a good summary of the issues; see also David Black's *Why Four Gospels: The Historical Origins of the Gospels* (Grand Rapids: Baker Academic, 2007) for an alternative view seeing Mark as the last gospel written. This endnote is a case in point for why I'll keep them to a minimum.

4. The statistical likelihood can be summed up like this: "This statement could statistically (practically) be true by estimating the number of possible variants of a snowflake and estimating the number of snowflakes that have ever existed." (I'm thankful for this and other contributions to this chapter from John Spears, a scientifically minded friend.)

5. I am not suggesting that philosophy is somehow inferior to science; I'm simply calling attention to the difference between the two disciplines and the need to distinguish them.

6. Lest there be any confusion, I'm referring to a Christian writer who happens to be a scientist, not a member of the Christian Science denomination.

7. David Wilkinson, *God, Time and Stephen Hawking: An Exploration into Origins* (Grand Rapids: Kregel, 2001), 77.

8. I credit R. C. Sproul with introducing me to this logical nicety in his Systematic Theology classes at Reformed Theological Seminary, Orlando, in the early 1990s. I have since seen it resurface in numerous writings and lectures.

9. For this section see Wilkinson, "The Proof of Science," *God, Time and Stephen Hawking*, 61–77 (ch. 4).

10. There is much more to this, of course. A concise lecture on quantum mechanics by Stephen Hawking can be found at www.hawking.org.uk/lectures/dice.html.

11. I borrowed this turn of phrase from my pastor, Scott Chapman.

12. Stephen Hawking, *A Brief History of Time: From the Big Bang to Black Holes* (New York: Bantam Books, 1990), 10. I again thank John Spears for pointing this out.

13. This is the conclusion of the lecture on Quantum Mechanics by Stephen Hawking in the site mentioned above (accessed 1/26/08).

14. For example, Roman Catholics accept several Jewish writings from the intertestamental era, which they label as "deuterocanonical," or "second canon" (the Eastern Orthodox Churches add a few more from that era). Protestants refer to these books as the Apocrypha, and since they were never included in the Hebrew Bible, reject them as Scripture, but nonetheless regard them as valuable sources from that era.

15. I'm referring to Bart Ehrman; more on him in a moment.

16. Dan Brown, *The Da Vinci Code* (New York: Doubleday, 2003). It is often pointed out that since *The Da Vinci Code* is a novel and thus fiction, Christians are getting their noses out of joint for no good reason. However, even though it is a work of fiction, it is presented as "historical fiction," a story spun around select historical facts.

17. The passages in the Dead Sea Scrolls that may refer to more than one Messiah are found in the community's sectarian documents, not in the Old Testament books.

18. I pinched this little phrase from Scot McKnight, "Who Is Jesus? An Introduction to Jesus Studies," in *Jesus under Fire: Modern Scholarship Reinvents the Historical Jesus*, edited by Michael Wilkins and J. P. Moreland (Grand Rapids: Zondervan, 1995), 56.

19. Bart Ehrman presents this view in a variety of his works; I'm here interacting with his *The New Testament: A Historical Introduction to the Early Christian Writings*, 3rd edition (Oxford: Oxford Univ. Press, 2004), 1–8.

20. Peter Stuhlmacher, *How to Do Biblical Theology* (Princeton Theology Monograph Series 38; Eugene, OR: Pickwick, 1995), 3.

21. See the article on "Canon" in *DLNT*, 135.

22. Elizabeth Clare Prophet, *The Lost Years of Jesus: Documentary Evidence of Jesus 17-Year Journey to the East* (Gardiner, MT: Summit Univ. Press, 1987).

23. Throughout this chapter I'll be interchanging the terms merely for the sake of variety. *Why* I can do this will be more fully explained below.

24. Literally: "You say," which is an affirmation along the lines of "You got *that* right."

25. N. T. Wright, "In Grateful Dialogue," *Jesus and the Restoration of Israel,* ed. Carey Newman (Downers Grove, IL: InterVarsity Press, 1999), 271.

26. Excluding, of course, his famous descendant, Jesus.

27. Jesse was David's father.

28. Jewish culture fun fact: the word "son" can refer to one's child, grandchild, or even a distant descendant. That is why Jesus is called "the son of David" as well as "the son of Abraham" in Matthew 1:1.

29. The term *Synoptic* means "seeing together," a reference to the fact that Matthew, Mark, and Luke follow the same basic outline. John affirms the claim of Jesus' messiahship as well, letting on that his being the Christ was suspected quite early on (John 1:41). Notice that the news is, "We have found the Messiah," which John translates for his Gentile audience "(that is, the Christ)." This indicates that this claim of Jesus' messianic identity goes back to the earliest days of the Aramaic-speaking church.

30. I'm assuming that the phrase belongs in the verse, though it is a text variant. However, it is not crucial to my point because of v.11.

31. Although "Christ" was a title meaning "anointed one," the identification of Jesus as "the Christ" par excellence quickly gave way to the use of "Jesus Christ" as a name. So "Jesus" and "Christ" were often used interchangeably in Christian writings.

32. The word "hanged" refers to being hanged on a cross as per Roman practice, not death by hanging from a gallows (Galatians 3:13, discussed below).

33. I'm grateful to Gary Habermas for this point; references in Going Deeper.

34. I am thankful for James Dunn for this reference from his article " 'A Light to the Gentiles': The Significance for the Damascus Road Christophany for Paul," in *The Glory of Christ in the New Testament: Studies in Christology in Memory of George Bradford Caird*, edited by L. D. Hurst and N. T. Wright (Eugene, OR: Wipf and Stock, 2006), 264. Incidentally, referring to the cross as a "tree" was a fairly common image, since crosses were upright poles made of wood, with a beam affixed resembling branches; see Acts 5:30; 10:39; 13:29; 1 Peter 2:24.

35. For the full quote in context refer to this site: newsweek.washingtonpost. com/onfaith/guestvoices/2007/02/crosson_bones_and_wounds.html.

36. John miraculously survived being boiled in oil, church tradition tells us, only to be exiled to a barren island (from which he wrote the book of Revelation).

37. This is, of course, a Protestant interpretation, that Mary and Joseph had children *after* the birth of Jesus. Roman Catholicism maintains that Mary remained a virgin her entire life.

38. Of the several men in the New Testament named James, Jesus' brother is the best candidate for the one assuming this leadership. For argumentation and citation of ancient sources see the commentaries on James by Doug Moo in The Pillar Commentary Series (Grand Rapids: Eerdmans, 2000) and David Nystrom, The NIV Application Commentary (Grand Rapids: Zondervan, 1997).

39. Contrary to popular belief, "Saul the persecutor" did not become "Paul the apostle" on the road to Damascus. In fact, he remained "Saul" for months and was still called that name several chapters *after* his conversion. "Saul" was his Jewish name; "Paul" was the Greek version, not mentioned until he was already on the first missionary journey to Gentile cities (Acts 13:9). From that point on

he's always called Paul, since he was the "apostle to the Gentiles" (Romans 11:13). There now, a myth tidily handled in an endnote.

40. I deal with this at length in chapter 18, so further comment will wait until then. I mention it here because it sets the pace for the rest of the book of Acts (if not the whole New Testament).

41. The Jehovah Witnesses are famous for rendering John 1:1c as "and the Word was a god." The issue involves details of Greek grammar, and though the translation "a god" may be *grammatically* permissible in a given context, it is highly unlikely in this one. *Theologically* speaking it's impossible. The gospel writer John is a Jew, for whom there is only one God. The mystery of the verse, how Jesus can be called God and yet not be an additional God, is precisely what this and the next chapter are all about.

42. Gordon Fee presents a different case for this verse. Though denying that Jesus is called "God" in this verse (as well as Romans 9:5), he demonstrates how Jesus assumes divine prerogatives in all of Paul's letters. See the Going Deeper section.

43. From Alfred Lord Tennyson's *In Memoriam*.

44. Those who didn't know Jesus in his earthly ministry relied on the eyewitness accounts and the further illumination of the Holy Spirit (see, e.g., Luke 1:1–4).

45. I am consciously bypassing the issue of whether or not these gifts are still available in our day. For anyone interested you can check out *Are Miraculous Gifts for Today?: 4 Views*, ed. Wayne Grudem (Grand Rapids: Zondervan, 1996).